The Lamentation over the Destruction of Sumer and Ur

MESOPOTAMIAN CIVILIZATIONS

1. *The Lamentation over the Destruction of Sumer and Ur*
   Piotr Michalowski

2. *Schlaf, Kindchen, schlaf! Mesopotamische Baby-Beschwörungen und -Rituale*
   Walter Farber

The Lamentation over the Destruction of Sumer and Ur

Piotr Michalowski

Eisenbrauns
Winona Lake
1989

Printed in the United States of America

Library of Congress Cataloging-in-Publication Data:

Lamentation over the destruction of Sumer and Ur.
English and Sumerian.
The lamentation over the destruction of Sumer and Ur.

(Mesopotamian civilizations; 1)
Bibliography: p.
Includes indexes.
Sumerian text; parallel translation and prefatory matter in English.
1. Elegiac poetry, Sumerian. 2. Sumerian language—Texts. I. Michalowski, Piotr. II. Title. III. Series.
PJ4065.L3 1988 899'.95 88-33386
ISBN 0-931464-43-9

Dla Miry i Jerzego

Contents

Preface

I began work on the *Lamentation over the Destruction of Sumer and Ur* in 1980 when Åke W. Sjöberg assigned the text to me as part of the Pennsylvania Sumerian Dictionary project, but it was only in 1985, after a generous Research Fellowship from the Rackham Fund of the University of Michigan allowed me to collate texts in Istanbul and in London, that I was able to proceed to finish the text edition. Throughout the time that I have worked on this text I have had much assistance from many friends and colleagues without whose help and advice this project could never have been finished.

Work with cuneiform tablets requires access to museum holdings throughout the world and it is my pleasure to thank the following scholars and institutions for allowing me access to the materials in their care and for permission to publish or collate original manuscripts. I am particularly indebted to Veysel Donbaz and Fatma Yıldız of the Museum of the Ancient Orient in Istanbul for their help and hospitality when I collated the tablets in Istanbul, to the Trustees of the British Museum for permission to study the Ur material, to William W. Hallo for permission to publish his copy of the text from the Yale Babylonian collection, to Åke W. Sjöberg for allowing me to study published and unpublished tablets from the University Museum of the University of Pennsylvania, as well as to Daniel Arnaud (epigrapher of the Larsa expedition) for sending me, and allowing me to publish here, a photograph of the Larsa tablet.

Others have helped me along the way with text identifications, advice, and hospitality: Herman Behrens, Miguel Civil, Irving Finkel, Markham J. Geller, Pamela Gerardi, Ulla Kasten, P. R. S. Moorey, Aaron Shaffer, and Christopher Walker. Brian Keck helped me to check all references. I owe special thanks to Samuel N. Kramer, who relinquished his interest in this text and permitted me to utilize his preliminary edition of the composition, and generously allowed the publication of his hand copies of some of the Nippur tablets. Jerrold S. Cooper and Peter Machinist offered valuable advice on an earlier version of the book.

I am particularly indebted to Miguel Civil, who read the final draft and provided many invaluable insights. Finally, I wish to acknowledge the support of the National Endowment for the Humanities, the American Philosophical Society, and the Rackham Fund of the University of Michigan for financial assistance that allowed me to collate and copy texts on two continents.

A word should be said on the preparation of this book. The major part of the manuscript was written on a personal computer using the FinalWord II word processing program. Stephen Tinney wrote a series of macros that converted the text into files that could be read directly by the typesetting equipment used by Eisenbrauns. He then converted the "score" into TEX and printed it on the APS-5 typesetter at the University of Michigan. This was a new experience for both of us, as well as for Jim Eisenbraun and his staff, and I am grateful to all of them for their help and their patience.

Abbreviations

1. **Bibliographical abbreviations** follow the usage of the *Chicago Assyrian Dictionary* and Borger, *HKL*, with the following additions.

Alster, *Dumuzi's Dream*
B. Alster. *Dumuzi's Dream: Aspects of Oral Poetry in a Sumerian Myth.* Copenhagen, 1972.

Alster, *Instructions*
B. Alster. *The Instructions of Suruppak: A Sumerian Proverb Collection.* Copenhagen, 1974.

Berlin, *Enmerkar*
A. Berlin. *Enmerkar and Ensuḫkešdana: A Sumerian Narrative Poem.* Philadelphia, 1979.

Castellino, *Two Šulgi Hymns*
G. R. Castellino. *Two Šulgi Hymns (BC).* Rome, 1972.

Charpin, *Ur*
D. Charpin. *Le clergé d'Ur au siècle d'Hammurabi (XIX*e*-XVIII*e *siècles av. J.-C.).* Geneva-Paris, 1986.

Cohen, *Balag Compositions*
M. E. Cohen. *An Analysis of the "Balag" Compositions to the God Enlil Copied in Babylon during the Seleucid Period.* Doctoral dissertation, University of Pennsylvania, 1972.

Cohen, *Enmerkar*
S. Cohen. *Enmerkar and the Lord of Aratta.* Doctoral dissertation, University of Pennsylvania, 1973.

Cohen, *Sumerian Hymnology*
M. E. Cohen. *Sumerian Hymnology: The Eršemma.* Cincinnati, 1981.

Cooper, *Agade*
J. S. Cooper. *The Curse of Agade.* Baltimore, 1983.

Farber-Flügge, *Inanna und Enki*
G. Farber-Flügge. *Der Mythos "Inanna und Enki" unter besonderer Berücksichtigung der Liste der me.* Rome, 1973.

Ferrara, *Nanna's Journey*
A. J. Ferrara. *Nanna-Suen's Journey to Nippur.* Rome, 1973.

Ferwerda, *Early Isin*
G. T. Ferwerda. *A Contribution to the Early Isin Craft Archive.* Leiden, 1985.

Frayne, *Historical Correlations*
D. R. Frayne. *The Historical Correlations of the Sumerian Royal Hymns (2400–1900 B.C.).* Doctoral dissertation, Yale University, 1981.

Green, *Eridu*
M. W. Green. *Eridu in Sumerian Culture*. Doctoral dissertation, University of Chicago, 1975.

Hall, *Moon God*
M. G. Hall. *A Study of the Sumerian Moon-God, Nanna/ Suen*. Doctoral dissertation, University of Pennsylvania, 1985.

Hallo and van Dijk, *Exaltation*
W. W. Hallo and J. J. A. van Dijk. *The Exaltation of Inanna*. New Haven, 1968.

Jacobsen, *The Harps*
T. Jacobsen. *The Harps That Once . . . : Sumerian Poetry in Translation*. New Haven, 1987.

Klein, *Three Šulgi Hymns*
J. Klein. *Three Šulgi Hymns: Sumerian Hymns Glorifying King Šulgi of Ur*. Ramat-Gan, 1981.

Kutscher, *Oh Angry Sea*
R. Kutscher. *Oh Angry Sea (a-ab-ba hu-luh-ha): The History of a Sumerian Congregational Lament*. New Haven, 1975.

Litke, *An=Anum*
R. L. Litke. *A Reconstruction of the Assyro-Babylonian God-Lists, An : ᵈA-nu-um and An : Anu šá amēli*. Doctoral Dissertation, Yale University, 1958.

Mélanges Birot
J.-M. Durand and J.-R. Kupper (eds.). *Miscellanea Babyloniaca: Mélanges offerts à Maurice Birot*. Paris, 1985.

Neumann, *Handwerk*
H. Neumann. *Handwerk in Mesopotamien*. Berlin, 1987.

PSD
The Sumerian Dictionary of the University Museum of the University of Pennsylvania, ed. Å. W. Sjöberg. Philadelphia, 1984–.

Riesman, *Two Neo-Sumerian Royal Hymns*
D. D. Riesman. *Two Neo-Sumerian Royal Hymns*. Doctoral dissertation, University of Pennsylvania, 1969.

Römer, *Bilgameš und Akka*
W. H. P. Römer. *Das sumerische Kurzepos "Bilgameš und Akka."* Neukirchen-Vluyn, 1980.

Sigrist, *Account Texts*
M. Sigrist. *Neo-Sumerian Account Texts in the Horn Archaeological Museum*. Berrien Springs, 1984.

Sladek, *Descent*
W. R. Sladek. *Inanna's Descent to the Netherworld*. Doctoral dissertation, University of Pennsylvania, 1974.

SLF
J. W. Heimerdinger. *Sumerian Literary Fragments from Nippur*. Philadelphia, 1979.

Steible, *Rīmsîn*

H. Steible. *Rīmsîn, mein König: Drei kultische Texte aus Ur mit der Schlussdoxologie ^{d}ri-im-^{d}sîn lugal-mu.* Wiesbaden, 1975.

Studies Reiner

F. Rochberg-Halton (ed.). *Language, Literature, and History: Philological and Historical Studies Presented to Erica Reiner.* New Haven, 1987.

Thomsen, *The Sumerian Language*

M.-L. Thomsen. *The Sumerian Language: An Introduction to its History and Grammatical Structure.* Copenhagen, 1984.

Volk, *Die Balağ-Komposition*

K. Volk. *Die Balağ-Komposition ÚRU ÀM-MA-IR-RA-BI: Eine bearbeitung der Tafeln 18 (19′ff.), 19, 20 und 21 der späten, kanonischen Version.* Doctoral dissertation, Albert-Ludwigs-Universität, Freiburg i. Br., 1985.

2. **Sumerian literary texts** that are extant in a single exemplar are cited according to the publication of the copy or the standard edition. For other texts the following abbreviations are used.

An-Anum

God list. Litke, *An=Anum.*

Angin

J. S. Cooper. *The Return of Ninurta to Nippur.* Rome, 1978.

Balag 44

J. A. Black. "A-še-er Gi$_6$-ta, a Balag of Inana." *ASJ* 7 (1985) 11–87.

Bird and Fish

Disputation between the Bird and the Fish. University Museum manuscript (M. Civil).

CA

Curse of Agade. Cooper, *Agade.*

Death of Ur-Namma

S. N. Kramer. "The Death of Ur-Nammu and His Descent to the Netherworld." *JCS* 21 (1967) 104–22. With additions by C. Wilcke, "Eine Schicksalsentscheidung für den toten Urnammu," in A. Finet, ed., *Actes de la XVIIe Rencontre Assyriologique Internationale: Université Libre de Bruxelles, 30 juin-4 juillet 1969* (Ham-Sur-Heure, 1970) 81–92, and unpublished Susa version courtesy M. Civil.

Dialog 2

Dialog between Enki-ḫegal and Enki-talu. University Museum manuscript (M. Civil).

ELA

Enmerkar and the Lord of Aratta. Cohen, *Enmerkar.*

Enki and Ninmaḫ

Enki and Ninmaḫ. C. E. Benito, *"Enki and Ninmah" and "Enki and the World Order."* Doctoral dissertation, University of Pennsylvania, 1969 (pp. 9–76).

Enki Letter

Letter of Sin-šamuḫ to Enki. W. W. Hallo. "Individual Prayer in Sumerian: The Continuity of a Tradition." *JAOS* 88 (1968) 82–88.

Enlil and Sud

M. Civil. "Enlil and Ninlil: The Marriage of Sud." *JAOS* 103 (1983) 43–66.

Eršemma 106

BE 30/1 12 and duplicate. Cohen, *Sumerian Hymnology* 70–71.

Eršemma 163.1

CT 15 pl. 11–12 and duplicates. Cohen, *Sumerian Hymnology* 121–24.

EWO

Enki and the World Order. C. E. Benito. *"Enki and Ninmah" and "Enki and the World Order."* Doctoral dissertation, University of Pennsylvania, 1969 (pp. 77–162).

Flood Story

PBS 5 1, ed. M. Civil in Lambert-Millard, *Atra-ḫasīs* 138–45; see also S. N. Kramer, "The Sumerian Deluge Myth," *AnSt* 33 (1983) 115–21.

Gilgameš and Ḫuwawa

S. N. Kramer. "Gilgamesh and the Land of the Living." *JCS* 1 (1947) 3–46.

Ḫaia Hymn

UET 6 101, in H. Steible, *Ein Lied an den Gott Ḫāja mit Bitte für den König Rīmsîn von Larsa.* Freiburg, 1967. New edition in Charpin, *Ur* 344–51.

Ḫendursanga Hymn

D. O. Edzard and C. Wilcke. "Die Ḫendursanga-Hymne." *AOAT* 25 (1976) 139–76.

Hoe and Plough

Disputation between Hoe and Plough. University Museum manuscript (M. Civil).

Inanna and Bilulu

T. Jacobsen. "The Myth of Inanna and Bilulu." *JNES* 12 (1953) 160–88.

Inanna and Ebiḫ

University Museum Manuscript (B. Eichler).

Inanna and Iddin-Dagan

Iddin-Dagan Hymn A. Riesman, *Two Neo-Sumerian Royal Hymns* 147–211.

Inanna and the Fire-Plant

S. N. Kramer. "Inanna and the *Numun*-Plant: A New Sumerian Myth." In G. Rendsburg et al., eds., *The Bible World: Essays in Honor of Cyrus H. Gordon*, 87–97. New York, 1980.

Inanna's Descent

Inanna's Descent to the Netherworld. Sladek, *Inanna* 100–224.

Inninšagura

Inanna Hymn C. Å. W. Sjöberg. "In-nin šà-gur$_4$-ra: A Hymn to the Goddess Inanna by the en-Priestess Enḫeduanna." *ZA* 65 (1975) 161–253.

Išbi-Erra A

Išbi-Erra Hymn A. *STVC* 62 + *STVC* 63 + Ni 9901 (*ISET* 1 210; for the join see M. Civil, *Or*, n.s. 41 [1972] 87), Ni 4328 (*ISET* 2 60), Ni 4390 (*ISET* 1 150), Ni 9784 (*ISET* 1 187), Ni 9957 (*ISET* 2 55).

Išme-Dagan A

Išme-Dagan Hymn A. *TCL* 15 9 and duplicates. University Museum manuscript (B. Eichler).

Išme-Dagan Z

Išme-Dagan Hymn Z (CBS 2253 and unpublished duplicates). University Museum manuscript (P. Michalowski).

Lahar and Ašnan

Dialog between Ewe and Grain. B. Alster and H. L. J. Vanstiphout. "Lahar and Ashnan: Presentation and Analysis of a Sumerian Disputation." *ASJ* 9 (1987) 1–43.

Letter B 8

Letter of Lugalnisag to a King. Ali, *Sumerian Letters* 92–95, with additional texts: *PRAK* B 88, UM 29-13-20, UM 29-13-24, Ni 9701 (*ISET* 2 114).

Letter B 11

Letter of an Ensi and a Sanga. Ali, *Sumerian Letters* 109–12, with additional texts: Ni 4574 (*ISET* 1 149), Ni 9701 (*ISET* 2 114), Ni 9705 (*ISET* 2 123).

LE

M. W. Green. "The Eridu Lament," *JCS* 30 (1978) 127–67.

LN

Lament over the Destruction of Nippur. Published sources listed by Wilcke, *Kollationen* 54, with additions by H. L. J. Vanstiphout, "Joins in Texts Published and Unpublished," *RA* 72 (1978) 82. University Museum manuscript (H. L. J. Vanstiphout).

LSUr

Lamentation over the Destruction of Sumer and Ur.

LU

Lament over the Destruction of Ur. S. N. Kramer. *Lamentation over the Destruction of Ur*. Chicago, 1940. Subsequently published texts listed by H. Sauren, "Zwei Duplikate zur Urklage des Musée d'Art et d'Histoire in Genf," *JNES* 29 (1970) 42; Wilcke, *Kollationen* 57; and H. L. J. Vanstiphout, *RA* 72 (1978) 81–82. New manuscript by H. L. J. Vanstiphout.

Lugalbanda 1

University Museum manuscript (S. Cohen, revised by M. G. Hall).

Lugalbanda 2

C. Wilcke. *Das Lugalbandaepos*. Wiesbaden, 1969.

Lugale

J. J. A. van Dijk. *LUGAL UD ME-LÁM-bi NIR-ĞÁL: Le récit épique et didactique des Travaux de Ninurta, du Déluge et de la Nouvelle Création*. Leiden, 1983.

LW

M. W. Green. "The Uruk Lament." *JAOS* 104 (1984) 253–79.

Message of Ludingira

Private manuscript based on the texts published in M. Civil, "The 'Message of Lu-dingir-ra to his Mother' and a Group of Akkado-Hittite 'Proverbs,'" *JNES* 23 (1964) 1–11; J. Nougayrol, *Ugaritica* 5 310–19; and M. Çığ and S. N. Kramer, "The Ideal Mother: A Sumerian Portrait," *Belleten* 40 (1976) 413–21.

Nanâ Hymn

E. Reiner. "A Sumero-Akkadian Hymn of Nanâ." *JNES* 33 (1974) 221–36.

Nanna's Journey to Nippur

Ferrara, *Nanna's Journey.*

Nanše Hymn

W. Heimpel. "The Nanshe Hymn." *JCS* 33 (1981) 65–139.

Nisaba Hymn

Nisaba Hymn A. W. W. Hallo. "The Cultic Setting of Sumerian Poetry." In A. Finet, ed., *Actes de la XVIIe Rencontre Assyriologique Internationale: Université Libre de Bruxelles, 30 juin-4 juillet 1969*, 123–33. Ham-Sur-Heure, 1970.

Nungal

Å. W. Sjöberg. "Nungal in the Ekur." *AfO* 24 (1973) 19–46.

Sumerian Lullaby

S. N. Kramer. "u$_5$-a a-ù-a: A Sumerian Lullaby." In *Studi in onore di Eduardo Volterra* 6, 191–205. Rome, 1969. And duplicates (see B. Alster, "On the Sumerian Lullaby," *RA* 65 [1971] 170–71).

Šulgi A

Šulgi Hymn A. Klein, *Three Šulgi Hymns* 167–217.

Šulgi B

Šulgi Hymn B. University Museum manuscript (G. Haayer).

Šulgi D

Šulgi Hymn D. Klein, *Three Šulgi Hymns* 50–123.

Šulgi F

Šulgi Hymn F. *TMHnf* IV 11 and duplicates; see Klein, *Three Šulgi Hymns* 40.

Šuruppak's Instructions

Alster, *Instructions.*

Temple Hymns

Sjöberg, *Temple Hymns* 1–154.

Udug ḫul (OB)

M. J. Geller. *Forerunners to Udug-ḫul: Sumerian Exorcistic Incantations.* Stuttgart, 1985.

Winter and Summer

Dialog between Winter and Summer. University Museum manuscript (M. Civil).

Chapter 1

Introduction

Background

During the twenty-fourth year of the reign of King Ibbi-Sin (2028–2004 B.C.) the city of Ur fell to an army from the east. The extensive empire that had been founded by Ur-Namma approximately one hundred years earlier and that had been brought to its highest point of internal cohesion and external expansion by his son Šulgi had already been tottering for over a generation, and this final act was nothing more than a *coup de grace* that affected only the old capital city and its immediate environs. Yet, in modern history writing and to a certain extent in ancient historiography, this story has acquired symbolic value that far outweighs the historical consequences that can be attached to this "event." In traditional terms, the causes and effects of the fall of Ur are difficult to assess. We have some evidence in contemporary economic documents as well as in the later copies of letters from the chancery of Ibbi-Sin that indicates economic and political instability.[1] It is clear, however, that the rise in prices and the breaking away of most of the provinces of the empire are only symptoms of an institutional crisis that is more difficult to comprehend. There can be little doubt that the root cause of the decline of the Ur III kingdom, a decline that had already begun during the reign of Ibbi-Sin's predecessor, Šu-Sin, must be sought in the very structure of the state and cannot be attributed solely to unpredictable outside forces.[2] But just as we know little about the complex events that preceded the downfall of the Ur III kingdom, we are likewise quite ignorant of the final moments of the capital city of Ur. The end of the dynasty can be established on the basis of the fact that Išbi-Erra, former underling of the last king of Ur and now founder of a new dynasty at Isin, named one of his years in commemoration of his expulsion of an Elamite garrison from the old capital.[3] All our other

[1] The classic statement is by T. Jacobsen, "The Reign of Ibbī-Suen," *JCS* 7 (1953) 36–47; see also W. W. Hallo, "A Sumerian Amphictiony," *JCS* 14 (1960) 88–114, and, most recently, T. Gomi, "On the Critical Economic Situation at Ur Early in the Reign of Ibbisin," *JCS* 36 (1984) 211–42.

[2] P. Steinkeller, "The Administrative and Economic Organization of the Ur III State: The Core and the Periphery," in M. Gibson and R. D. Biggs, eds., *The Organization of Power: Aspects of Bureaucracy in the Ancient Near East* (Chicago, 1987) 19–41.

[3] Išbi-Erra year name "26": mu elam šà uri$_5^{ki}$-ma durun-a ba-dab$_5$ / im-ta-e$_{11}$; the year dates of this king are cited according to the scheme of M. Van De Mieroop, *Sumerian Administrative Documents from the Reigns of Išbi-Erra and Šū-ilišu* [=*BIN* 10] (New Haven, 1987) 2–3.

sources of information are literary. The "Sumerian King List" records the change of hegemony from Ur to Isin,[4] and later omens associate the last king of the Ur III dynasty, Ibbi-Sin, with one concept—turmoil, disaster.[5] Royal hymns of the first king of the successor state at Isin contain some information on the last days of the Ur III dynasty.[6] All these sources agree that the final blow to Ur was dealt by an army from the east, from the lands of Elam and Šimaški. The process that led up to this event is, however, impossible to reconstruct, for the history of the relationships between Ur and Šimaški is not sufficiently documented at present.[7] We only know that lands that had been subservient to Ur were instrumental in the final downfall of the kingdom. The Empire struck back.

Moreover, the relationships between Ur and its eastern neighbors—Elam and Šimaški—are unequally documented. Much of the written information at our disposal comes from the territories under the direct control of the kingdom of Ur and thus, by necessity, the perspective that dominates modern historical accounts of the period is heavily influenced by Sumerian ideological prejudices. Slowly, however, we are learning more about the history of the Iranian highlands in the first half of the second millennium. New texts, as well as new interpretations of previously known data, can now be utilized to determine the outlines of the political history of western Iran during the time that the Third Dynasty of Ur held power in Sumer. The most important component in the new views on these matters is P. Steinkeller's identification of LÚ.SU(.A) as a writing of Šimaški.[8] This identification, combined with the evidence of two newly discovered historical texts, provides us with new information on the interactions of the Šimaškian and Ur III states.

An important role in these affairs was played by the last ruler of the Dynasty of Awan: Puzur-Inšušinak. According to one of his own inscriptions, he received homage from the king of Šimaški and brought under his control a sizable territory that included Susa as well as the highlands to the north.[9] Our view of these events has now acquired new perspective as a result of the discovery, at Isin, of an Old Babylonian copy of an inscription of Ur-Namma that mentions the defeat of Puzur-Inšušinak.[10] Traditionally, the reign of the last ruler of Awan had been dated at least half a century earlier, to the time

[4] On the historiographical reflexes of this fact see my "History as Charter: The Sumerian King List Revisited," *JAOS* 103 (1983) 237–48.

[5] Akkadian *šaḫluqtum, saḫmaštum*; see A. Goetze, "Historical Allusions in Old Babylonian Omen Texts," *JCS* 1 (1947) 262, and Edzard, *Zwischenzeit* 50 n. 227.

[6] See Frayne, *Historical Correlations* 301–63.

[7] The literary sources for some of these interconnections have now been surveyed by S. N. Kramer, "Ancient Sumer and Iran: Gleanings from Sumerian Literature," *Bulletin of the Asia Institute*, n.s. 1 (1987) 9–16.

[8] P. Steinkeller, "On the Identity of the Toponym LÚ.SU(.A)," *JAOS* 108 (1988) 197-202.

[9] Sollberger and Kupper, *Inscriptions Royales* 126 (IIG2e).

[10] Published by C. Wilcke, "Die Inschriftenfunde der 7. und 8. Kampagnen (1983 und 1984)," in B. Hrouda, ed., *Isin-Išān Baḥrīyāt III: Die Ergebnisse der Ausgrabungen 1983-1984* (Munich, 1987) 108–11.

following the reign of Šar-kali-šarri of Akkad (2217–2193 B.C.).[11] Susa was known to be under the control of Ur by the time of Šulgi, but it is possible that the conquest took place earlier during the reign of Ur-Namma.[12] The defeat of Puzur-Inšušinak probably allowed a local dynasty to take control of Šimaški, the dynasty that follows upon the list of Awan kings in the "king list" from Susa.[13] These rulers eventually became clients of Ur in the reign of Šu-Sin (2037–2029 B.C.) and some of their names, hitherto known primarily from Iranian sources, are now attested in Ur III administrative documents.[14] The sixth ruler of Šimaški, Kindattu, was able to renounce any dependence on Ur, together with all the other eastern provinces, early in the reign of Ibbi-Sin. Finally, Elam and Šimaški clashed with their former overlords and Kindattu was able to bring an end to the reign of the Third Dynasty of Ur.[15]

The end of the Ur III kingdom was alluded to and mentioned in Sumerian literature. There is only one ancient composition, however, that purports to deal extensively with this historical moment, and this text is the one that is known by its modern title as the *Lamentation over the Destruction of Sumer and Ur*.[16]

History of Research

Parts of the lament had been published as early as 1914,[17] but the first major contribution to the study of the composition was published in 1950 when A. Falkenstein edited the first fifty-four lines.[18] Although fragments of the text were already available in hand copies of Nippur tablets, it was only with the study of the Ur material that the approximate length and the scope of the whole lament could be established.[19] S. N. Kramer, with the assistance

[11] See, most recently, E. Carter and M. W. Stolper, *Elam: Surveys of Political History and Archaeology* (Berkeley, 1984) 15.

[12] In addition to the Isin text mentioned above, there is evidence of battles with Elam in another recently published inscription of the founder of the Ur III state; see M. Civil, "On Some Texts Mentioning Ur-Namma," *Or*, n.s. 54 (1985) 27–32.

[13] A detailed exposition of the history of Šimaški is found in M. W. Stolper, "On the Dynasty of Šimaški and the Early Sukkalmaḫs," *ZA* 72 (1982) 42–67.

[14] P. Steinkeller, *JAOS* 108 (1988) 201–2.

[15] Some of these events were described in a fragmentary hymn of Išbi-Erra of Isin, published by J. J. A. van Dijk, "Išbiʾerra, Kindattu, l'homme d'Elam et la chute de la ville d'Ur," *JCS* 30 (1978) 189–208. Note that P. Amiet, *L'âge des échanges inter-iraniens 3500–1700 avant J.-C.* (Paris, 1986) 149, ascribes the conquest of Ur to Kindattu's successor, Idadu I.

[16] The Sumerian title was its incipit: u_4 šu-bal aka-dè. The text has been variously referred to as the *Ibbi-Sin Klage* and the *Zweite Urklage*, the latter a reference to the text known as the *Lament over the Destruction of Ur*.

[17] Sources V and U, published in hand copy as texts 2 and 3 in S. Langdon, *Historical and Religious Texts from the Temple Library of Nippur* (*BE* 31; Munich, 1914).

[18] "Die Ibbīsîn-Klage," *WO* 1 (1950) 377–84.

[19] While preparing his copies of the Ur texts C. J. Gadd published "The Second Lamentation for Ur," in D. W. Thomas and W. D. McHardy, eds., *Hebrew and Semitic Studies Presented to Godfrey Rolles Driver* (Oxford, 1963) 59–71. This article

of M. Civil, established a preliminary set of sources.[20] Kramer prepared an unpublished edition of the composition and presented a translation in 1969.[21] Subsequently, D. O. Edzard, in a review in 1970 of a volume of copies from Ur, provided a list of published sources, which was updated by C. Wilcke in 1976.[22] Further new text identifications and joins have been made by M. Civil, H. L. J. Vanstiphout,[23] and me.

City Laments

The very title that modern scholars have appended to the text under study here has determined its interpretation from the outset. Like all other Sumerian literary compositions *LSUr*, as I shall refer to this text for convenience, has no ancient title and was referred to in antiquity by its incipit u_4 šu-bal aka-dè, 'To overturn the (appointed) time.' By designating it as a "lament" we have, automatically, assigned it to a textual genre, and thus have assured certain interpretations that follow from the expectations associated with modern Western notions of generic identity.[24] Generic categorizations, however, are closely linked with reception, and the reading of ancient texts, when no continuous tradition of reading has survived, presents particular problems that are different from those encountered in old texts belonging to a living stream of interpretation. Faced with bare texts, with no ancient meta-discourse about them, we simply read them as if they were strictly referential, or more precisely, as if strictly referential texts were possible. By placing together certain texts we create a close and closed intertextuality, which, in turn, provides us with a false sense of security in reading. *LSUr* serves as a first-class case in point. Because a different text, commonly called the *Lament over the Destruction of Ur* (*LU*), was well known to modern scholarship, and had been well edited forty-five years ago, *LSUr* was at one time designated as the *Second Lament over Ur*.[25] Even though that label was abandoned, the

---

included an edition of U.16900B, which was later published in copy as *UET* 6 131 (text HH of this edition).

[20] See the remarks in *UET* 6/2 1. As Kramer noted there, the Ur texts for the first time allowed scholars to reconstruct one text rather than two separate compositions, as had been previously proposed.

[21] In J. B. Pritchard, ed., *Ancient Near Eastern Texts Relating to the Old Testament* (3d ed.; Princeton, 1969) 611–19.

[22] D. O. Edzard, *AfO* 23 (1970) 92; Wilcke, *Kollationen* 59–60.

[23] H. L. J. Vanstiphout, "Joins in Texts Published and Unpublished," *RA* 72 (1978) 82.

[24] The very word "lamentation" immediately imposes connections that otherwise would not even come to mind, as is best exemplified by the spurious attempts to connect the Sumerian "city laments" with the biblical book of Lamentations; see, conveniently, D. R. Hillers, *Lamentations: A New Translation with Introduction and Commentary* (Garden City, 1972) xxviii-xxx. For an overview of the Sumerian laments see now also S. N. Kramer, "The Weeping Goddess: Sumerian Prototypes of the *Mater Dolorosa*," *BA* 46 (1983) 69–80.

[25] S. N. Kramer, *Lamentation over the Destruction of Ur* (Chicago, 1940). Newer translations were published S. N. Kramer, *ANET*^{3} 455–63, and Jacobsen, *The Harps* 447–74.

almost logical primacy of *LU* has remained. At least four other compositions were likewise designated as city laments: *The Nippur Lament* (*LN*),[26] *The Eridu Lament* (*LE*),[27] *The Uruk Lament* (*LW*),[28] and a fragmentary composition known as the *Ekimar Lament*.[29] The general characteristics of these texts, with reference to the older literature on the subject, have been discussed at length by M. W. Green in her doctoral dissertation on the city of Eridu.[30]

Of all these compositions only three are complete: *LSUr*, *LU*, and *LN*. Thus Assyriology is here doubly hampered by a lack of theoretical reflection on generic taxonomy, as well as by the fact that the putative class of texts includes fragmentary compositions. Moreover, if city laments are to be taken as a class, does that mean that they are part of a larger set of texts that can be designated as laments? In view of the fact that other Sumerian texts have been called laments in the literature, the answer will have to be positive.[31] In a recent article devoted to the problem of genre in Mesopotamian literature, H. L. J. Vanstiphout has argued for the validity of generic criticism as applied to cuneiform literature.[32] In his defense of genre Vanstiphout has drawn on a new tradition that has overturned the general skepticism toward such studies that followed in the wake of Vico's rejection of any such analysis. As an example of historically oriented genre criticism he proposes a possible line of development of the "lament genre." He suggests that *LSUr* was the primary text that served as a model for further developments: historical phases in the life of the form during which changes took place but some sort of generic identity was maintained. The Ur Lament followed, and in turn gave birth to the Eridu and Uruk laments. The Nippur Lament was the last in this series and in turn gave rise to "literary laments."[33]

From the formal point of view the texts that have been grouped together under the label of "city laments" are not homogeneous. Except for the fact that they depict in great detail the fall and destruction of cities and states, as

[26] S. N. Kramer, "Lamentation over the Destruction of Nippur: A Preliminary Report." *Eretz-Israel* 9 (1969) 89–93; H. L. J. Vanstiphout, "Een sumerische Stadklacht uit de oudbabylonische Periode: Turmenuna, of de Nippurklacht," in K. R. Veenhof, ed., *Schrijvend Verleden: Documenten uit het oude nabije Oosten vertaald en Toegelicht* (Leiden, 1983) 330–41. H. L. J. Vanstiphout, who is preparing an edition of this composition, has kindly put his preliminary manuscript at my disposal.

[27] M. W. Green, "The Eridu Lament," *JCS* 30 (1978) 127–67.

[28] M. W. Green, "The Uruk Lament," *JAOS* 104 (1984) 253–79.

[29] *SLTN* 103; see Edzard, *Zwischenzeit* 51.

[30] Green, *Eridu* chap. 9: "Sumerian Lamentations," 277–325.

[31] See, for example, J. Krecher, "Klagelied," *RlA* 6 (1984) 1–6.

[32] H. L. J. Vanstiphout, "Some Thoughts on Genre in Mesopotamian Literature," in K. Hecker and W. Sommerfeld, eds., *Keilschriftliche Literaturen. Ausgewählte Vorträge der XXXII. Rencontre Assyriologique Internationale. Münster, 8.-12.7.1985* (Berlin, 1986) 1–11.

[33] T. Jacobsen, review of *Lamentation over the Destruction of Ur*, by S. N. Kramer, *AJSL* 58 (1941) 222, first proposed, writing of *LU*, that "although not expressly so labeled, the general character of this composition classes it as a balag, a characteristic genre within Sumerian literature specializing in lament for major public disasters." He viewed this composition as a cultic text that was used during the ceremonies that attended the rebuilding of Ur under the Isin kings (p. 223).

well as a decision by the gods to undo the disaster, they have little in common. All the known examples are divided into sections called ***kirugu*** but the number and size of these sections differ in individual compositions, although the fragmentary state of *LE* and *LW* makes it difficult to generalize in this matter. *LSUr* stands out as unique, for it is divided into five (in some versions four) such sections, *LU* has eleven, *LN* twelve, *LE* at least eight, and *LW* at least twelve. Only *LN* and *LW* mention a historical restoration, for they specifically name Išme-Dagan (1953–1935 B.C.), the fourth member of the Isin dynasty, as the ruler responsible for the rebuilding of the city. This is an important fact as these are the only city laments that can be precisely dated. Moreover, these texts do not stand alone but are linked to other compositions that depict, in highly literary style, the destruction and restoration of Sumer during the reign of that king. Most important here is the evidence of *Išme-Dagan A*, a long text that concentrates on the connections between the king and the city of Nippur.[34] There is also a distinct possibility that *LE* was composed as well during the reign of Išme-Dagan, although the time of Nur-Adad can by no means be ruled out.[35] The dating of possibly three of the five extant major city laments provides a new perspective on the generic history proposed by Vanstiphout; it strengthens his chronology and allows one to take a fresh look at *LSUr*, presumably the first text in the series.

To be sure, the temporal ordering of these texts is still hypothetical, but in the absence of a firm chronology one can only speculate and some guesses are better than others. Let us assume that *LSUr* is indeed the first in the series. It is difficult to state when the text was written, but at least we know the specific events that it purports to describe and interpret. There can be little doubt that the composition, whatever its primary cultic or ritualistic use, is to be understood within the broad context of Isin dynasty historiography and legitimization. In view of the fact that I have discussed these matters in detail elsewhere, I shall only outline the main lines of my position here.[36] The dynasty founded by the *homo novus* Išbi-Erra at Isin had little claim to traditional forms of ideological legitimization. Moreover, new historical circumstances required a claim of continuity with the state that had just toppled—the "empire" ruled from Ur. To create the fiction that Išbi-Erra and his followers were the true sovereigns of Sumer and Akkad, his scribes imitated the style of Ur III propaganda and composed literary texts that stressed connections with the successors of Ur-Namma.[37] Already under Išbi-Erra there is evidence for such scribal activity in at least two attempts to link the reign of the new king with the times of the new rulers' old masters. Primary here are two royal

[34] For a discussion of the events of this time see Edzard, *Zwischenzeit* 80–82, 86–90.

[35] See the discussion of M. W. Green, *JCS* 30 (1978) 128–30.

[36] "History as Charter: Some Observations on the Sumerian King List," *JAOS* 103 (1983) 237–48.

[37] See my "Charisma and Control: On Continuity and Change in Early Mesopotamian Bureaucratic Systems," in M. Gibson and R. D. Biggs, eds., *The Organization of Power: Aspects of Bureaucracy in the Ancient Near East* (Chicago, 1987) 55–68.

hymns, Išbi-Erra Hymns A and B.[38] Both are fragmentary and must therefore be used with caution, particularly *Išbi-Erra A*. Even in a bad state of preservation, however, these texts reveal something of the ideological strategies of the early Isin composers. Hymn A constantly utilizes the language of legitimization; all the gods bestow attributes upon the new king, who is the shepherd of the masses.[39] The same text appears to enumerate some military activities against the Gutians,[40] thus echoing the exploits of Utu-hegal, Ur-Namma, and Šulgi, as they were recounted in an inscription of the first, and in the hymns of the latter two kings. Hymn B, which in the preserved sections has much more precise historical detail, is unique, for it is a "hymn" (divided into *kirugus*) that actually mentions at least one historical figure, Kindattu, the ruler of Elam.[41] The text appears to deal with the specific events that place at the fall of took Ur and the enemies that are mentioned in *LSUr*—Elam, Anšan, and Šimaški—all appear there.[42]

From the fragmentary evidence of these hymns one could conclude that Išbi-Erra is portrayed as one who took part in the defense of the homeland against external enemies, and avenged the downfall of Ur, thus becoming the keeper of the tradition and legacy of the dynasty of Ur-Namma. Of course, the Old Babylonian scribes who copied these texts during the time of Rim-Sin and Samsu-iluna also knew of other texts describing the less glorious activities of Išbi-Erra, particularly his blackmail of Ibbi-Sin and his machinations for power over the cities of Isin and Nippur. The royal letters of Ibbi-Sin as well as those of Išbi-Erra himself, reshaped, copied, and recopied in the Old Babylonian scribal schools, kept alive a different picture of these events.[43] The important thing to keep in mind, however, is the fact that during the reign of the first king of the Isin dynasty, there was a concentrated effort to provide a form of *apologia* for the new royal lineage and the new seat of power. *LSUr* undoubtedly played a part in these ideological posturings, and, even if we cannot in any way prove that it was composed at the time of Išbi-Erra, the text was undoubtedly part of the attempt to legitimize the new dynasty. The global structure of the text is specifically organized toward this aim: a long description of destruction and calamity that affected the whole central territory of the state and, finally, the capital city of Ur[44] is followed by a decision of the gods to restore Sumer and to curse the enemies that brought about its

[38] Published sources for the former are enumerated in the abbreviations list. For an edition of the latter see J. J. A. van Dijk, "Išbiʾerra, Kindattu, l'homme d'Elam, et la chute de la ville d'Ur," *JCS* 30 (1978) 189–208. See now also D. R. Frayne, "New Light on the Reign of Išbi-Erra," *Vorträge gehalten auf der 28. Rencontre Assyriologique Internationale in Wien, 6.-10. Juli 1981* (Horn, 1982) 26–32.

[39] See, for example, Ni 4390 (*ISET* 1 150) iii 1′: sipa un šá[r-ra . . .]; and 5′: un lu-a sipa x[. . .].

[40] *STVC* 63 iv 10′–12′: gu-ti-um^{ki} [. . .], ^{d}iš-bi-è[r-ra . . .], elam.⌜ki⌝ [. . .].

[41] Line iii 28′. On Kindattu see M. W. Stolper, *ZA* 72 (1982) 46–48.

[42] Reading iii 29′ as an-ša$_4$-an^{ki}-e LÚ.SU^{ki} sig$_{11}$ ba-ab-gi$_4$ kur im-ma-an-te, collated.

[43] See T. Jacobsen, *JCS* 7 (1953) 36–47; and my "Königsbriefe," *RlA* 6 (1984) 51–59, and idem, *The Royal Correspondence of Ur*, forthcoming.

[44] The geographical *topoi*, which may have already been used in other texts, become almost standardized in the other laments; see C. Wilcke, "Der aktuelle Bezug

downfall. The successor state is never mentioned, but the last king of Ur is announced by name. But while the general structure of the text is clear, its genealogy is not. For where, one may ask, did the poets of Sumer find the inspiration and model for such a complex creation?

The Lamentation over the Destruction of Sumer and Ur and The Curse of Agade

On first glance one is tempted to propose the famous apology of Uruinimgina as a source for *LSUr*.[45] This repetitive text begins with a statement to the effect that the ruler of Umma burned down the Antasura, an important cultic site in the Lagaš state. This is followed by a litany of statements on the burning and plundering of cult places and temples in the Lagaš area, ending with a curse on Lugalzagesi, the king of Umma who was, in Uruinimgina's view, responsible for these acts. In general terms, the outline just given is *LSUr* in a nutshell. Unfortunately, there are great difficulties in connecting texts from the Early Dynastic rulers of Lagaš with the Old Babylonian corpus known to us from Nippur, Ur, and other sites. There can be no doubt, however, that some texts from the earlier time and area were incorporated into the later tradition, the best known examples being *Lugale* and the *Nanše Hymn*. The date when these texts entered the Old Babylonian school curriculum is unknown. However, one scholar has argued that these traditions were brought in by the kings of Larsa,[46] and hence would probably have surfaced too late for the composition of *LSUr*. Moreover, the very purpose and context of the Uruinimgina composition are unknown. Unlike most of the non-administrative Girsu documents the composition does not appear to have been a monumental text; the only surviving manuscript was written on a tablet, and we have no clues concerning its origins or its possible cultic use.

Nonetheless, one cannot dismiss the Uruinimgina text out of hand, for it is possibly but a singular survivor of a more common type of text from the Early Dynastic period. While keeping that in mind, we must, at present, look elsewhere for the "prior text" to *LSUr*. There is only one real candidate for this role: the *Curse of Agade* (*CA*), a poem written sometime during the Ur III period, or perhaps even earlier. Here was a patent historical fiction that shortened the length of the Akkad dynasty, and ascribed horrendous deeds to Naram-Sin. None of these deeds, as far as we know, bear any relationship to the truth, yet they were set down in clay and entered into the scribal curricu-

---

der Sammlung der sumerischen Tempelhymnen und ein Fragment eines Klagesliedes," *ZA* 62 (1972) 35–61.

[45] Ukg. 16: *NFT* 47 = H. Steible, *Die altsumersichen Bau- und Weihinschriften* (Wiesbaden, 1982), 1:333–37; English translation in J. S. Cooper, *Sumerian and Akkadian Royal Inscriptions* (New Haven, 1986), 1:78–79. On this inscription, "which in some respects is a precursor of the later Sumerian lamentations over destroyed cities," see J. S. Cooper, *Reconstructing History from Ancient Inscriptions: The Lagash-Umma Border Conflict* (Malibu, 1983) 16 (with an English translation on p. 52).

[46] W. W. Hallo, "Choice in Sumerian," *JANES* 5 (1973) 171.

lum within one or two generations after the actual demise of the dynasty of Agade.[47] *CA* ends with the fall of the kingdom, as ordained by the gods, and contains a curse on the capital city, which is never to rise again. The author of *LSUr* used much of this structure, but reshaped it for new purposes. The final curse was turned around and directed against the enemies of the state, and, most importantly, the role of the earthly ruler was changed. While in *CA* Naram-Sin was a guilty ruler, one whose own impatience and hubris brought about the calamity that afflicted his kingdom, in *LSUr* Ibbi-Sin was a simple victim of fate. The time for the end of his dynasty had come—it is as simple as that. The seeds of this view are already there in *CA*; the beginning of the end of Akkad is found in the denial of favorable omens to the king and in the unexplained decision by the goddess Inanna to abandon her seat of power in Agade. The switch of accent, from guilty to innocent protagonist, from curse upon the destroyed city to a curse upon those who fulfilled the destiny pronounced by the gods and who took part in the destruction of Sumer, is a fundamental element in the relationship between the two compositions and is the key to the intertextual nature of this type of writing. *LSUr* cannot really be understood without recourse to *CA*, for the relationship between the two is truly dialectical with mutual contradictions bound to similarities.[48] The new order results from a change in perspective but this change can only be grasped against the evidence of the older text.

Seen in this light, it would be difficult to consult *LSUr* as a literal historical source, a text to be mined for information on the fall of the Ur III empire. As a poetic text that creates a portrait primarily oriented toward ideological goals it must be read as a symbolic act. True, Ibbi-Sin was a historical figure and Ur did fall, but the details of the end of the dynasty must be sought in the complex interrelationship of historical, economic, organizational, and propagandistic factors of the Ur III state. It is clear that, ultimately, this history will be written primarily from administrative texts. Because the laments, in general, work within a generic set of symbols of destruction and rebirth, it would be, I believe, a mistake to attempt to read the texts literally and to infer the reasons for the fall of states from such evidence.[49]

[47] The literary memory of Naram-Sin's reign grew quite complex in the Old Babylonian period. "Epic" texts based on royal inscriptions were composed and omens connected with his name were copied, in addition to copies of original inscriptions. See, most recently, J.-J. Glassner, "Narām-Sîn poliorcète: les avatars d'une sentence divinatoire," *RA* 77 (1983) 3–10.

[48] On the level of poetic language note the similarities of diction between *CA* and the laments, as demonstrated by Cooper, *Agade* 20–26. Cooper (p. 20), however, argues against the association of the two texts and states that "the *Curse of Agade*'s willingness to name names, and its treatment of the rise and fall of a of a specific dynasty, approaches the character of the tradition of literary-historical texts. . . ."

[49] It has been proposed recently that the Sumerian city laments depict pestilence and plague and that this was the primary reason for the calamities described in these texts (H. L. J. Vanstiphout, "Was een Pestepidemie de Oorzaak van de Ondergang van het Nieuwsumerische Rijk?" *Phoenix* 20 [1974] 351–70; idem, "The Death of an Era:

The Structure of LSUr

The comparative study of the laments must await the publication of the new editions of *LN* and *LU*. For the present edition I reluctantly offer a general summary of *LSUr*. My reluctance is dictated by an uneasiness about the very act of describing the "contents" and "structure" of a fictive text. One critic remarked that a full description, in the traditional sense, could only be a word-for-word repetition of the original composition, and thus questioned the very act of description.[50] The following summary, therefore, is offered only in order to provide the reader with a guide to the kinds of philological choices that I have made in the preparation of this edition. This is an important matter, for the current state of our understanding of Sumerian morphology, syntax, and poetics is such that one can offer wildly different translations and provide justifications, of a sort, for all of them. The editor must make choices and cannot offer every imaginable lexical interpretation without regard to context. A recent case in point is the edition of the *Curse of Agade* by J. S. Cooper. Some reviewers have provided discussions of alternate translations of individual passages without taking into account the fact that Cooper chose specific solutions on the basis of his overall interpretation of the text.[51] Therefore, what follows is an outline of the structure of the text that is intended as a guide to the translation and makes only limited interpretive claims.

Kirugu 1

The first *kirugu* is poetically the most complex part of the composition. The text begins with an introduction of fifty-five lines that contains only two finite verbal clauses: lines 2 and 55. Scholars have differed on the syntactic analysis of this passage; some have interpreted lines 1–2 as a separate unit,[52] while others have viewed lines 1 and 2–54 as dependent on 55, with line 2 as a parenthetical clause modifying line 1.[53] I shall argue here that the former interpretation is correct.

The whole first section of the text is one large subordinate clause. The difficulties in rendering this complex into English arise partly from the fact that in Sumerian, as is typical for SOV languages, subordinate clauses precede

---

The Great Mortality in the Sumerian City Laments," in B. Alster, ed., *Death in Mesopotamia: Papers Read at the XXVIe Rencontre assyriologique internationale* [Copenhagen, 1980] 83–89). As is apparent from the foregoing discussion, my own skepticism toward such an approach is basically methodological and therefore, while it would be wrong to reject this hypothesis out of hand, the position taken here cannot be reconciled with such an interpretation of the texts.

[50] T. Todorov, "Poétique," in O. Ducrot et al., *Qu'est-ce que le structuralisme* (Paris, 1968) 100.

[51] P. Attinger, "Remarques à propos de la 'Malédiction d'Accad,'" *RA* 78 (1984) 99–121; W. P. Römer, *Or*, n.s. 55 (1986) 459–564.

[52] Thus A. Falkenstein, *WO* 1 (1950) 380, and Green, *Eridu* 290–91.

[53] So, apparently, H. G. Güterbock, *ZA* 42 (1934) 39; S. N. Kramer, *ANET*[3] 611; and Thomsen, *The Sumerian Language* 266–67.

main clauses.[54] Thus, in a language like Sumerian, the sentence "I kissed the man who came to dinner" would have to have the form "The man who came to dinner, I kissed him." Moreover, to date there has been little work done on the understanding of subordination in Sumerian.[55] All of the three general types of subordinate clauses—complements, relative clauses, and adverbial clauses—are represented in the opening section of *LSUr*. For convenience, I quote the following definition:

> We can distinguish three types of subordinate clauses: those which function as noun phrases (called complements), those which function as modifiers of nouns (called relative clauses), and those which function as modifiers of verb phrases or entire propositions (called adverbial clauses).[56]

The first two lines are composed of a complement and a head clause:

1. u$_4$ šu-bal aka-dè giš-ḫur ḫa-lam-e-dè
   To overturn the (appointed) time, to forsake the (preordained) plans,
2. u$_4$-dè mar-ru$_{10}$-gin$_7$ ur-bi ì-gu$_7$-e
   The storms gather to strike like a flood.

This couplet sets up the whole syntactic pattern of the first ***kirugu***, which will contain poetic reflexes of parts of this complex. First of all, line 2 is repeated as the "antiphone" (giš-gi$_4$-gal) of the whole ***kirugu***, that is, the last line of the first section of the poem (line 113).[57] Second, the latter part of line 1 (giš-ḫur ḫa-lam-e-dè) is repeated as the verbal phrase of line 21.[58] And, finally, the first part of the line (šu-bal aka-dè) is used as the final part of line 3, which begins a new syntactic unit. In fact, lines 1 and 3 are structured in a way that is typical of Sumerian poetry:

1. u$_4$ šu-bal aka-dè giš-ḫur ḫa-lam-e-dè
3. me ki-en-gi-ra šu-bal aka-dè

Note that the identity of the first part of line 1 and the end of 3 is balanced by the synonymity of giš-ḫur and me. The major difference is the fact that line 3 introduces the major topic of the section that is to follow: the fate of ki-en-gi, that is, Sumer. More importantly, however, these lines establish the major

[54] See J. H. Greenberg, "Some Universals of Grammar with Particular Reference to the Order of Meaningful Elements," in J. H. Greenberg, ed., *Universals of Language* (Cambridge, 1966) 84.

[55] Certain aspects of the matter, such as relative and temporal adverbial clause formation, have been discussed by G. G. Gragg, "Sumerian and Selected Afro-Asiatic Languages," in P. M. Parenteu et al., eds., *The Chicago Which Hunt: Papers from the Relative Clause Festival* (Chicago, 1972) 153–56, and idem, "A Class of 'When' Clauses in Sumerian," *JNES* 32 (1973) 124–34.

[56] S. A. Thompson and R. E. Longacre, "Adverbial Clauses," in T. Shopen, ed., *Language Typology and Syntactic Description II: Complex Constructions* (Cambridge, 1985) 172.

[57] Note that this line is preceded by three subordinate clauses in lines 109–11.

[58] See Green, *Eridu* 291.

theme of the whole text: the destiny of the city of Ur. The whole ***kirugu*** is, in fact, nothing else but an enumeration of the divine plans and decrees (me and giš-ḫur) that are the objects of these two lines.

Beginning with line 3 the text introduces an unprecedented series of complements and adverbial phrases that are governed by a solitary line: an ^{d}en-líl ^{d}en-ki ^{d}nin-maḫ-bi nam-bi ḫa-ba-an-tar-re-eš, '(The gods) An, Enlil, Enki, and Ninmaḫ decided its fate' (line 55). Thus, the pattern that was briefly introduced in 1 and 2 is now extended over fifty-three lines of poetry. The internal structure of this enormous subordinate construction is quite complex, however. The verbal morphology of Sumerian provides additional poetic devices that are exploited here, for while complements end with verbal forms that are constructed on the pattern R-e-dè, temporal adverbial clauses contain final predicates built on the pattern PREFIXES—R-a-ba, thus providing a form of final rhyme for the section. The first nineteen complements (lines 3–21) lead from the major topic, Sumer and its institutions, to the natural world that is crucial for the maintenance of the state (6–11), from the familial institutions of mankind (12–16) to the institution of kingship (17–21). In line 21 we find a reprise of line 1 (through the repetition of giš-ḫur ḫa-lam-e-dè) and an anticipation of the final line of the complex (through the invocation of the decree of An and Enlil). This leads to a series of adverbial clauses that describe the actions carried out by the major gods of the pantheon, who play out their role in the preparations for the destruction of Ur (22–27). The topic, Sumer, is brought back in line 27, which now contains echoes of both lines 1 and 3:

1. u_4 šu-bal aka-dè giš-ḫur ḫa-lam-e-dè
3. me ki-en-gi-ra šu-bal aka-dè
27. ki-en-gi-ra me-bi ḫa-lam-e-dè giš-ḫur-bi kúr-ru-dè

This synopsis of the whole section that dealt with Sumer provides the opportunity to move from the general to the particular, from the land of Sumer to the center, to the primary topic of the text: the city of Ur. Eventually, the text returns to the topic of Sumer, which now includes Ur as the center. The complements that follow describe the intention to destroy the people and the civilization of the city (28–51), beginning with the most important matter, the divine right to hegemony over Sumer, through the person of the king, the physical surroundings of the city, the norms of civilization, and the fertility of the land. The climax of the whole series is found in the relative clauses in lines 52–54, which are themselves dependent on the main clause in line 55.

Lines 55 and 56 are the center of the *kirugu*, in terms of the architectural and narrative structure. This section of the poem contains exactly 112 lines—we shall not count the rubrics in 112 and 114—so that 55 and 56 are the exact middle of the *kirugu*. Line 55 looks back, dominating the preceding section; line 56 opens the way for the declarative sentences that are to follow. The subordinate structure of the first half has provided a series of linked topics that were introduced by means of different types of subordination. The impersonal, agentless storm that destroys the timeless norms (giš-ḫur and me) as well as the gods in line 55 are the subjects of main clauses. When the gods are introduced in embedded form in lines 22–26, they are the subjects not of complements but of adverbial clauses, which modify the whole sentence of line 55, and hence function as coordinate topics. When the attention of the text is centered properly on Ur in line 52, it is followed by a relative clause, which modifies only the subject of the preceding clause, and thus stresses the new topic. In this manner the primary actors in the drama—the "storm" and the gods—are juxtaposed against three major topics: fate, in the form of the plans and decrees, Sumer as a whole, and finally Ur.

All of this is only the beginning, however. In the lines that follow, the destruction that was predicted in such a complex manner is realized in the form of declarative sentences but in a way that is almost parallel to the previous section. Most of the second half of the *kirugu* repeats, with different words, and with different rhetoric, what was predicted in the first section. The gods carry out their destructive tasks, the kingship of the land and the very person of the king are carried off, and, finally, the storm reaches Ur. As M. W. Green has summarized it:

> The *kirugu* is constructed with a three-part structure, first describing the destruction that was intended (1–55), then narrating the onslaught (56–75), finally describing in retrospect the destruction which did occur. The last two parts follow the same pattern as the first, with a long passage concerning Sumer followed by a brief passage concerning Ur.[59]

Kirugu 2

At the beginning of the second *kirugu* the focus shifts once again away from Ur toward the state as a whole, beginning with the northern part of the core of the empire, in the region of Kish and Kazallu. The basic theme is divine abandonment and destruction: the principal gods leave their dwellings and the goddesses set up a bitter lament.[60] The general movement is from north to south and while there are similarities between each subsection and recurring refrains, the poet has taken great pains to introduce variety in the description of each individual city.[61] Once the destruction reaches the Lagaš region, the overall pattern changes. After the description of the abandonment of Girsu and Urukug, the voice of the narrator steps in line 163 in the form of the rhetorical question: 'On that day the word (of Enlil) was an attacking storm—who could fathom it?' This is the same device that had been used earlier in *kirugu* 1 to switch the primary topic and to interject the voice of the narrator. In answer to this question an agent of divine displeasure, the

[59] Ibid.

[60] On the recurring motif of divine abandonment and the ideological uses of the theme see P. Machinist, "Literature as Politics: The Tukulti-Ninurta Epic and the Bible," *Catholic Biblical Quarterly* 38 (1976) 462–64, with previous literature.

[61] For a discussion of the order of cities in the laments see C. Wilcke, *ZA* 62 (1972) 35–61.

"Elamites," is introduced (line 166). What follows is a return to the enumeration of abandoned cities leading along the major canals from the Lagaš region toward Ur. The pattern stops at Eridu and then appears an embedded minor lament over the destruction of Eridu (lines 221–50). After the long passage concerning Eridu, dangerously close to the capital city, the narrator takes a pause and introduces an interlude concerning the paralyzing effects that the news of the destruction of the land has had in Ur (251–59). The final line of this passage demonstrates how far the narrative has gone, for it contains a contrasting reference to line 52, in which the city of Ur was first introduced in the poem. The difference is striking:

52. uri_5^{ki} am gal ù-na-gub-ba ní-bi-ta nir-gál
The city of Ur is a great charging aurochs, confident in its own strength.

259. uri_5^{ki} am gal ù-na-gub-ba-gin, gú ki-š[è ba-ab-gar]
Ur, like a great charging aurochs, bowed its neck to the ground.

Once again the abandonment of cities resumes. The end of the *kirugu* is not preserved, however, and it is impossible to reconstruct it.

Kirugu 3

The third *kirugu* is broken at the very beginning; by the time the text becomes intelligible it turns out that the destruction has reached Ur. The largest part of the section is devoted to an enumeration of the horrors that have been inflicted on the capital of Sumer. This enumeration provides a structural equivalent of the lists in *kirugus* 1 and 2. As the city and the surrounding regions are abandoned and destroyed, yet another voice is introduced: that of the chief deity of Ur, Nanna. The prayer of Nanna (lines 341–56), addressed to Enlil, contains a brief description of the plight of Ur, followed by a plea for the restitution of the city. The final line (356) is typical of prayers for the absolution of sins and thus provides a generic reference for the plea of the moon god:[62]

me ki-en-gi-ra ba-da-ḫa-lam-e ki-bi ḫa-ra-ab-gi_4-gi_4
May you restore the (divine) decrees of Sumer that have been forgotten!

Notice that this prayer ends with a plea for the restitution of the very elements that began the composition: the divine rights and decrees of Sumer.

Kirugu 4

After a brief interjection of the narrator's voice, in the form of the "antiphone" of the preceding section, the fourth *kirugu* begins with the answer of Enlil (lines 361–70). This speech is the ideological high point of the

[62] Lines ending with ki-bi . . . gi_4 'to make as it once was' are found, most often, in the concluding parts of *dingir-šà-dib-ba* incantations, eršaḫunga prayers, and some letter-prayers; that is, the kind of text described in detail by W. W. Hallo, "Individual Prayer in Sumerian: The Continuity of a Tradition," *JAOS* 88 (1968) 71–89.

whole piece, for it provides the justification for the fall of the Ur III state that the gods decreed at the outset of the poem. This is where the Isin dynasty concept of a succession of dynasties that reigned one after another over Sumer is explained in specific terms, just as it was demonstrated through simple enumeration in a contemporary historiographic composition, *The Sumerian King List*.[63] The gods have made their decision and Ur must fall, for it is time for a new dynasty to take over; no fault is implied, this is simply how things are. Isin's time has come, for (366–70):

> "Ur was indeed given kingship (but) it was not given an eternal reign.
> From time immemorial, since the land was founded, until the population multiplied,
> Who has ever seen a reign of kingship that would take precedence (for ever)?
> The reign of its kingship had been long indeed but had to exhaust itself.
> O my Nanna, do not exert yourself (in vain), leave your city!"[64]

Upon hearing his father's reply Nanna too finally abandons Ur, as does his spouse Ningal and all the Anunna gods. Now the final onslaught on the city comes and it is described in a long, vivid passage (lines 377–448). Once again the moon god prays to his father Enlil (451–56) and asks him to reconsider the deadly verdict. Without hesitation Enlil relents and addresses two favorable pronouncements, one in reply to Nanna (461–69), and another one that must be understood as a legal order that ends the destruction (471–74). Upon hearing this Nanna and Ningal reverse their decision to abandon the city and return to their dwelling places. The decision has been taken to spare Ur, but in narrative terms all is not yet over. The "antiphone" provides the contrasting view, for, as it tells us, there is still mourning in the city (479–81).

Kirugu 5

There is mourning in the city, but it has not been utterly destroyed. The last section of the poem consists of one long discourse addressed by the voice of the narrator against the agent of destruction, the "storm" sent by Enlil and the gods. Part incantation, part blessing, this invocation harks back to the opening lines of the first *kirugu* by enumerating all the positive things that are now to happen in Sumer, and thus invokes the restoration of the plans and decrees that had been altered at the beginning of the text.

[63] I have dealt with this issue in full in my study "History as Charter: The Sumerian King List Revisited," *JAOS* 103 (1983) 237–48.
[64] Lines 366–70.

Chapter 2

Manuscripts

Provenience and Date

LSUr is preserved on forty-seven tablets, all dating from the Old Babylonian period. Thirty-one of the sources originated from Nippur, thirteen from Ur, one from Larsa, and two from unknown sites.[1] The preserved exemplars are roughly contemporary, and it is likely that the majority of these tablets were written sometime during the reigns of Rim-Sin of Larsa and Samsu-iluna of Babylon. Unfortunately, only a handful of these tablets have exact archaeological contexts. Of the Nippur sources only three tablets derive from excavations for which stratigraphic information is available. Texts QQ, RR, and SS were discovered during the 1951–52 season, the first and last in room TA 205, which contained a large number of literary tablets that had been reused as bricks and fill. It is quite probable that these texts come from the time of the rebellion of Rim-Sin II in the South, that is, approximately, the ninth year of Samsu-iluna's reign (c. 1740 B.C.).[2] The same date is the most likely context for text RR, which was found in room 191, floor X, level 1.

Find spots are known for only four of the Ur texts. Sources BB, HH, II, and KK were registered as being found in the Old Babylonian house that Woolley dubbed No. 1 Broad Street. Text EE, which was undoubtedly written by the same scribe who inscribed text BB, must also derive from that address. In fact, according to Woolley, almost two thousand tablets were found there.[3]

> Some hundreds of these were of the regular "school exercise" type, the flat bun-shaped tablets used for fair copies, etc.; there were very many religious texts perhaps used for dictation or for learning by rote, some historical texts, mathematical tablets, multiplication tables, etc. as well as a quantity of business records apparently referring to temple affairs.[4]

[1] Texts A and PP. There is no information on the provenience of these tablets. The one thing that can be stated for certain is that they did not come from Nippur.

[2] See M. Civil, *MSL* 14 8.

[3] The tablet finds from No.1 Broad Street have now been studied extensively by D. Charpin, *Ur* 438–86, who points out that this number was greatly exaggerated by the excavator. Charpin's analysis of the nonliterary texts found in the house indicates that no text was found there dated after Rim-Sin 35 (p. 484).

[4] C. L. Woolley, "Excavations at Ur, 1930–1," *The Antiquaries Journal* 11 (1931) 365–66.

An analysis of the literary texts found in No. 1 Broad Street indicates that the core instructional base of the "school" was represented by the recovered materials. There are occasional discrepancies between the contemporary Ur and Nippur curricula, such as the different redactions of *Enki and Ninḫursag* or of the *Lisina Lament*, but in general outline one can posit that there was a uniformity of schooling, in the South at least, during the middle part of the Old Babylonian period. It is difficult, however, to specify the role that *LSUr* played in the educational process, except to state that it was part of the central curriculum and was copied as part of the daily exercises of schoolboys.

The tablet from Larsa (source TT) was excavated in secondary context in a room in the Ebabbar temple. It was found, together with two other literary texts, both written in Akkadian, in room no. 3 of the temple, together with a large group of administrative texts:

> Sur ce sol plus ancien fut retrouvé, le long du mur nord-ouest, un lot abondant de tablettes du XVIIIe siècle, échelonnées de Rim-Sin à Samsu-iluna.[5]

The administrative tablets that had been abandoned in this room clearly derive from a variety of separate archives. The last dated text (no. 171) bears the year-date of Samsu-iluna year 11. One can only conjecture the circumstances surrounding the collection and abandonment of these disparate texts, but the dating of the last text suggests the broad historical context of this abandonment. The rebellion against Babylonian rule in the South, which took place in the eighth year of Samsu-iluna, was put down within a year and a half or so, and thus in many places texts reappear with dates of the year Si 10 mentioning the Babylonian king.[6] The restoration of Babylonian rule was short-lived, however, for there is no evidence at present suggesting that Samsu-iluna managed to retain his hold on some of the southern cities, including Larsa, after his eleventh year.[7] Nippur, on the other hand, was retained by Babylon for more than a decade.[8] In view of these events, it may be tempting to speculate that the reorganization or, more probably, the cleaning out of archives at the Ebabbar took place during the takeover of Larsa by new rulers after the break with Babylon during the latter part of

[5] Y. Calvet, D. Charpin, S. Cleuziou, J. D. Forest, sous la direction de J.-L. Huot, "Larsa. Rapport préliminaire sur la sixième campagne de fouilles," *Syria* 53 (1976) 18.

[6] See, most recently, M. Stol, *Studies in Old Babylonian History* (Istanbul, 1976) 44–58, and D. Charpin, *Archives familiales et propriété privée en babylonie ancienne: Étude des documents de "Tell Sifr"* (Geneva, 1980) 194–95.

[7] Discussed, on the basis of the Ṣilli-Šamaš archive, by W. F. Leemans, "Tablets from Bad-Tibira and Samsuiluna's Reconquest of the South," *JEOL* V/15 (1957/58) 214–18, and Charpin, *Archives familiales* 194–95.

[8] The last known OB tablet from Nippur dated by a year-name of a king of Babylon is Si 29 (E. C. Stone, "Economic Crisis and Social Upheaval in Old Babylonian Nippur," in L. D. Levine and T. C. Young, Jr., eds., *Mountains and Lowlands: Essays in the Archaeology of Greater Mesopotamia* [Malibu, 1977] 281). The last extant text from nearby Isin is dated Si 28 (AO 11135, published by J. Nougayrol, *RA* 73 [1979] 76; see D. Charpin and J.-M. Durand, *RA* 75 [1981] 27).

Samsu-iluna year 11. There is reason to believe, however, that many of the cities south of Nippur, including Larsa and Ur, were abandoned after Si 11, while at Nippur itself a serious economic and social crisis severely afflicted the city.[9] In light of this, it is quite probable that the pile of Old Babylonian tablets in room E of the Ebabbar was the work of Kassite workmen who were involved in the rebuilding of the temple.[10] It is therefore impossible to establish the date of source TT, except that it was written before Samsu-iluna 12, a fact that could have been predicted on other grounds.

The foregoing discussion has highlighted the difficulties in arriving at a precise dating of those texts of *LSUr* that have known find spots. Moreover, such tablets constitute only a minority of the relevant texts. Nevertheless, on the basis of what we know about the historical realities of the time of Samsu-iluna it is possible to state that all the Larsa and Ur sources must antedate his twelfth year. The excavated tablets from the third postwar season at Nippur may also have to date from just before Si 9 or one or two years later. The remaining Nippur texts, for which no excavation information is available, must, at the latest, have been written before Si 29, when Nippur appears to have been abandoned for three centuries.[11]

If one assumes that school tablets were not kept for a long period of time, then one may posit that the contexts of the excavated Nippur and Larsa texts of *LSUr* were almost contemporary while the Ur texts must be dated one generation earlier. The foregoing discussion, however, highlights the difficulties of establishing more precise dating parameters.

Tablet Types

The majority of the manuscripts of *LSUr* are one-column exercise tablets that contained, when complete, from thirty to sixty or so lines of text. This type of tablet, which in the native Sumerian terminology was designated *im-gíd-da*, appears to have been the standard vehicle for daily student exercises at the intermediate and perhaps higher levels of instruction. Among the Nippur manuscripts there are only four or five tablets that had more than one column per side: texts J, N, V, UU, and probably W. It is not possible to establish the complete form of AA. Thus of the thirty-one Nippur manuscripts twenty-six or twenty-seven are of the *im-gíd-da* type. The multicolumn texts are all broken but the best estimate is that they were all three-column tablets that contained approximately 250–300 lines each in columns of approximately fifty lines. In other words, these tablets represent what may be termed two tablet redactions of the composition.

Among the Ur sources the one-column tablets likewise predominate. The only text that definitely had more than one column is source DD, which

[9] This has been argued in detail by Stone, "Economic Crisis," 267–89.

[10] This is the suggestion of D. Arnaud, *Syria* 53 (1976) 78, who proposes that this happened during the time of Burna-buriaš II (1359–1333 B.C.).

[11] More precisely, after the two year reign of Iluma-ilu at Nippur. See Stone, "Economic Crisis," 281.

contains lines 1 though 69 repeated three times.[12] Most of the one-column tablets probably had sixty lines but at least one, text BB, had seventy-four. The sole Larsa text is a two-column text and the two isolated unprovenienced manuscripts are *im-gíd-das*.

It is difficult to draw any conclusions from the distribution of tablet types of this composition. The main reason for this is the fact that comparison with other contemporary literary compositions is impeded by a lack of proper descriptions of the physical characteristics of sources in many contemporary text editions. Without, therefore, a thorough reexamination of all texts in museums, it is not possible to establish a taxonomy of tablet types and literary exercises for the majority of Old Babylonian school texts.[13]

Redactional Questions

It is impossible to speak properly of redactions of a text that does not exist in a single complete manuscript. This, and related problems, have been discussed above. Here, I shall only be concerned with apparent differences between texts.

One major difference between two sources is found in a passage that follows after line 80. Two texts PP (of unknown provenience) and TT (from Larsa) contain two lines, designated in the edition as 80α and 80β. Two tablets omit these lines: A (of unknown origins) and RR (from Nippur). If one were to posit, for the sake of the argument, that there were two redactions of this passage, Larsan and Nippurean, then one would have to conclude that the unprovenienced texts were split in their loyalties, one following Nippur and the other Larsa. A study of other variants, however, indicates that it is impossible to group PP with TT and A with RR on this basis. Here, as in other instances, we again witness the independent nature of individual variations.

The principal redactional differences that can be traced in this composition are between the texts from Ur and Nippur. As a rule, the main difference is the existence of lines in the Ur texts that are not present in the Nippur material. In this edition, such lines have been designated as a, b, c, and d lines. This difference is, indeed, quite consistent. With one notable exception, which will be discussed separately below, all such additional Ur lines are present in all manuscripts from that site, and absent from any Nippur texts whenever there is more than one source for a given line from each site. There are also lines that are extant in Nippur texts but are not attested in the Ur exemplars.[14] This type of variation is of a different order.

The first lines omitted in the Ur texts are lines 10 and 11, which are absent in source DD and are present in BB and CC, both also from Ur. Line 26 is

[12] This text may have omitted line 26.

[13] The situation is slowly being remedied. The round tablets have now been studied by R. F. Falkowitz, "Round Old Babylonian School Tablets from Nippur," *AfO* 29/30 (1983/84) 18–45.

[14] I exclude from this discussion the occasional omission or difference in line order of repeated formulas.

omitted in BB but is written in DD. The opposite situation is found in line 45, which is present in BB but not in DD. Text KK omits lines 454–56 and 459, but in their places contains blank lines, indicating that the scribe was aware of the fact that these lines existed, while another Ur witness, JJ, simply omits 452–55 and 457, without blank lines. The technique of leaving blank lines to indicate missing portions is not limited to Ur, however, for the Nippur tablet I uses the same method for lines 173–81. KK also omits the passage between lines 478–82, including the formula for noting the end of the fourth *kirugu* as well as the appropriate *gišgigal*. The same omission, however, is also found in a Nippur text: source O.[15] Otherwise, the Ur texts do not differ substantially from the Nippur ones, adhering more to the patterns found in texts such as *LU* or *CA*, which show little variation, as opposed to texts such as *Enki and Ninḫursag* (*UET* 6, 1) or *LE*, which are quite different from the extant Nippur versions.[16] For convenience, I provide here a list of all omitted and blank lines. The texts marked by an asterisk are from Ur, the rest come from Nippur.

10	DD*	190	EE*
11	DD*	339	HH*
26	BB*	349	HH*
45	DD*	379	E
67	RR	448	JJ*
126	N, LL*	452–55, 477	JJ*
142	N, V	461	JJ*
145	N, V	478–82	O, KK*
154	N, EE*		

An attempt to study the variation in spelling and the use of verbal affixes failed to reveal any significant pattern that would allow for the reconstruction of manuscript families. Among the Nippur tablets, only three, QQ, RR, and SS, come from modern excavations during which specific find spots were recorded. Two of these tablets were found at the same locus, TA 205 XI-1, but they do not overlap so it is impossible to analyze the presence or absence of variation within one "school." Likewise, of the texts found at Ur, only four have known provenience, for they were registered as coming from No. 1 Broad Street. Unfortunately, for our purposes, none of them cover the same lines of the text. It is impossible to establish where the rest of the Ur tablets of *LSUr* were found but it is possible that many of the unprovenienced texts were also excavated at No. 1 Broad Street. In those sections of the composition where Ur texts overlap, however, there is a noticeable degree of variation in spelling as well as in choice of words.

15 This Nippur tablet also does not have the preceding line (477a).

16 On the whole there is a good deal of uniformity between Ur and Nippur exemplars of the major school exercises. Texts that show major discrepancies, such as *Enki and Ninḫursag* or *LE*, are not well attested at either site.

The Present Edition

The present edition contains a reconstruction of an idealized text together with a "score," or *Partitur*, of the individual manuscripts, arranged in such a way that the reader can reconstruct the exact wording of each individual witness. There are obvious drawbacks to this type of edition, but at the present time there is no other practical way of presenting a text such as *LSUr*. With some modifications I have followed here the example of J. S. Cooper's recent edition of *CA*. Practical reasons may account for the way in which one edits a text but the result inevitably does violence to an ancient composition and therefore, even if we must perform such acts, some words of justification are in order. This is particularly important since there has been very little attention paid in the literature of Sumerology to the problem of textual editing.[17] Other fields with similar problematics such as Classics, Medieval, and Biblical Studies, have dedicated much time and effort to the discussion of questions of textual editing and reconstruction and it is undoubtedly high time that our own field should begin to reflect more critically on such issues. The following observations are in no way intended to fulfill that need, but are only intended to outline some of the general problems within the context of the present edition.

Textual criticism is, of course, as old as written literature itself. Although modern textbooks on the subject invariably hark back to the collectors of the Alexandria library in the search for first examples, the scribes of Mesopotamia were involved in such endeavors at a much earlier period. As with so much of ancient Near Eastern scribal activity, however, we are at a loss here for there is not a trace of their own attitudes toward the matter in the texts; only the results of their labor have been preserved. The theories that concerned many later editors are similarly undocumented, and it is only in the last two centuries that theoretical discussion as well as practical editing have been discussed in earnest.[18] For a long time the role of the editor was understood as an effort to reconstruct an authoritative text that would be as close as possible a reconstruction of the author's intentions. The techniques for such reconstruction were first outlined by Lachmann and have been modified by various authors since then. This method, which is concerned with tracing common errors through individual manuscripts and manuscript traditions, was well established in various fields of philology and has been followed, to a certain extent, by

[17] For a brief discussion see D. O. Edzard, "Zur sumerischen Hymne auf das Heiligtum Keš," *Or*, n.s. 43 (1974) 103–13, especially 105–6, M. Powell, "Ukubi to Mother . . . The Situation is Desperate: A Plaidoyer for Methodological Rigor in Editing and Interpreting Sumerian Texts with an Excursus on the Verb taka: da_x-da_x (TAG_4)," *ZA* 68 (1978) 163–95; and H. L. J. Vanstiphout, "Towards a Reading of 'Gilgamesh and Agga,'" *Aula Orientalis* 5 (1987) 129–41.

[18] For an excellent overview see G. Pasquali, *Storia della tradizione e critica del testo* (Florence, 1934). An important recent contribution to the debate is J. J. McGann, *A Critique of Modern Textual Criticism* (Chicago, 1983).

some Assyriologists.[19] The first to attempt to trace manuscript genealogies of a Mesopotamian composition was T. Jacobsen, who in his 1939 edition of the *Sumerian King List* attempted to trace back all the extant manuscripts to a single source.[20] Similar questions were, for the most part, ignored by Assyriologists for thirty years until W. W. Hallo and J. J. A. van Dijk attempted to trace manuscript traditions in their discussion of the Sumerian Inanna hymn nin-me-šár-ra.[21] These authors were working with a much more complicated text with many more exemplars and their provisional conclusions were much more limited: they proposed to trace back three original manuscript families with the interesting conclusion that "the family distribution seems independent of the provenience of the manuscripts, for exemplars from both Ur and Nippur figure equally in all three families."[22] The goal of achieving even a hypothetical reconstruction of a common source manuscript becomes ever more elusive as the number of manuscripts increases and the history of transmission is extended, as can best be seen on the evidence of the recent edition of *Lugale*.[23]

The Lachmannian tradition was not without critics, however, and early in this century the principal alternatives to this type of editing were found in the work of J. Bédier. Briefly stated, Bédier proposed that, in the absence of an original authorial manuscript, the editor should not follow a hypothetical reconstructed text, but rather should rely on the best extant copy. As a result, "since the best manuscript is presumed to be the most faithful to the author, Bédierist editions have gradually led to the identification of the work with the basic manuscript, often to the detriment of the author's interests."[24] Further refinements and reactions against both the Lachmannian and Bédierist traditions resulted in various proposals, including positions that advocated the separate treatment of all extant manuscripts.[25] It is interesting to note, however, that although such debates were taking place in a variety of philological fields, there has been relatively little contact between scholars in separate disciplines, who have often had to face similar problems, yet have often remained ignorant of each others work.[26]

[19] The classic statement of these principles was outlined by the classicist P. Maas, *Textual Criticism* (trans. B. Flowers; Oxford, 1958).

[20] T. Jacobsen, *Sumerian King List* (Chicago, 1939) 13.

[21] Hallo and van Dijk, *Exaltation* 39–43. On the difficulties of working with large numbers of nearly contemporary copies of OB Sumerian texts see J. S. Cooper, "Gilgamesh and Agga: A Review Article," *JCS* 33 (1981) 230–31.

[22] Hallo and van Dijk, *Exaltation* 42.

[23] See the discussion of the manuscript tradition of this text by J. J. A. van Dijk, *LUGAL UD ME-LÁM-bi NIR-G̃ÁL: Le récit épique et didactique des Travaux de Ninurta, du Déluge et de la Nouvelle Création* II (Leiden, 1983) 1–9.

[24] M. B. Speer, "Wrestling with Change: Old French Textual Criticism and *Mouvance*," *Olifant* 7 (1980) 314.

[25] For a convenient summary of these works see A. Foulet and M. B. Speer, *On Editing Old French Texts* (Lawrence, 1980), and M. B. Speer, "Textual Criticism Redivivus," *L'Espirit Créateur* 23 (1983) 38–48.

[26] G. T. Tanselle, "Classical, Biblical, and Medieval Textual Criticism and Modern Editing," *Studies in Bibliography* 36 (1983) 21–68.

The problems that beset the editor of a text are practical as well as theoretical. On the simplest level one must simply decide how to present the variations in differing manuscripts, so that the edition can be published in an accessible manner. How to do this, however, is a matter that involves not only practical matters such as the layout and presentation of variant readings but invokes, at the deepest levels, the very problem of the nature of textuality. How one views a manuscript tradition depends very much on how one approaches text as text, and on how one interprets the nature of textual transmission in a given society. Even after the invention of printing, which brought about immense changes in textual presentation, matters of textual editing persisted. For even when a relatively modern text is preserved in multiple editions and even when corrected author's proofs are extant, it is not at all an easy matter to reconstruct "authorial intentions." How these putative "intentions" are defined is a debatable question and one that brings philosophy and literary theory into the debate.[27]

Any attempt to reconstruct an original manuscript, or to proceed in such a manner as to recreate a text that is as close as possible to an "authoritative" text, must rest on the assumption that a more or less continuous scribal transmission is responsible for the existence of errors and misreadings that can be traced back through the sources. This holds true primarily for a written, scribal culture in which texts were copied and recopied through the years. In recent years, however, there has been some discussion on the nature of textual transmission and of the role that oral tradition plays in societies that have acquired writing. The dichotomy of oral and written cultures is no longer as distinct as it used to be, and this, in turn, has called for a reexamination of the role that oral transmission played in the preservation of texts that were originally composed in writing. Moreover, the breakdown of the clear dichotomy between fluid oral texts and fixed written ones was instrumental in the reexamination of the very nature of written composition. Perhaps nowhere has this been as important as in the study of medieval French texts, where the interest in such matters led to a new conceptualization of the life history of texts and to the notion of *mouvance*. This term, originally coined by P. Zumthor, has been discussed and redefined by Zumthor and others.[28] For Zumthor, a medieval composition was a fluid, ever changing creation, without authorial authority, realized anew by performers and copyists. In the index to his book, Zumthor offered the following definition of his neologism:

> mouvance: "le caractère de l'oeuvre qui, comme telle, avant l'âge du livre, ressort d'une quasi-abstraction, les textes concrets qui la réalisent présentant, par le jeu

[27] See M. Foucault, "What is an Author?" in J. V. Harari, ed., *Textual Strategies: Perspectives in Post-Structuralist Criticism* (Ithaca, 1979) 141–60.

[28] P. Zumthor, *Essai de poétique médiévale* (Paris, 1972) 65–75. As noted by M. B. Speer, "Wrestling with Change: Old French Textual Criticism and *Mouvance*," *Olifant* 7 (1980) 317, the concept, and a similar term, had already been discussed by J. Rychner, *Contribution à l'étude des fabliaux: variantes, remaniements, dégradations* (Neuchâtel, 1960), 1:131. See also P. Zumthor, "Intertextualité et mouvance," *Littérature* 41 (1981) 8–16, and idem, *Speaking of the Middle Ages* (Lincoln, 1986) 61.

> des variantes et remaniements, comme une incessante vibration et une instabilité fondamentale."[29]

The concept of *oeuvre* is reminiscent here of Chomsky's deep structure, and one must keep in mind that we are dealing here with a book published in 1972. The realizations of this *oeuvre* are the individual texts and none of them takes precedence over another, as they are all recreations of the quasi-abstract, underlying *oeuvre*. I do not wish to argue that we must accept this concept of *mouvance* and adapt it without modification for the study of Mesopotamian literary texts. Nevertheless, I do think that this conceptualization of medieval writing has much to offer to Assyriology. The fluid, largely anonymous, titleless literary creativity of early Mesopotamia has many analogies with the literature of medieval Europe. To be sure, there are enormous differences in the practice and perception of literacy, as well as in the uses to which this art was put, but there are also similarities. One important consequence of such an attitude toward textuality, however, and one that is directly pertinent to the present discussion, is the necessary abandonment of any attempt to privilege any particular manuscript. This undoubtedly creates problems for the textual editor and one must search for ways of presenting a text that do not violate the spirit of this position.

The issues discussed above have a direct bearing on the process of textual editing and raise specific problems that are of prime importance for the present edition of *LSUr*. To recapitulate: the manuscripts come from disparate sources, are imprecisely dated, and most probably represent the work of at least two generations of students. Moreover, there is not a single extant text from any site that covered more than a fraction of the composition. This, combined with the theoretical issues raised above, makes it difficult for the editor to proceed with the task of textual reconstruction.

The problems encountered in editing *LSUr* are by no means unique. Most longer Old Babylonian Sumerian literary texts have similar problems: the roughly contemporary sources come primarily from Nippur, with a smaller number of manuscripts from Ur and a sprinkling of tablets from other, often undocumented sites. There is uneven coverage of the text as some sections are documented by multiple sources while in some parts one has only two or even one manuscript to use. The editor therefore has no choice: one must reconstruct the poem from disparate, often contradictory sources. Moreover, he or she must face the fact that there are no established criteria that would allow one to choose one variant over another, or even one witness over another one. Simply speaking, one chooses variants on the basis of one's concepts of the "proper" grammar and orthography of Old Babylonian Sumerian.

The result, therefore, must be an eclectic text and there is really no alternative, no matter what theoretical stance one assumes. I have therefore taken the traditional Assyriological attitude; I have decided to provide the reader with a composite text that can be translated into English, and I have appended a "score" of all the surviving sources, thereby providing the simplest

[29] *Essai de poétique médiévale*, 507.

possible presentation of each individual witness. Anyone who would like to reconstruct the text differently has all the evidence for such an operation, complete with the results of collations of the original tablets. The resulting composite text, however, is an ideal reconstruction that makes no pretense at any recreation of a putative archetype. It does not represent an imaginary *Urtext*, for there is no guarantee that such a text ever existed, nor does it reconstruct a putative underlying deeper structure. Rather it is an intellectual construct, a compromise that is presented only for practical reasons. The result is a text that may be quoted with an agreed line numbering but one can be quite certain that a text such as the one presented here never existed.

The Reconstruction of the Composite Text

The line numbering of this edition differs slightly from that of the published translation of S. N. Kramer and from the numbering of an earlier manuscript by the author that was cited in volume B of the *Pennsylvania Sumerian Dictionary*. The numbering offered here is not final, and may require further changes as new manuscripts are discovered that provide better documentation for badly preserved passages.[30] All the lines have been assigned numbers, although ancient scribes never counted section rubrics such as *kirugu* or *gišgigal* as separate lines. The reasons for providing such line numbers was twofold: first, the current practice is to count all lines and, second, it is difficult to refer to such divisions unless they have been marked in a specific manner.

The changes in the ordering of lines resulted primarily from joins and collations of the original tablets. The most serious was the estimation of the number of missing lines in two lacunas. The first one, at the beginning of *kirugu* 2, was reconstructed on the basis of N. The only other manuscript at this point, text A, ends with the first line of the section, line 115. N, a multicolumn tablet, has the remains of three more lines and then breaks off, to resume again in what is now line 124. At this point it overlaps with F, which has one line before it. On the basis of the examination of N, I have estimated that three lines are broken, 119, 120, and 121.[31] This means that between the description of the abandonment of Kiš and that of nearby Kazallu, there was probably a short section about another city, possibly Apiak or GÍR.KAL^{ki}.[32] A

[30] For practical purposes, the reconstruction, as well as the line numbering, follow the Nippur sources. Additional lines from Ur are provided with a, b, and c extensions; lines from texts from other sites have extensions from the Greek alphabet. The principles used in choosing variants are, in essence, those outlined in Cooper, *Agade* 47–48.

[31] It is equally possible that one should only look for two missing lines here.

[32] Note the order of cities in the so-called Ur-Namma Code: Akšak, Marad, GÍR.KAL, Kazallu (see my "Mental Maps and Ideology: Reflections on Subartu," in H. Weiss, ed., *The Origins of Cities in Dry-Farming Syria and Mesopotamia in the Third Millennium* B.C. [Guilford, 1986] 141 n. 22). It is also possible that the missing lines contained a long description of the events at Kazallu and that no other city was mentioned at this point.

problem is created, however, by the evidence of a fragmentary Ur text, source LL. The copy of this text is to appear in *UET* 6/3 and therefore, for the convenience of the reader, the text is transliterated here in full (LL = *UET* 6/3 *21 + *22):

1′. [. . .] x [. . .]
2′. [. . . k]i ur-s[ag . . .]
3′. [. . . á]g-gá-ni gir[i$_3$ . .]
4′. [. . .].ki-mu im-⌜me⌝ a [. . .]
5′. [. . .].ki ní-ba lu-a šu [. . .]
6′. [. . .] ⌜ki⌝-tuš ki-ág-gá-⌜ni⌝ [. . .]
7′. [. . .] ^{d}⌜nam⌝-⟨ra⟩-at munus sa$_6$-g[a . . .]
8′. [. . . s]u$_{13}$-ga i-im-gál ⌜a⌝ [. . .]
9′. [. . . k]i-ke$_4$ nam ba-an-k[u$_5$ . . .]
10′. [. . .] nu-un-gál [. . .]
11′. [. . . -g]in$_7$ ba-ḫur-ḫur [. . .]

Lines 5′–11′ of this fragment are equivalent to 123–30 of the composite text that includes, on the basis of the calculation described above, a short lacuna before these lines. One would have hoped, therefore, that lines 1′–3′ of the Ur tablet would provide clues to the proper identification of the city that was described between Kiš and Kazallu. This is unlikely, however. One suspects that the scribe who wrote this tablet did not get things completely right and that lines 1′–3′ are in fact improperly placed. The reconstruction of these lines is dependent on the restoration of 2′. One interpretation is to see ur-sag as a dictation error for ḫur-sag and to view 2′–3′ as a badly written version of lines 115–16, with omission of the next passage. There is a more probable scenario, however. These lines may in fact be a remnant of the misplaced lines, that read:

159. gír-su^{ki} uru^{ki} ur-sag-gá-e-ne-ke$_4$ im-gír-e ba-ab-dug$_4$
160. ^{d}nin-gír-su-ke$_4$ é-ninnu-ta giri$_3$ kúr ba-ra-an-dab$_5$

The reason for this confusion is not difficult to ascertain: it is caused by the fact that the goddess Bau occurs in *LSUr* as both spouse of Zababa of Kiš and of Ningirsu of Girsu.

The second major lacuna is found between lines 284 and 288. There was no indication of the length of this lacuna until five tablets were joined to create text X. Although the tablet is still not complete, the reconstructed piece has a summary on the left edge, indicating that the complete piece contained eighty-five lines. On the basis of this reconstituted source, text GG was placed correctly, and the gap between 284 and 288 was properly reconstructed.

The examination of the originals greatly helped in the proper analysis of badly documented passages, particularly in the case of lined tablets that had been copied without indication of the lines. This was particularly important for the numbering of lines following 90, which are primarily attested through source N. The copyist had not indicated where the line rulings were and thus indented lines appeared to be separate units. Finally, there is a possibility that the preserved manuscripts have omitted a line after 219, a matter discussed in the commentary to line 220. The collations resulted in new readings and in the confirmation of doubtful passages. Nevertheless, this is only a preliminary edition of *LSUr*, and the transliterations and translations contained in the following pages will doubtless eventually be superseded as a result of the labors of other Sumerologists and the discovery of new manuscripts.

The Score of LSUr

In the "score," or tabulation of the contents of individual manuscripts, a dash (-) represents a sign identical with the one in the composite text and an asterisk (*) is used when a particular sign is not present. A slash (/) represents an indented line. Since all but one of the individual manuscripts were collated, it would have been impractical to indicate each and every case in which a reading was corrected for that would have resulted in an unreadable conglomeration of symbols. Thus, whenever the score is different from a published hand copy, it is different as a result of personal inspection of the original. The composite text does not contain half brackets that symbolize a partially preserved grapheme; this convention is reserved for the score only. One should note here that this is the most subjective element in the transcription of the text from three-dimensional inscribed signs to two-dimensional transliteration, and repeated collations of the same tablet often result in a different use of this symbolism. One further difficulty encountered in reinvestigating tablets that were originally copied some time ago is the deterioration of certain originals. Thus, unless otherwise indicated, signs that were attested in hand copies but are no longer extant on the original are still transliterated in the score. Finally, a note should be added on the translation. The English version offered here is a conservative rendering and I have not attempted to give approximate partial translations of certain lines that I do not understand.

Chapter 3

Sources

Unless otherwise noted all texts are from Nippur, with the exception of BB–NN, which are from Ur. All texts were collated on originals with the exception of M and TT (the latter was read from a photograph). Many of the published texts have deteriorated since they were first copied and therefore collations could not in every case confirm the accuracy of the original publication. The asterisked numbers from Ur are the preliminary numbers from the forthcoming *UET* 6/3, which will contain copies by A. Shaffer.

Source	*Museum Numbers and Publication*	*Description*	*Lines*
A	Ash. 1926,396 (*OECT* 5 11) (pl. 1)	One-column tablet. Damaged at bottom. Provenience unknown.	65–88, 100–115
B	CBS 2154 (*PBS* 10/4 6) (pl. 2)	One-column tablet. Damaged at top. Possibly by same scribe as C.	160–210
C	CBS 2222 (*PBS* 5 20) + CBS 2279 (*STVC* 31) (both pl. 3)	One-column tablet. Damaged on right bottom half and left top third.	210–65
D	CBS 2307 + CBS 9204 (*SEM* 96) + CBS 9878 (*SEM* 95) + N 2430 (all fig. 1 and pl. 4)	One-column tablet. Slightly damaged on right top.	483–519
E	CBS 2359 (*PBS* 10/2 19) (pl. 5)	One-column tablet. Damaged on right top and bottom. Original has deteriorated since first copy.	371–400, 402–28
F	CBS 4577 (*PBS* 10/2 4) (pl. 6)	One-column tablet.	123–55

Source	*Museum Numbers and Publication*	*Description*	*Lines*
G	CBS 4593 (*STVC* 25) (pl. 7)	One-column tablet. Bottom left half. May be part of the same tablet as S (N 3626). Left edge: 80.	347–87
H	CBS 8324 (*STVC* 27) (pl. 7)	One-column tablet. Right top corner. Complete tablet contained lines 1–60.	1–13, 49–60
I	CBS 9245 (fig. 2) + CBS 13112 (*STVC* 28) (both pl. 8)	One-column tablet. The second number in the join has deteriorated since it was copied by E. Chiera and therefore only the new piece is presented in copy here. Nine lines blank on obverse (= 173–81).	168–205
J	CBS 10342 (*STVC* 29) (pl. 9)	Upper left part of three-column tablet. Many signs now missing. Summary at bottom of rev. i: 49.	52, 97–104, 182, 185–91, 242–43
K	CBS 12671 (*STVC* 26) (pl. 9)	One-column tablet. Lower left corner.	340–57
L	CBS 15178 (*PBS* 5 21) + CBS 15305 (both pl. 10)	One-column tablet. Central fragment. Original has deteriorated since first copy.	246–61, 271–82
M	HS 1523 (*TMH* 4 28) + HS 1525 (*TMH* 4 26) + HS 2508 + HS 2551 (new copy by J. Oelsner in Wilcke, *Kollationen* 62–63)	One-column tablet. Top half, damaged on top left and bottom right.	430–70

Source	*Museum Numbers and Publication*	*Description*	*Lines*
N	N 1735 + N 1764 + N 1783 + N 6287 (all fig. 3, copy by S. N. Kramer and P. Michalowski; all pls. 11, 12) + Ni. 4414 (*ISET* I, 153)	Three-column tablet. Left upper corner missing, broken on top and bottom.	28–37, 60–77, 90–97, 99–118, 124–27, 136–48, 152–59, 178–99, 231–34, 236–47
O	N 1778 + N 1781 (both fig. 4, copy by S. N. Kramer; both pls. 13, 14)	One-column tablet. Top half. Omits lines (the end of the fourth *kirugu* and the beginning of the fifth). Summary on left edge: 103. Obverse badly worn.	406–30, 468–72, 476–93
P	N 2624 + N 3084 (both fig. 5 and pl. 14)	One-column tablet. Small top central piece, obverse only.	493–500
Q	N 3123 (fig. 6 and pl. 14)	One-column tablet. Top central fragment, obverse only. Possibly part of the same tablet as Z.	51–60
R	N 3253 (fig. 7 and pl. 15)	One-column tablet. Lower right fragment.	366–75
S	N 3626 (fig. 8, copy by S. N. Kramer; pl. 15)	One-column tablet. Top left corner. Obverse only, remnant of the final line of the reverse. May be part of the same tablet as G (CBS 4593).	327–32
T	N 6722 (fig. 9 and pl. 15)	One-column tablet(?). Fragment of left bottom edge of reverse(?).	419–29
U	Ni. 350 (*BE* 31 3)	One-column tablet. Damaged at bottom. Complete tablet contained lines 1–51.	1–26, 32–51

Source	Museum Numbers and Publication	Description	Lines
V	Ni. 1578 (*BE* 31 2)	Three-column tablet. Part of right part of reverse. Three lines on right edge of obverse not in S. Langdon's copy.	99–102, 138–50, 192–98
W	Ni. 2281 (*SLTN* 100)	Probably a multi-column tablet. Central fragment, obverse only.	182–91
X	Ni. 2519 (*SRT* 51) (+) Ni. 4079 (*ISET* 2 5) (+) Ni. 4277 (*ISET* 1 143) (+) Ni. 4279 (*ISET* 1 143) + Ni. 9951 (*ISET* 2 61)	One-column tablet. Damaged on top right corner and bottom right side. Summary on left edge: 85.	239–46, 248–80, 292–327
Y	Ni. 4203 (*ISET* 1 137) + Ni. 9637 (*ISET* 1 176) + Ni. 9461 (*ISET* 1 228)	One-column tablet.	300–316, 327–41
Z	Ni. 4281 (*ISET* 1 143)	One-column tablet. Bottom right fragment, obverse(?) only. Possibly part of the same tablet as P.	508–11
AA	Ni. 9944 (*ISET* 1 204)	Small fragment of edge of obverse(?) of a multi-column(?) tablet. Edge includes an extra line that I cannot place. Reverse(?) contains traces of four unidentified lines.	209–19
BB	U 16900E (*UET* 6 124)	One-column tablet. From No. 1 Broad St. Complete tablet contained lines 1–75 (except 26). Has ten-marks. The tablet has deteriorated since the original copy was made.	1–75

Source	Museum Numbers and Publication	Description	Lines
CC	*UET* 6 125	One-column tablet. Top central fragment. Colophon: 60, [im-gí]d-da 1-kam-ma. Complete tablet contained lines 1–61, omitting one line (possibly 26).	1–12, 58–61
DD	*UET* 6 126 + *UET* 6 127 (+) *UET* 6 *24 + *UET* 6 *139 + *UET* 6 *242 + *UET* 6 *434 (pl. 16)	Two-column tablet. Central part broken. Repeats beginning of text three times. Complete tablet contained lines 1–69, 1–69, and 1–9+.	DD: 1–16, 20–27, 35–49 DDa: 19–46, 66–69 DDb: 1–9
EE	*UET* 6 128	One-column tablet. Slightly broken on top and bottom left. Has ten-marks.	146–221
FF	*UET* 6 129	One-column tablet. Broken on top right and bottom left and right, obverse. Reverse almost completely destroyed except for a few isolated signs and a final line half an inch from the bottom.	221–48
GG	*UET* 6 130 + *UET* 6 *157	One-column tablet. Central lower fragment. Tablet larger than other Ur one-column exemplars.	289–325
HH	U 16900B (*UET* 6 131)	One-column tablet. From No. 1 Broad St. Catchline, colophon: 1 šu-si, im-gíd-da *dam-qí-ì-lí-šu*, iti ab-è u_4 12-kam. Has ten-marks.	296–360

Source	*Museum Numbers and Publication*	*Description*	*Lines*
II	U 16900H (*UET* 6 132)	One-column tablet. Slightly damaged on top left of obverse. From No. 1 Broad St. Colophon: 1 šu-si 6?. Has ten-marks.	360–418
JJ	*UET* 6 133	One-column tablet. Slightly damaged on top left of reverse. Obverse eroded in the center. Catch line, colophon: iti še-kin-$kuru_5$ $u_4 2$ 18-kam.	418–83
KK	U 16858 (*UET* 6 134)	One-column tablet. Bottom two-thirds. From No. 1 Broad St.	439–91, 516–19
LL	*UET* 6 *21 + *UET* 6 *22 (both pl. 17)	One-column tablet(?). Central fragment. There are seven illegible lines before 95.	95–98, 123–30
MM	*UET* 6 *26 (pl. 17)	One-column tablet(?). Right bottom fragment. Obverse completely destroyed except for the ends of two lines on right edge.	414–15, 418–27
NN	*UET* 6 *272 (pl. 17)	One-column tablet(?). Central fragment.	335–47
OO	UM 29-15-414 (fig. 10 and pl. 18)	One-column tablet. Central fragment.	191–208, 237–52
PP	YBC 4610 (fig. 11, copy by W. W. Hallo; pl. 19)	One-column tablet. Provenience unknown.	42–80β
QQ	3 N-T 318B (A 302118B) + 3 N-T 321 (UM 55-21-305) (both fig. 12 and pls. 20, 21)	One-column tablet. Top half, broken at left top. From TA 205 XI-1.	397–409, 428–31

Source	Museum Numbers and Publication	Description	Lines
RR	3 N-T 666 (IM 58605) + 3 N-T 917, 386 (*SLF* pl. 12) + 3 N-T 917, 402 (*SLF* pl. 12) (all fig. 13 and pls. 22, 23)	One-column tablet. Broken on top half. Omits lines 67–68. From TA 191 X-1	62–94
SS	3 N-T 900, 3 (*SLF* pl. 12) (pl. 23)	One-column tablet. Lower central fragment. From TA 205 XI-1.	411–18, 420–22
TT	L 74.150 (pl. 24)	Right left part of two-column tablet. From Larsa, the Ebabbar temple, room 3. See D. Arnaud, *Syria* 53 (1976) 76–77.	?, 53–84, ?
UU	Ni. 1089	Three-column tablet. From a transliteration by S. N. Kramer.	46–52, 86–89, 159–68

Chapter 4

Composite Text and Translation

1. u$_4$ šu-bal aka-dè giš-ḫur ḫa-lam-e-dè
2. u$_4$-dè mar-ru$_{10}$-gin$_7$ ur-bi ì-gu$_7$-e
3. me ki-en-gi-ra šu-bal aka-dè
4. bala sa$_6$-ga é-ba gi$_4$-gi$_4$-dè
5. uru$_2$ gul-gul-lu-dè é gul-gul-lu-dè
6. tùr gul-gul-lu-dè amaš tab-tab-e-dè
7. gud-bi tùr-bi-a nu-gub-bu-dè
8. udu-bi amaš-bi-a nu-dagal-e-dè
9. íd-bi a mun$_4$-na tùm-ù-dè
10. gán-né zi-dè ^{ú}KI.KAL mú-mú-dè
11. eden-né ^{ú}a-nir mú-mú-dè
12. ama dumu-ni-ir ki nu-kin-kin-dè
13. ad-da a dam-mu nu-di-dè
14. dam banda$_3$ úr-ra nu-ḫúl-le-dè
15. tur-tur du$_{10}$-ba nu-bulug$_3$-gá-e-dè
16. umeda-e u$_5$-a nu-di-dè
17. nam-lugal-la ki-tuš-bi kúr-ru-dè
18. eš-bar kin-gá šu lá-e-dè
19. nam-lugal kalam-ma kar-kar-re-dè
20. igi-bi ki šár-ra gá-gá-dè
21. inim du$_{11}$-ga an ^{d}en-líl-lá-ta giš-ḫur ḫa-lam-e-dè
22. u$_4$ an-né kur-kur-ra sag-ki ba-da-an-gíd-da-ba
23. ^{d}en-líl-le igi-ni ki kúr-ra ba-an-gar-ra-a-ba
24. ^{d}nin-tu-re níg-dím-dím-ma-ni zag bí-in-tag-a-ba
25. ^{d}en-ki-ke$_4$ ^{íd}idigna ^{íd}buranun-na šu bí-in-bal-a-ba
26. ^{d}utu ḫar-ra-an kaskal-e nam ba-an-kud-a-ba
27. ki-en-gi-ra me-bi ḫa-lam-e-dè giš-ḫur-bi kúr-ru-dè

28. uri$_5$^{ki}-ma me nam-lugal-la bala-bi sù-sù-ud-dè
29. dumu-nun-na é-kiš-nu-gál-la-na šu pe-el-lá di-dè

1. To overturn the (appointed) time, to forsake the (preordained) plans,
2. The storms gather to strike like a flood.
3. To overturn the (divine) decrees of Sumer,
4. To lock the favorable reign in its abode,
5. To destroy the city, to destroy the temple,
6. To destroy the cattle pen, to level the sheep fold,
7. That the cattle not stand in the pen,
8. That the sheep not multiply in the fold,
9. That its watercourses carry brackish water,
10. That weeds grow in the fertile fields
11. That "mourning" plants grow in the steppe,
12. That the mother does not seek out her child,
13. That the father not say, "Oh, my (dear) wife!"
14. That the junior wife not take joy in (his) embrace,
15. That the young child not grow vigorous on (her) knee,
16. That the wetnurse not sing lullabies,
17. To change the location of kingship,
18. To defile the rights and decrees,
19. To take away kingship from the land,
20. To cast the eye (of the storm) on all the land,
21. To forsake the divine decrees by the order of An and Enlil,
22. After An had frowned upon all the lands,
23. After Enlil had looked favorably on an enemy land,
24. After Nintu had scattered the creatures that she had created,
25. After Enki had altered (the course of) the Tigris and Euphrates,
26. After Utu had cast his curse on the roads and highways,
27. In order to forsake the divine decrees of Sumer, to change its (pre-ordained) plans,
28. To alienate the (divine) decrees of the reign of kingship of Ur,
29. To defile the Princely Son in his (temple) Ekišnugal,

30. ^{d}nanna un u$_{8}$-gin$_{7}$ lu-a-na igi te-en-bi si-il-le-dè
31. uri$_{5}$^{ki} èš nindaba gal-gal-la nindaba-bi kúr-ru-dè

32. un-bi ki-tuš-ba nu-tuš-ù-dè ki erim$_{2}$-e šúm-mu-dè

33. LÚ.SU^{ki} elam^{ki} lú kúr-ra ki-tuš-bi tuš-ù-dè

34. sipa-bi é-gal ní-te-na lú erim$_{2}$-e dab$_{5}$-bé-dè
35. ^{d}i-bí-^{d}en.zu kur elam^{ki}-ma-šè ^{giš}búr-ra túm-mu-dè
36. iši za-bu gaba a-ab-ba-ka-ta zag an-ša$_{4}$-an^{ki}-šè

37. buru$_{5}$^{mušen} é-bi ba-ra-an-dal-a-gin$_{7}$ uru-ni-šè nu-gur-re-dè
38. ^{íd}idigna ^{íd}buranun-na gú $^{min_{6}}$min-a-ba ú ḫul mú-mú-dè
39. kaskal-la giri$_{3}$ nu-gá-gá-dè ḫar-ra-an nu-kin-kin-dè
40. uru á-dam ki gar-gar-ra-ba du$_{6}$-du$_{6}$-ra šid-dè
41. un sag-gi$_{6}$ lu-lu-a-ba ^{giš}ḫaš-šè aka-dè
42. gán-né zi-dè ^{giš}al nu-ru-gú-dè numun ki nu-tag-dè

43. e-el-lu šìr gud su$_{8}$-su$_{8}$-ba eden-na nu-di-dè

44. é-tùr-ra i̯à gara$_{2}$ nu-aka-dè šurim ki nu-tag-e-dè

45. sipa-dè ^{giš}šukur-ra amaš kù-ga šu nu-nigin-dè
46. i-lu-lam-ma du$_{9}$-du$_{9}$ ^{dug}šakir$_{3}$-ra amaš-a nu-di-dè
47. eden-na máš-anše tur-re-dè níg-zi-gál til-le-dè
48. níg-úr limmu$_{2}$ ^{d}šakan$_{2}$-na-ke$_{4}$ šurim ki-a nu-tag-ge-dè
49. ambar-ra šu ki-in-dar di-dè numun nu-tuk-tuk-dè

50. ^{giš}gi gi sag-ḫul mú-mú-dè ḫáb-ba til-e-dè

51. pú ^{giš}kiri$_{6}$ ú gibil-lá nu-me-a ní-ba šú-šú-dè

52. uri$_{5}$^{ki} am gal ù-na-gub-ba ní-bi-ta nir-gál
53. uru numun i-i nam-en nam-lugal-la ki sikil-la dù-a

54. gud-gin$_{7}$ saman ul$_{4}$-la-bi šub-bu-dè gú ki-šè lá-e-dè
55. an ^{d}en-líl ^{d}en-ki ^{d}nin-maḫ-bi nam-bi ḫa-ba-an-tar-re-eš
56. nam-tar-ra-bi níg nu-kúr-ru-dam a-ba šu mi-ni-íb-bal-e
57. inim du$_{11}$-ga an ^{d}en-líl-lá-ka sag a-ba mu-un-gá-gá

30. To break up the unity of the people of Nanna, numerous as ewes,
31. To change the food offerings of Ur, the shrine of magnificent food offerings,
32. That its people no longer dwell in their quarters, that they be given over (to live) in an inimical place,
33. That (the soldiers of) Šimaški and Elam, the enemy, dwell in their place,
34. That its shepherd be captured by the enemy, all alone,
35. That Ibbi-Sin be taken to the land of Elam in fetters,
36. That from the mountain Zabu, which is on the edge of the sealand, to the borders of Anšan,
37. Like a bird that has flown its nest, he not return to his city,
38. That on the two banks of the Tigris and Euphrates "bad weeds" grow,
39. That no one set out for the road, that no one seek out the highway,
40. That the city and its settled surroundings be razed to ruins,
41. To slaughter its numerous black-headed people,
42. That the hoe not attack the fertile fields, that seed not be planted in the ground,
43. That the sound of the song of the one tending the oxen not resound on the plain,
44. That butter and cheese not be made in the cattle pen, that dung not be laid on the ground,
45. That the shepherd not enclose the sacred sheep fold with a fence,
46. That the song of churning not resound in the cattle pen,
47. To decimate the animals of the steppe, to finish off (all) living things,
48. That the four-legged creatures of Šakan not lay dung on the ground,
49. That the marshes (be so dry as to) be full of cracks, that it not have any (new) seed,
50. That *saghul*-reeds grow in the canebrake, that they be covered by a stinking morass,
51. That there be no new growth in the orchards, that it all collapse by itself—
52. The city of Ur is a great charging aurochs, confident in its own strength,
53. It is the primeval city of Lordship and Kingship, built on sacred ground—
54. To quickly subdue it like a yoked ox, to bow its neck to the ground,
55. (the gods) An, Enlil, Enki, and Ninmaḫ decided its fate.
56. Its fate, which cannot be changed, who can overturn it—
57. Who can oppose the commands of An and Enlil?

58. an-né ki-en-gi ki-tuš-ba bí-in-ḫu-luḫ un-e ní bí-in-te
59. ^{d}en-líl-le u$_4$ gig-ga mu-un-zal uru-a me bí-íb-gar
60. ^{d}nin-tu-re ama$_5$ kalam-ma-ka ^{giš}ig-šu-úr im-mi-in-DU
61. ^{d}en-ki-ke$_4$ ^{íd}idigna ^{íd}buranun-na a im-ma-da-an-kéš
62. ^{d}utu níg-si-sá inim gi-na ka-ta ba-da-an-kar
63. ^{d}inanna-ke$_4$ mè šen-šen-na ki bal-e ba-an-šúm
64. ^{d}nin-gír-su-ke$_4$ ki-en-gi ga-gin$_7$ ur-e ba-an-dé
65. kalam-ma ga-ba-ra-ḫum im-ma-an-šub níg lú nu-zu-a

66. níg igi nu-gál-la inim nu-gál-la níg šu nu-te-gá-dam

67. kur-kur-re ní-te-a-bi-a šu sùḫ-a ba-ab-dug$_4$
68. uru^{ki} dingir-bi ba-da-gur sipa-bi ba-da-ḫa-lam
69. nam-lú-u$_{18}$-lu ní-te-bi-a zi gig mu-un-pa-an-pa-an
70. u$_4$-dè šu-ne-ne ba-dù-dù u$_4$ nu-mu-un-ne-gi$_4$-gi$_4$
71. u$_4$ gi$_4$-a mu-un-ne-tuk-àm u$_4$ dab$_5$-bé-šè nu-DU
72. ^{d}en-líl sipa sag gi$_6$-ga-ke$_4$ a-na bí-in-ak-a-bi
73. ^{d}en-líl-le é zi gul-gul-lu-dè lú zi tur-re-dè
74. dumu lú zi-da-ke$_4$ dumu sag-e igi ḫul dím-me-dè
75. u$_4$-ba ^{d}en-líl-le gu-ti-um^{ki} kur-ta im-ta-an-è
76. DU-bi a-ma-ru ^{d}en-líl-lá gaba-gi$_4$ nu-tuku-àm
77. im gal eden-na eden-e im-si igi-šè mu-un-ne-DU
78. eden níg-dagal-ba sìg ba-ab-dug$_4$ lú nu-mu-ni-in-dib-bé
79. u$_4$ kukku$_2$-ga šika bar$_7$-bar$_7$-ra sa-šè ba-ab-DU
80. u$_4$ babbar-re izi gi$_6$ eden-na ba-da-an-tab-tab
80α. u$_4$ mud-e KA ì-dub-dub sag ì-dab$_5$-dab$_5$
80β. u$_4$ ^{giš}gana$_2$-ùr an-ta è-dè uru ^{giš}al-e ba-ab-ra-aḫ

81. u$_4$-ba an ba-dúb ki ba-sìg igi u$_4$-da ba-lim

82. an ba-sùḫ-sùḫ gissu ba-an-lá kur-re ur$_5$ mi-ni-ib-ša$_4$

83. ^{d}utu an úr-ra i-in-ná saḫar kur-ra zal-àm
84. ^{d}nanna an-[pa]-a i-in-ná un-e ní bí-in-te
85. uru^{ki} ba-an-d[ug$_4$$^{?}$ k]i-tuš ba-ab-bé-dè bar-ta ba-da-gub
86. kur-kur-re uru^{ki} lú-bi nu-til-la i-im-sar-sar-re-ne
87. giš maḫ úr-bi-a mu-un-bal-e giš tir-ra guruš$_5$-i
88. pú ^{giš}kiri$_6$ gurun-ba mu-un-su$_{13}$-su$_{13}$ ligima ì-bu-re

58. An frightened the (very) dwelling of Sumer, the people were afraid,
59. Enlil blew an evil storm, silence lay upon the city,
60. Nintu bolted the door of the storehouses of the land,
61. Enki blocked the water in the Tigris and Euphrates,
62. Utu took away the pronouncement of equity and justice,
63. Inanna handed over (victory in) strife and battle to a rebellious land,
64. Ningirsu wasted Sumer like milk poured to the dogs.
65. Revolt descended upon the land, something that no one had ever known,
66. Something unseen, which had no name, something that could not be fathomed.
67. The lands were confused in their fear,
68. The god of that city turned away, its shepherd vanished.
69. The people, in fear, breathed only with difficulty,
70. The storm immobilizes them, the storm does not let them return,
71. There is no return for them, the time of captivity does not pass.
72. This is what Enlil, the shepherd of the black-headed people did:
73. Enlil, to destroy the loyal household, to decimate the loyal man,
74. To put the evil eye on the son of the loyal one, on the first-born,
75. Enlil then sent down Gutium from the mountains.
76. Their advance was as the flood of Enlil that cannot be withstood,
77. The great storm of the plain filled the plain, it advanced before them,
78. The teeming plain was destroyed, no one moved about there.
79. The dark time was roasted by hailstones and flames,
80. The bright time was wiped out by a shadow.
80α. On that bloody day, *mouths* were crushed, heads were crashed,
80β. The storm was a harrow coming from above, the city was struck (as) by a hoe.
81. On that day, heaven rumbled, the earth trembled, the storm worked without respite,
82. The heavens were darkened, they were covered by a shadow, the mountains roared,
83. The sun lay down at the horizon, dust *passed over* the mountains,
84. The moon lay at the zenith, the people were afraid.
85. The city . . . stepped outside.
86. The foreigners in the city (even) chase away the dead.
87. Large trees were being uprooted, the forest growth was ripped out,
88. The orchards were being stripped of their fruit, they were being cleaned of their offshoots,

89. buru$_{14}$ išin-bi-a mu-un-su-su ^{d}ašnan ì-tur-re

90. [. . .]-la sag [. . . -i]n-bal-bal-e
91. [. . . ba-da]-kar-ra-bi [. . . ba-a]b-DU
92. [. . . ^{ú}]numun$_{2}$ x ba-da-kar-ra-bi [^{ú}]numun$_{2}$ x ba-ab-DU
93. [. . . zur-r]e-eš mu-un-du$_{8}$-du$_{8}$ [. . . za]r-re-eš mu-un-sal-sal-e-eš
94. [. . . í]d.buranun-na ad$_{6}$ ì-me-a [. . . sag]-gaz ì-ak-e

95. [ad-da dam-a-ni-t]a ba-da-gur dam-mu nu-im-me
96. [ama dumu-ni-t]a ba-da-gur dumu-mu nu-im-me
97. é zi-da-ke$_{4}$ é-a-ni mu-un-šub é-mu nu-im-me
98. níg-gur$_{11}$ tuku níg-gur$_{11}$-ra-ni-ta giri$_{3}$ kúr ba-ra-an-[dab$_{5}$]
99. u$_{4}$-ba nam-lugal kalam-ma-ka šu pe-el-lá ba-ab-dug$_{4}$
100. aga men sag-gá gál-la-bi ur-bi ba-ra-a[n- . . .]
101. kur-kur-re du$_{10}$-ús dili dab$_{5}$-ba-bi igi te-en-bi ba-si-il

102. uri$_{5}^{ki}$ èš nindaba gal-gal-la-ka nindaba-bi ba-d[a$^{?}$-kúr$^{?}$]

103. ^{d}nanna un u$_{8}$-gin$_{7}$ lu-a-na šu bal ba-an-da-ab-ak
104. lugal-bi é-gal ní-te-na zi im-ma-ni-in-gi$_{4}$
105. ^{d}i-bí-^{d}en.zu é-gal ní-te-na i-si-iš ba-ni-in-lá-lá
106. é-nam-ti-la šà ḫúl-la-ka-na ér gig mu-un-še$_{8}$-še$_{8}$
107. a-ma-ru du$_{6}^{!}$(ki) al-ak-e šu im-ùr-ùr-re
108. u$_{4}$ gal-gin$_{7}$ ki-a ur$_{5}$ mi-ni-ib-ša$_{4}$ a-ba-a ba-ra-è
109. uru gul-gul-lu-dè é gul-gul-lu-dè
110. lú lul lú zi-da an-ta nú-ù-dè
111. uri$_{3}$ lú lul-e lú zi-ra ugu-a-na DU-šè
112. ki-ru-gú 1-a-kam
113. u$_{4}$-dè mar-ru$_{10}$-gin$_{7}$ ur-bi ì-gu$_{7}$-e
114. giš-gi$_{4}$-gál ki-ru-gú-da-kam
115. é kiš^{ki}-a ḫur-sag-kalam-ma-ka šu ḫul ba-e-dug$_{4}$
116. ^{d}za-ba$_{4}$-ba$_{4}$ ki-tuš [ki-ág-gá-ni giri$_{3}$ kúr ba-ra-an-dab$_{5}$]
117. ama ^{d}ba-Ú é u[ru-kù-ga-na ér gig mu-un-še$_{8}$-še$_{8}$]
118. a uru [gul-la é gul-la-mu gig-ga-bi im-me]
119. x [. . .]
120. [. . .]
121. [. . .]
122. [a uru gul-la é gul-la-mu gig-ga-bi im-me]

89. The crop was drowning while it was still on the stalk, the (yield) of the grain was being diminished.
90. . . .
91. . . .
92. . . .
93. [. . .] they piled up in heaps [. . .] they spread out like sheaves.
94. There were corpses (floating) in the Euphrates, brigands roamed [the roads].
95. [The father turned away from his wife], he says not, "Oh, my wife!"
96. [The mother turned away from her child], she says not, "Oh, my child!"
97. (The one) who had a productive estate [says not], "Oh, my estate!"
98. The rich left his possessions and took an unfamiliar path.
99. In those days the kingship of the land was defiled,
100. The crown that had been on the head (of the king) [. . .] by itself.
101. The lands that had taken the same road (in obedience to Ur), were split into factions,
102. The food offerings of Ur, the shrine (that received) magnificent food offerings, were changed (for the worse).
103. Nanna traded away his people numerous as ewes.
104. Its king sat immobilized in the palace, all alone.
105. Ibbi-Sin was sitting in anguish in the palace, all alone.
106. In the Enamtila, the palace of his delight, he was crying bitterly.
107. The devastating flood was leveling (everything),
108. Like a great storm it roared over the earth, who could escape it?
109. To destroy the city, to destroy the temple,
110. That traitors would lay on top of loyal men, and
111. The blood of traitors flow upon loyal men,
112. *The first kirugu.*
113. The storms gather to strike like a flood.
114. *—the antiphone of the kirugu.*
115. The temple of Kiš, Ḫursagkalama, was destroyed,
116. Zababa took an unfamiliar path away from his beloved dwelling,
117. Mother Baʾu was lamenting bitterly in her Urukug,
118. "Alas, the destroyed city, my destroyed temple!" bitterly she cries.
119. [. . .]
120. [. . .]
121. [. . .]
122. ["Alas, the destroyed city, my destroyed temple!" bitterly she cries.]

123. ka-z[al-l]u^{ki} uru ní-ba lu-a šu sùḫ-a ba-ab-dug$_4$
124. ^{d}nu-muš-da uru ki-tuš ki-ág-gá-ni giri$_3$ kúr ba-ra-an-dab$_5$

125. nitadam-a-ni ^{d}nam-ra-at munus sa$_6$-ga-a ér in-še$_8$-še$_8$-e
126. a uru$_2$ gul-la é gul-la-mu gig-ga-bi im-me
127. íd-bi šà-sù-ga ì-gál a nu-un-dé
128. íd ^{d}en-ki-ke$_4$ nam-ku$_5$-rá-gin$_7$ ka-bi-a ba-úš
129. a-šà-ga še gu-nu nu-gál un-e nu-gu$_7$-e
130. pú ^{giš}kiri$_6$-bi gir$_4$-gin$_7$ ba-ḫur-ḫur eden-bi ság ba-ab-di

131. máš-anše níg-úr limmu$_2$ níg-zi-gál nu-mu-un-bu-e
132. níg-úr limmu$_2$ ^{d}šakan$_2$-ke$_4$ ní nu-mu-ni-ib-te-en-te-en
133. ^{d}lugal-marad-da-ke$_4$ uru-ni-ta bar-ta ba-da-gub
134. ^{d}nin-zu-an-na ki-tuš ki-ág-gá-ni giri$_3$ kúr ba-ra-an-dab$_5$
135. a uru$_2$ gul-la é gul-la-mu gig-ga-bi im-me
136. i-si-in^{ki} èš kar-re nu-me-a a-e ba-e-dar
137. ^{d}nin-in-si-in-na ama kalam-ma-ke$_4$ ér gig mu-un-še$_8$-še$_8$
138. a uru gul-la é gul-la-mu gig-ga-bi im-me
139. ^{d}en-líl-le dur-an-ki-ka ^{giš}middu$_2$-a ba-an-sìg
140. ^{d}en-líl-le uru-ni èš nibru^{ki}-a a-nir ba-ab-gar
141. ama ^{d}nin-líl nin ki-ùr-ra-ke$_4$ ér gig mu-un-še$_8$-še$_8$
142. a uru$_2$ gul-la é gul-la-mu gig-ga-bi im-me
143. kèš^{ki} an eden-na dili dù-a šu líl-lá ba-ab-dug$_4$
144. adab^{ki}-bu é íd-dè lá-a-ri a-e ba-da-ab-bu$_x$(PI)
145. muš kur-ra-ke$_4$ ki-ná ba-ni-ib-gar ki bala-šè ba-ab-dug$_4$

146. gu-ti-um^{ki} šà ba-ni-ib-bal-bal numun ba-ni-ib-i-i
147. ^{d}nin-tu-re níg-dím-dím-ma-ni-šè ér gig mu-un-še$_8$-še$_8$
148. a uru gul-la é gul-la-mu gig-ga-bi im-me
149. ki zabala^{ki}-a gi-gun$_4$-na kù-ga šu líl-lá ba-ab-dug$_4$
150. unug^{ki}-ta ^{d}inanna ba-da-an-kar ki erim$_2$-e ba-ab-gin
151. é-an-na èš gi$_6$-par$_4$ kù-ga erim$_2$-e igi i-ni-in-bar
152. gi$_6$-par$_4$ kù nam-en-na-ba šu ba-e-lá-lá
153. en-bi gi$_6$-par$_4$-ta ba-da-an-kar ki erim$_2$-e ba-ab-de$_6$

154. a uru$_2$ gul-la é gul-la-mu gig-ga-bi im-me
155. umma^{ki} sig$_4$-kur-šà-ba-ke$_4$ u$_4$ gig-ga ba-e-dal

123. Kazallu, the city of teeming multitudes, was wrought with confusion,
124. Numušda took an unfamiliar path away from the city, his beloved dwelling,
125. His wife Namrat, the beautiful lady, was lamenting bitterly,
126. "Alas, the destroyed city, my destroyed temple!" bitterly she cries.
127. Its river bed was empty, no water flowed,
128. Like a river cursed by Enki, its opening channel was dammed up,
129. On the fields fine grains grew not, people had nothing to eat,
130. The orchards were scorched like an oven, its (surrounding) steppe was scattered,
131. The wild animals, the four legged creatures did not run about,
132. The four legged creatures of Šakan could find no rest.
133. Lugalmarada stepped outside his city,
134. Ninzuana took an unfamiliar path away from her beloved dwelling,
135. "Alas, the destroyed city, my destroyed temple!" bitterly she cries.
136. Isin, the shrine that was not a quay, was split by (onrushing) waters,
137. Ninisina, the mother of the land, wept bitter tears,
138. "Alas, the destroyed city, my destroyed temple!" bitterly she cries.
139. Enlil smote Duranki with a mace,
140. Enlil established lamenting in his city, the shrine of Nippur,
141. Mother Ninlil, the lady of the Kiur, wept bitter tears,
142. "Alas, the destroyed city, my destroyed temple!" bitterly she cries.
143. Keš, built all alone on the high steppe, was haunted,
144. Adab, which stretches out along the river, was deprived of water.
145. The snake of the mountain made his lair there, it became a rebellious land;
146. The Gutians bred there, issued their seed.
147. Nintu wept bitter tears over her creatures that she had created,
148. "Alas, the destroyed city, my destroyed temple!" bitterly she cries.
149. In Zabala the sacred Giguna was haunted,
150. Inanna abandoned Uruk, went off to enemy territory.
151. In the Eanna the enemy laid his eyes upon the sacred Gipar shrine.
152. The sacred Gipar of the *en*-ship was defiled,
153. Its En priest was snatched from the Gipar (and) carried off to enemy territory.
154. "Alas, the destroyed city, my destroyed temple!" bitterly she cries.
155. A violent storm blew over Umma, *the brickwork in the midst of the "highland,"*

156. [^{d}šara$_{2}$ é]-maḫ k[i-tuš] ki-ág-gá-ni giri$_{3}$ kúr ba-ra-an-dab$_{5}$

157. [^{d}n]in-mul-e uru^{ki} ḫul-lu-a-na ér gig mu-un-še$_{8}$-še$_{8}$
158. [uru^{ki}-mu$^{?}$] la-la-bi lú nu-un-gi$_{4}$-a-mu gig-ga-bi im-me

159. gír-su^{ki} uru^{ki} ur-sag-gá-e-ne-ke$_{4}$ im-gír-e ba-ab-dug$_{4}$
160. ^{d}nin-gír-su-ke$_{4}$ é-ninnu-ta giri$_{3}$ kúr ba-ra-an-dab$_{5}$
161. ama ^{d}ba-ú é uru-kù-ga-na ér gig mu-un-še$_{8}$-še$_{8}$
162. a uru gul-la é gul-la-mu gig-ga-bi im-me
163. u$_{4}$-ba inim u$_{4}$-dam al-du$_{7}$-du$_{7}$ šà-bi a-ba-a mu-un-zu

164. inim ^{d}en-líl-lá zi-da gil-èm-dè gùb-bu zu-zu-dè
165. ^{d}en-líl lú nam-tar-tar-re-dè a-na bí-in-ak-a-ba
166. ^{d}en-líl-le elam^{ki} lú kúr-ra kur-ta im-ta-an-è
167. ^{d}nanše dumu gi$_{7}$ uru bar-ra mu-un-na-TUŠ-àm
168. ^{d}nin-mar^{ki}-ra èš gú-ab-ba-ka izi im-ma-da-an-te
169. kù ^{na_4}za-gìn-bi má gal-gal-la bala-šè ì-ak-e
170. nin níg-gur$_{11}$-ra-ni ḫul-lu ti-la-àm kù ^{d}nin-mar^{ki}-ke$_{4}$

171. u$_{4}$-ba u$_{4}$ KA.NE-gin$_{7}$ bar$_{7}$-ra-àm im-ma-da-ab-TAR-re
172. ki-lagaša^{ki} elam^{ki} šu-ni-a im-ma-ši-in-gi$_{4}$
173. u$_{4}$-bi-a nin-e u$_{4}$-da-a-ni sá nam-ga-mu-ni-ib-dug$_{4}$
174. ^{d}ba-Ú lú-u$_{18}$-lu-gin$_{7}$ u$_{4}$-da-a-ni sá nam-ga-mu-ni-ib-dug$_{4}$
175. me-li-e-a u$_{4}$-dè šu-ni-a im-ma-ši-in-gi$_{4}$
176. u$_{4}$ uru$_{2}$ gul-gul-e šu-ni-a im-ma-ši-in-gi$_{4}$
177. u$_{4}$ é gul-gul-e šu-ni-a im-ma-ši-in-gi$_{4}$
178. ^{d}dumu-zi-abzu é-bi ki-nu-nir-šà-ba-ke$_{4}$ ní im-ma-da-an-te
179. ki-[nu]-nir-šà^{ki} uru nam-dumu gi$_{7}$-ra-ka-ni kar-kar-re-dè ba-ab-dug$_{4}$
180. ^{d}nanše uru-ni AB×ḪA^{ki}-a kur-re ba-ab-gar
181. sirara$_{3}^{ki}$ ki-tuš ki-ág-gá-ni ḫul-gál-e ba-an-šúm
182. a uru gul-la é gul-la-mu gig-ga-bi im-me
183. gi$_{6}$-par$_{4}$ kù nam-en-na-ba šu ba-e-lá-lá
184. en-bi gi$_{6}$-par$_{4}$-ta ba-da-an-kar ki erim$_{2}$-e ba-ab-de$_{6}$

185. gú íd-nun-na-^{d}nanna-ka á dugud ba-ši-in-DU
186. maš-gana$_{2}$ maš-gana$_{2}$ é-dana-^{d}nanna-ka tùr dugud-gin$_{7}$ ba-gul

187. lú kar-ra-bi maš kar-ra-gin$_{7}$ ur im-me-da

156. Šara took an unfamiliar path away from the Emaḫ, his beloved dwelling,
157. Ninmul cried bitter tears over her destroyed city,
158. "O my city, whose charms can no longer satisfy me!" bitterly she was crying.
159. Girsu, the city of heroes, was afflicted with a lightning storm,
160. Ningirsu took an unfamiliar path away from the Eninnu,
161. Mother Baʾu wept bitter tears in her Urukug,
162. "Alas, the destroyed city, my destroyed temple!" bitterly she cries.
163. On that day the word (of Enlil) was an attacking storm—who could fathom it?
164. The word of Enlil is destruction on the right, is . . . on the left,
165. This is what Enlil did in order to decide the fate of mankind:
166. Enlil brought down the Elamites, the enemy, from the highlands.
167. Nanše, the Noble Son, was settled outside the city.
168. Fire approached Ninmar in the shrine Guabba,
169. Large boats were carrying off its precious metals and stones.
170. The lady—sacred Ninmar—was despondent because of her perished goods.
171. Then the day, burning like . . . ,
172. The province of Lagaš was handed over to Elam.
173. And then the Queen also reached the end of her time,
174. Baʾu, as if she were human, also reached the end of her time:
175. "Woe is me, he (Enlil) has handed over (the city to the) storm,
176. He has handed (it) over to the storm that destroys cities,
177. He has handed (it) over to the storm that destroys temples!"
178. Dumuziabzu was full of fear in the temple of Kinunirša,
179. Kinunirša, the city of her noble youth, was ordered to be plundered.
180. The city of Nanše, AB×ḪA^{ki}, was delivered to the foreigners,
181. Sirara, her beloved dwelling, was handed over to the evil ones,
182. "Alas, the destroyed city, my destroyed temple!" bitterly she cries.
183. Its sacred Gipar of *en*-ship was defiled,
184. Its En priest was snatched from the Gipar (and) carried off to enemy territory.
185. A mighty arm was set over the bank(s) of the Idnuna-Nanna canal,
186. The settlements of Edana-Nanna were destroyed like a mighty cattle pen.
187. Its refugees, like stampeding goats, were *chased by* dogs.

188. ga-eš^{ki} ga-gin$_7$ ur-e ba-an-dé ì-gul-gul-lu-ne
189. alam dím-ma SIG$_7$.ALAM sa$_6$-ga-bi im-zé-er-zé-re-e-ne
190. a uru gul-la é gul-la-mu gig-ga-bi im-me
191. gi$_6$-par$_4$ kù nam-en-na-ba šu ba-e-lá-lá
192. en-bi gi$_6$-par$_4$-ta ba-da-an-kar ki-erim$_2$-e ba-ab-de$_6$

193. bara$_2$ an-na-da gíd-da-bi a-nir ba-da-an-di
194. ^{giš}gu-za an-na-bi nu-ub-gub sag me-te-a-aš li-bí-ib-gál
195. ^{giš}nimbar-gin$_7$ gú-gur$_5$ ba-ab-dug$_4$ ur-bi ba-ra-an-kad$_4$
196. aš-šu^{ki} é íd-dè lá-a-ri a-e ba-da-ab-bu

197. níg-erim$_2$ nu-dib ^{d}nanna-ka lú erim$_2$-e ba-an-dib
198. é ḫur-re-àm a-na-àm ab-ak
199. é pu-úḫ-ru-um-ma šà-sù-ga ba-ab-gar
200. KI.ABRIG$_2$^{ki}-a áb lu amar lu-a-ri tùr dugud-gin$_7$ ba-gul

201. ^{d}nin-gublaga-ke$_4$ gá-bur-ta giri$_3$ kúr ba-ra-an-dab$_5$
202. ^{d}nin-i̭à-gara$_2$-ke$_4$ ní-te-na ér gig mu-un-še$_8$-še$_8$
203. a uru gul-la é gul-la-mu gig-ga-bi im-me
204. gi$_6$-par$_4$ kù nam-en-na-ba šu ba-e-lá-lá
205. en-bi gi$_6$-par$_4$-ta ba-da-an-kar ki erim$_2$-e ba-ab-de$_6$

206. ^{d}nin-a-zu é-gíd-da-ke$_4$ ^{giš}tukul ub-ba i-ni-in-gub
207. ^{d}nin-ḫur-sag é-nu-tur-ra-ke$_4$ u$_4$ ḫul ba-an-da-dal
208. tu^{mušen}-gin$_7$ ab-làl-ta ba-da-an-dal eden-na bar bí-íb-gub
209. a uru^{ki} gul-la é gul-la-mu gig-ga-bi im-me
210. giš-bàn-da é ér-re gál-la-ri gi ér-ra ba-an-mú

211. ^{d}nin-giz-zi-da giš-bàn-da giri$_3$ kúr ba-ra-an-dab$_5$
212. ^{d}á-zi-mú-a nin uru-a-ke$_4$ ér gig mu-un-še$_8$-še$_8$
213. a uru$_2$ gul-la é gul-la-mu gig-ga-bi im-me
214. u$_4$-bi-a u$_{18}$-lu lú gi$_6$-a ba-an-dúr-ru-ne-eš
215. kuʾara^{ki} ḫul-ḫul-lu-dè lú gi$_6$-a ba-an-dúr-ru-ne-eš
216. ^{d}nin-é-ḪA-ma ní-te-na ér gig mu-un-še$_8$-še$_8$
217. a uru$_2$ gul-la é gul-la-mu gig-ga-bi im-me
218. ^{d}asar-lú-ḫi ul$_4$-ul$_4$-la túg ba-an-mu$_4$ LUL.KU mu-un-DU
219. ^{d}lugal-bàn-da ki-tuš ki-ág-gá-ni giri$_3$ kúr ba-ra-an-dab$_5$
219′. ⌜d⌝[nin-sún . . .]

188. They destroy Gaeš like milk poured out to dogs,
189. Its finely fashioned statues they shatter,
190. "Alas, the destroyed city, my destroyed temple!" bitterly she cries.
191. Its sacred Gipar of *en*-ship was defiled,
192. Its En priest was snatched from the Gipar (and) carried off to enemy territory.
193. A lament was raised at the dais that stretches out toward heaven,
194. Its heavenly throne was not set up, it was not fit *to be crowned*,
195. Was cut down as if it were a date palm and tied together.
196. Aššu, the estate that stretches out along the river, was deprived of water,
197. At the place of Nanna where evil had never walked, the enemy walked,
198. Thus the temple was treated.
199. The Epuḫruma was emptied,
200. Kiabrig, which used to be filled with numerous cows and numerous calves, was destroyed like a mighty cattle pen,
201. Ningublaga took an unfamiliar path away from the Gabur,
202. Niniagara wept bitter tears all alone,
203. "Alas, the destroyed city, my destroyed temple!" bitterly she cries.
204. Its sacred Gipar of *en*-ship was defiled,
205. Its En priest was snatched from the Gipar (and) carried off to enemy territory.
206. Ninazu deposited (his) weapon in a corner in the Egida.
207. An evil storm swept over Ninḫursag at the Enutura,
208. Like a dove she flew from the window, she stood away on the plain.
209. "Alas, the destroyed city, my destroyed temple!" bitterly she cries.
210. In the Gišbanda, the temple that was filled with lamentation, "lamentation" reeds grew,
211. Ningizzida took an unfamiliar path away from the Gišbanda,
212. Ninazimua, the queen of the city, wept bitter tears,
213. "Alas, the destroyed city, my destroyed temple!" bitterly she cries.
214. On that day, the storm forced people to live in darkness,
215. In order to destroy Kuʾara, it forced people to live in darkness.
216. Nineḫama in fear wept bitter tears,
217. "Alas, the destroyed city, my destroyed temple!" bitterly she cries.
218. Asarluḫi put his robes on with haste . . . ,
219. Lugalbanda took an unfamiliar path away from his beloved dwelling,
219′. Ninsun [. . .],

220. a uru$_2$ gul-la é gul-la-mu gig-ga-bi im-me
221. eridu^{ki} a gal-la diri-ga a nag-e ba-àm-ugun$^?$
222. bar-ba eden líl-e dù-a x x [. . .]
223. lú zi ki lul-la x x [. . .]
224. ^{d}KA-ḫé-gál-la ^{d}igi-ḫé-gál-la [. . .]
225. guruš me-en u$_4$ nu x la x x mu [x (x)] gul [. . . .]
226. u$_4$ nu-gul-la ḫi-li nu-til-la me-en [. . .] mu-u[n- . . .]
227. x x-gin$_7$ su$^?$ sa$_6$-ga-meš ì-[x]-ge-dè-[en-dè-en]
228. x x-gin$_7$ igi gùn-gùn-meš ì-[x-x]x-dè-en-dè-en
229. alan-gin$_7$ kùš-kùš-a dé-a-meš ì-[sì-g]e-dè-en-dè-en
230. [gu]-ti-um^{ki} lú ḫa-lam-ma-ke$_4$ me-zé-er-zé-re-ne
231. [a-a ^{d}e]n-ki-ra abzu eridu^{ki}-šè šu-a ba-en-dè-en-gi$_4$
232. [. . .] a-na im-me-en-da-na a-na bí-in-daḫ-e-da-na
233. [. . .]x a-na im-me-en-da-na a-na bí-in-daḫ-e-da-na
234. [. . .] eridu^{ki}-ga-ta ḫé-em-da-è$^?$-da-na
235. [. . .]x ba-gub-bu-da-na gissu ba-x-mu
236. gi$_6$-a x x-ke$_4$ ḫa-ba-gub-bu-da-na u$_4$-dè ba-ra-an-tuku
237. u$_4$-da-gub sag sìg-ge-me-a-a-na šu ba-ni-ti-en-dè-en
238. gi$_6$-da-gub ù nu-ku-me-a-a-na ú-gu me-dé-dè-en-dè-[en]
239. ^{d}en-ki-ke$_4$ uru$_2$-zu nam ḫa-ba-da-an-ku$_5$ ki erim$_2$-e ḫa-ba-an-šúm
240. me-en-dè eridu^{ki}-ta gál-la-da a-na-aš mu-e-dè-lá-e-ne$^?$
241. ^{giš}nimbar-gin$_7$ šu nu-du$_{11}$-ga-me a-na-aš mu-e-gul-gul-lu-ne
242. ^{giš}má gibil-gin$_7$ sa pil-lá nu-ak-e a-na-aš mu-e-zé-er-zé-re-ne
243. ^{d}en-ki-ke$_4$ igi-ni ki kúr-ra ba-an-gar-ra-ba
244. u$_4$$^?$ x x nam-tag dugud-da-ke$_4$ giš ḫul mu-un-ne-šum
245. [. . .] UM/DUB$^?$ ba-da-an-zi-ge-eš-a ildu$_2$-ba mu-un-sa$_4$$^?$-eš
246. [^{d}en-ki]-ke$_4$ eridu^{ki}-ga-ta giri$_3$ kúr ba-ra-an-dab$_5$
247. [^{d}dam-gal]-nun-na ama é-maḫ-a ér gig mu-un-še$_8$-še$_8$
248. a uru$_2$ gul-la é gul-la-mu gig-ga-bi im-me
249. gi$_6$-par$_4$ kù nam-en-na-ba šu ba-e-lá-lá
250. en-bi gi$_6$-par$_4$-ta ba-da-an-kar ki erim$_2$-e ba-ab-de$_6$

251. uri$_5$^{ki}-ma lú ú-šè nu-gin lú a-šè nu-gin
252. ú-šè gin-bi ú-ta ba-gin ur$_5$ nu-ni-ib-gur-ru

253. a-šè gin-bi a-ta ba-gin ur$_5$ nu-ni-ib-gur-ru

254. sig-šè elam^{ki}-ma ba-ši-in-gub-bu gaz-dè ì-TIL-e

220. "Alas, the destroyed city, my destroyed temple!" bitterly she cries.
221. Eridu, floating on great waters, *was deprived* of drinking water,
222. In its outer environs, which had turned into haunted plains . . . ,
223. The loyal man in a place of treachery . . .
224. (The gods) Kaḫegala and Igiḫegala . . .
225. "I am a young man . . . ,
226. . . .
227. . . .
228. . . .
229. "We are spilled out like figurines being cast in molds,
230. We are being wiped out by the Gutians, the vandals.
231. We turned to Enki in the Abzu of Eridu:
232. [. . .] what can we say, what more can we add?
233. [. . .] what can we say, what more can we add?"
234. [. . .] went out from Eridu.
235. [. . .] . . . a shadow . . .
236. By night [. . .] . . . by day . . .
237. ". . .
238. . . .
239. Enki, your city has been cursed, it has been given to an enemy land.
240. We . . .
241. Like a palm tree we . . . , why are we being destroyed?
242. Like a new boat that . . . why are we being destroyed?"
243. After Enki has cast his eyes on a foreign land,
244. . . .
245. . . .
246. Enki took an unfamiliar path away from Eridu,
247. Damgalnuna, the mother of the Emaḫ, wept bitter tears,
248. "Alas, the destroyed city, my destroyed temple!" bitterly she cries.
249. Its sacred Gipar was defiled,
250. Its En priest was snatched from the Gipar (and) carried off to enemy territory.
251. In Ur no one went to fetch food, no one went to fetch drink,
252. (But) the one who went to fetch food went away from the food, and so will not return,
253. The one who went to fetch drink went away from the drink, and so will not return.
254. To the south, the Elamites stepped in, slaughtering . . . ,

255. nim-šè ḫa-al-ma lú kúr-ra-ke$_4$ šu-ni [. . .]x x
256. ti-id-nu-um^{ki}-e u$_4$-šú-uš ^{giš}middu$_2$-a úr-ra ba-ni-in-gar
257. sig-šè elam^{ki}-ma ú-a è-a-gin$_7$ KU-bi im-[. . .]x-le
258. nim-šè in-dal im dal-la-gin$_7$ eden-n[a . . .]x
259. uri$_5$^{ki} am gal ù-na-gub-ba-gin$_7$ gú ki-š[è ba-ab-gar]
260. ^{d}en-líl-le lú nam tar-tar-re-dè a-na [bí-in-ak-a-ba]
261. mìn-kam-ma-šè elam^{ki} lú kúr-ra kur-t[a ba-ra-è]

262. é sag-kal-la giri$_3$ dù-a um-ma-[. . .]
263. kisiga^{ki} ḫul-ḫul-lu-dè lú 10 l[ú 5 . . .]
264. u$_4$ 3-e gi$_6$ 3-e la-ba-da-te$^{?}$ x x [. . .] uru^{giš}al-e ba-ab-r[a-aḫ]

265. kisiga^{ki} ^{d}dumu-zi sag-gin$_7$$^{?}$ ba-r[a-è] šu-ni ba-da-ab-[dù]

266. é-šè kù giri$_3$[. . .] a KA [. . .]
267. zi-ga u$_5$ [. . . z]i-ga u$_5$ [. . .] x
268. [. . .]-un-DU zi-ga u$_5$ [. . .]
269. [. . . s]i gal-gal ba-an-u$_5$-bi x[. . .]x-DU-eš
270. [. . .] si tur-tur máš igi-du-gin$_7$ x[. . . da]b$_5$$^{?}$-bé-eš
271. níg-gur$_{11}$-ra-ni-ta ba-da-u$_5$ kur-šè ba-gin
272. i-lu kur kiš-nu-gál-la-ba gal-gal-bi m[i-ni-in-di]
273. ga-ša-an-mèn níg-gur$_{11}$-gá ga-ba-da-[u$_5$ ki]-ba gi$_4$-in dè-mèn

274. kù ^{na_4}za-gìn-mu-ta ga-ba-e-[da]-u$_5$ ki-ba gi$_4$-in dè-mèn

275. ki-ba na-ág-gi$_4$-in nam-lú-ulu$_3$ [x]x SAG a-ba-a ba-ab-ús-e
276. ki-ba na-ág-gi$_4$-in elam^{ki} [x] x a-ba-a ba-ab-ús-e
277. a uru gul-la é gul-la-mu gig-[ga]-bi im-me
278. nin-mu lú kur nu-me-a ku[r$^{?}$-r]e$^{?}$ ba-ab-gin
279. ^{d}[ama-ušum$_2$-ga]l-an-na kisiga[^{ki} . . .]-gá
280. [x-m]u$^{?}$ uru$_2$-gin$_7$ nu-x[. . .]x
281. ki-r[u-gú 2-kam-ma]
282. [. . .] x x [. . .]
283. [. . .]
284. [giš-gi$_4$-gál ki-ru-gú-da-kam]
285. [. . .]
286. [. . .]
287. [. . .]

255. To the north, the vandals, the enemy . . . ,
256. The Tidnumites daily strapped the mace to their loins,
257. To the south, the Elamites, like an onrushing wave, were . . . ,
258. To the north, like chaff blowing in the wind, [they . . .] over the steppe,
259. Ur, like a great charging aurochs, bowed its neck to the ground.
260. This is what Enlil, the one who decides the fates, then did:
261. For the second time he sent down the Elamites, the enemy, from the mountains.
262. The foremost temple, firmly founded . . . ,
263. In order to destroy Kisiga, ten, [nay five me]n . . . ,
264. Three days and three nights did not pass [. . .] the city was raked (as by) a hoe,
265. Dumuzi went out of Kisiga like a prisoner of war, his hands were fettered.
266. . . .
267. "Rise up, ride away [. . .] rise up, ride away [. . .]!
268. [. . .] rise up, ride away [. . .]!"
269. Small . . . had ridden away . . .
270. Large . . . , like a lead goat . . . captured.
271. She rode away from her possessions, she went to the mountains,
272. She loudly sang out a lament over those brightly lit mountains:
273. "I am a Lady, (but) I had to ride away from my possessions, and now I am a slave in these parts,
274. I had to ride away from my precious metals and stones, and now I am a slave in these parts,
275. There, slavery, . . . people, who can . . . it?
276. There, slavery, Elam . . . , who can . . . it?"
277. "Alas, the destroyed city, my destroyed temple!" bitterly she cries.
278. Her Majesty, though not the enemy, went to *enemy land*.
279. Amaušumgalana [. . .] Kisiga,
280. [. . .] like a city [. . .]
281. [*The second*] *k*[*irugu*.]
282. [. . .]
283. [. . .]
284. [*—the antiphone of the kirugu.*]
285. [. . .]
286. [. . .]
287. [. . .]

288. [. . .]
289. [. . .] ú-a ba-š[i-in . . .]
290. [. . . ú]-a ba-ši-in-x[. . .]
291. [. . . gu]b-bu-bi kur$_6$ maḫ-gin$_7$ ba-e-x[. . .]
292. ^{d}en-líl-le abul-la maḫ-ba ^{giš}ig im-ma bí-[in-gub]
293. uri$_5$^{ki}-ma lú ú-šè nu-gin lú a-šè nu-gin
294. un-bi a túl-a dé-a-gin$_7$ šu ì-nigin$^{?}$-ne
295. usu-bi ní-bi-a nu-gál giri$_3$-bi ba-ra-an-dab$_5$
296. ^{d}en-líl-le šà-gar lú níg-ḫul uru-a ba-ra-an-dab$_5$
297. níg uru gul-gul-e níg é gul-gul-e uru-a ba-an-da-dab$_5$

298. níg igi-bi-šè ^{giš}tukul-e la-ba-gub-bu-a uru-a ba-an-da-dab$_5$

299. šà nu-si-si igi nigin$_2$-bi uru-a ba-an-da-dab$_5$
300. uri$_5$^{ki}-ma gi dili dù-a-gin$_7$ sag sìg-ge nu-gá-gá
301. un-bi ku$_6$ šu dab$_5$-ba-gin$_7$ zi-bi mi-ni-in-túm-túm-mu
302. tur maḫ-bi ì-bara$_3$-bara$_3$-ge-eš lú nu-um-zi-zi-zi
303. LUGAL.BI.GUB dub-lá-a u$_5$-a níg-gu$_7$ la-ba-na-gál
304. lugal níg-sa$_6$-ga gu$_7$-gu$_7$-a kur$_6$-re im-ma-an-dab$_5$

305. u$_4$ im-šú-šú igi im-lá-e šà-ka-tab ì-zu-zu

306. é-lunga-na kaš nu-un-gál munu$_3$-bi nu-um-gál

307. é-gal-la-na níg-gu$_7$ la-ba-na-gál tuš-ù-bi nu-ub-du$_7$

308. gá-nun maḫ-a-ni še nu-um-si-si zi-bi la-ba-ši-in-túm-túm-mu

309. gur$_7$-du$_6$ gur$_7$-maš-a ^{d}nanna-ka ^{d}ašnan nu-un-gál
310. kin-sig unu$_2$ gal dingir-re-e-ne-ke$_4$ šu ba-e-lá-lá
311. unu$_2$ gal-bi kaš kurun làl mùš im-ma-[ab$^{?}$]-de$_6$
312. gír-pa-a gud udu gu$_7$-a ú-šim-e ba-[da$^{?}$]-ná

313. gir$_4$ maḫ-ba gud udu ì-ak-e ir nu-mu-un-ur$_5$-ur$_5$-e

314. bur-sag á sikil ^{d}nanna-ka za-pa-ág-bi ba-ra-gul
315. é gud-gin$_7$ gù bí-íb-du$_{11}$-ga-a-ri si-ga-bi ba-dù
316. mu-un-DU kù-ga si nu-un-sá-e gar-ra-bi ba-sù-ud
317. ^{na_4}kikkin ^{giš}naga$_3$ ^{giš}gan-na ì-dúr-dúr lú nu-um-ši-gam-e

288. [. . .]
289. . . .
290. . . .
291. . . . like a great ration . . .
292. Enlil threw open the door of the grand gate to the wind.
293. In Ur no one went to fetch food, no one went to fetch drink,
294. Its people rush around like water *churning* in a well,
295. Their strength has ebbed away, they cannot (even) go on their way.
296. Enlil afflicted the city with an inimical famine.
297. He afflicted the city with something that destroys cities, that destroys temples,
298. He afflicted the city with something that cannot be withstood with weapons,
299. He afflicted the city with dissatisfaction and treachery.
300. In Ur, which was like a solitary reed, there was not (even) *fear*,
301. Its people, like fish being grabbed (in a pond) sought shelter,
302. Everyone lay spread about, no one could rise.
303. At the *royal station* that was on top of the platform there was no food,
304. The king who was used to eating marvelous food grabbed at a (mere) ration,
305. (As) the day grew dark, the eye (of the sun) was eclipsing, (the people) experienced hunger,
306. There was no beer in his (the king's) beer-hall, there was no more malt (for making) it,
307. There was no food for him in the palace, it was made unsuitable to live in,
308. Grain filled not his lofty storehouse, he could not (send there for supplies) to save his life.
309. The grain stacks and grain depots of Nanna held no grain,
310. The evening meal in the great dining hall of the gods was defiled,
311. Beer, wine, and honey ceased (to flow) in the great dining hall,
312. The butcher knife that used to slay sheep and oxen lay hungry in the grass,
313. Its mighty oven no longer processed sheep and oxen, it no longer emitted the aroma (of roasting meat).
314. The sounds of the Bursag of Nanna were stilled,
315. The temple, which used to bellow like a bull, was silenced,
316. Its holy deliveries were no longer fulfilled, its . . . were alienated,
317. The mortar, pestle, and grinding stone lay idle, no one bends down (to use them).

318. kar-za-gìn-na ^{d}nanna-ka a-e ba-da-lá
319. a ^{giš}má-sag-gá-ke$_4$ gù nu-mu-un-gi$_4$-gi$_4$ asil$_3$-lá nu-mu-un-šub

320. unu$_2$-RI-bàn-da ^{d}nanna-ka saḫar ba-da-dub-dub
321. ^{ú}numun$_2$ ba-da-mú ^{ú}numun$_2$ ba-da-mú gir-re-e ba-an-mú

322. má má-gur$_8$-ra kar-za-gìn-na mùš im-ma-ab-de$_6$
323. íd má-gur$_8$-ra ba-ab-du$_7$-a-za á nu-un-sù-sù-e
324. ezen ki garza-ka giš-ḫur-bi ba-da-kúr
325. má nisag-gá a-a ugu-na-ka nisag nu-mu-un-na-ab-túm

326. ^{ninda}nindaba-bi ^{d}en-líl nibru^{ki}-šè nu-mu-da-an-ku$_4$-ku$_4$
327. íd-bi šà-su$_{13}$-ga ì-gál má-gur$_8$ nu-mu-un-dib-bé
328. gú ^{min_6}min-a-bi giri$_3$ nu-gál ú gíd-da ba-àm-mú

329. é-tùr dagal-la ^{d}nanna-ka dub-ba-an-bi ba-si-il
330. gi-sig ^{giš}kiri$_6$-ka šu ba-e-[lá$^{?}$]-lá gú-giri$_{16}$ ba-an-gar-gar
331. áb šilam-ma amar-bi ba-[da-a]b-dab$_5$ ki erim$_2$-e ba-ab-de$_6$

332. áb ^{ú}munzer-e eden ki nu-zu-bi giri$_3$ kúr ba-ra-an-dab$_5$-bé-eš

333. ^{d}ga-a-a-ú lú áb ki-ág-gá ^{giš}tukul šurim-ma ba-šub
334. ^{d}šu-ni-dùg i̯à ga-àr-ra du$_6$-ul-du$_6$-ul-e i̯à ga-àr-ra nu-du$_6$-ul-du$_6$-ul

335. i̯à-bi lú i̯à nu-zu-ne ì-dun$_5$-dun$_5$-ne
336. ga-bi lú ga nu-zu-ne ì-im-mùš-mùš-ù-ne
337. é-tùr-ra ^{dug}šakir$_3$-e dun$_5$-dun$_5$-e gù nun nu-mu-ni-ib-bé
338. ne-mur dugud-gin$_7$ ì-ra-a-ri i-bí-bi ba-gul
339. [. . .]x unu$_2$ gal ^{d}nanna-ka [. . .]
340. ^{d}en.zu-e a-a-ni ^{d}en-líl-ra ér mu-un-na-še$_8$-še$_8$
341. a-a ugu-mu uru^{ki}-mu a-na-ra-dù$^{?}$ a-na-aš ba-e-da-gur-re-en

342. ^{d}en-líl uri$_5$^{ki}-mu a-na-ra-dù$^{?}$ a-na-aš ba-e-da-gur-re-en

343. má nisag-gá a-a ugu-na-šè nisag nu-mu-un-na-ab-tùm

344. nindaba-zu ^{d}en-líl nibru^{ki}-šè nu-mu-un-na-da-an-ku$_4$-ku$_4$
345. en uru bar-ra en uru šà-ga líl-e ḫa-ba-ab-laḫ$_5$-e-eš

318. The Shining Quay of Nanna was silted up.
319. The sound (of water lapping against) the prow of the boat ceased, there was no rejoicing,
320. The UnuRIbanda of Nanna was heaped with dust.
321. The rushes grew, the rushes grew, the "mourning reeds" grew (and as a result),
322. Boats and ships ceased docking at the Shining Quay.
323. Nothing moved on the watercourse that was fit for large ships.
324. The rites of the festivals at the place of the "plans" were altered,
325. The boat with first fruit-offerings no longer brings the first fruit offerings to the father who begat him (Nanna),
326. Its food offerings could not be taken to Enlil in Nippur.
327. Its watercourse was empty, (and so) ships could not travel,
328. There were no paths on both of its banks (for) long grasses grew (there).
329. The reed fence of the fecund cattle pen of Nanna was torn out,
330. The garden huts were overrun, (their) walls were breached,
331. The cow and her young were captured (and) carried off to enemy territory.
332. The *munzer*-fed cows took an unfamiliar path, in a steppe that they did not know,
333. Gaa̭u, who loves cows, dropped his weapon in the dung,
334. Šunidu, who stores the butter and cheese, did not store the butter and cheese.
335. Those who are unfamiliar with butter were churning the butter,
336. Those who are unfamiliar with milk were . . . ing the cream.
337. The sound of the churning vat did not resound in the cattle pen,
338. Like mighty fire that used to burn (but now) its smoke is extinguished,
339. [. . .] the great dining hall of Nanna [. . .],
340. Suʾen wept to his father Enlil:
341. "O father who begot me, why have you turned away from Ur the city that *was built for you*?
342. O Enlil, why have you turned away from Ur, the city that *was built for you*?"
343. The boat with first fruit-offerings no longer brings the first fruit offerings to the father who begot him,
344. Its food offerings could no longer be brought to Enlil in Nippur."
345. The En-priests of the city and of the countryside were carried off by phantoms,

346. uri$_5^{ki}$ uru^{ki} ^{giš}al-e ri-a-gin$_7$ du$_6$-du$_6$-da ba-šid

347. ki-ùr ki ní-dúb-bu ^{d}en-líl-lá èš líl-lá ba-ab-gar
348. ^{d}en-líl uru-zu igi-zu igi ba x é-ri-a sù-ga
349. nibru^{ki} uru-zu igi-zu x[. . . é-ri-a sù-ga]
350. uri$_5^{ki}$-ma ur-bi úr bàd-da si-im-si-im nu-mu-un-ak-e
351. túl sag bulug-ga ganba-bi-a ki li-bi-ib-ri-ri-ge

352. a-a ugu-mu uru-mu dili-bi-ta á-zu-šè nigin$_2$-àm-ši-ib

353. ^{d}en-líl uri$_5^{ki}$-mu dili-bi-ta á-zu-šè nigin$_2$-àm-ši-ib
354. é-kiš-nu-gál-mu dili-bi-ta á-zu-šè nigin$_2$-àm-ši-ib
355. uri$_5^{ki}$-ma numun ḫa-ra-ni-ib-è un ḫu-mu-ra-ab-dagal-la
356. me ki-en-gi-ra ba-da-ḫa-lam-e ki-bi ḫa-ra-ab-gi$_4$-gi$_4$

357. ki-ru-gú 3-kam-ma
358. a é zi é zi a lú-bi lú-bi

359. giš-gi$_4$-gál-bi-im
360. ^{d}en-líl-le dumu-ni ^{d}en.zu-ra mu-un-na-ni-ib-gi$_4$-gi$_4$
361. uru$_2$ líl-lá šà-bi a-nir-ra gi ér-ra ba-àm-mú
361a. [šà-b]i a-še-ra gi ér-ra ba-àm-mú
362. šà-bi-a a-nir-ra u$_4$ mi-ni-ib-zal-zal-e
362a. [dumu-m]u dumu gi$_7$ IM.ZA-bi-me-en ér-ra ⟨a$^?$⟩-na-bi-me-en
363. ^{d}nanna dumu gi$_7$ IM.ZA-bi-me-en ér-ra ⟨a$^?$⟩-na-bi-me-en

364. di-til-la inim pu-úḫ-ru-um-ma-ka šu gi$_4$-gi$_4$ nu-gál
365. inim du$_{11}$-ga an ^{d}en-líl-lá-ka šu bal-e nu-zu
366. uri$_5^{ki}$-ma nam-lugal ḫa-ba-šúm bala da-rí la-ba-an-šúm
367. u$_4$ ul kalam ki gar-ra-ta zag un lu-a-šè

368. bala nam-lugal-la sag-bi-šè è-a a-ba-a igi im-mi-in-du$_8$-a

369. nam-lugal-bi bala-bi ba-gíd-e-dè šà-kúš-ù-dè
370. ^{d}nanna-mu na-an-kúš-kúš-ù-dè uru^{ki}-zu è-bar-ra-ab
371. u$_4$-ba lugal-mu dumu gi$_7$-ra ur$_5$-ra-ni ba-an-BAD

372. en ^{d}aš-ím-babbar dumu gi$_7$-ra šà ḫul-lu im-ma-an-dím
373. ^{d}nanna lú uru^{ki}-ni ki-ág-gá uru^{ki}-ni ba-ra-è

346. Ur, like a city that has been wrought by the hoe, became a ruined mound,

347. The Kiur, the place of Enlil's flour offerings, became a haunted shrine.

348. O Enlil, your city . . . an empty wasteland,

349. Nippur, your city . . . an empty wasteland.

350. The dogs of Ur no longer sniff at the base of the city wall.

351. The one who (used to) drill large wells, (now just) scratches the ground in the market place.

352. "My father who bore me, my city, which is all alone, return to your embrace,

353. Enlil, my (city of) Ur, which is all alone, return to your embrace,

354. My Ekišnugal, which is all alone, return to your embrace!

355. May you bring forth offspring in Ur, may you multiply (its) people,

356. May you restore the (divine) decrees of Sumer that have been forgotten!"

357. *The third kirugu.*

358. Oh, the righteous temple, the righteous temple! Oh, its people, its people!

359. *—the antiphone of the kirugu.*

360. Enlil then answers his son Suʾen:

361. "There is lamentation in the haunted city, 'mourning' reeds grow there,

361a. In its midst there is lamentation, 'mourning' reeds grow there,

362. In it (the population) pass their days in sighing.

362a. My son, the Noble Son . . . , why do you concern yourself with crying?

363. O Nanna, the Noble Son . . . , why do you concern yourself with crying?

364. The judgment of the assembly cannot be turned back,

365. The word of An and Enlil knows no overturning,

366. Ur was indeed given kingship (but) it was not given an eternal reign.

367. From time immemorial, since the land was founded, until the population multiplied,

368. Who has ever seen a reign of kingship that would take precedence (for ever)?

369. The reign of its kingship had been long indeed but had to exhaust itself.

370. O my Nanna, do not exert yourself (in vain), leave your city!"

371. Then, (upon hearing this), His Majesty, the Noble Son, became distraught,

372. Lord Ašimbabbar, the Noble Son, grieved,

373. Nanna, who loves his city, left his city,

374. ^{d}en.zu-e uri$_5^{ki}$ ki-ág-gá giri$_3$-ni ba-ra-an-dab$_5$
375. ^{d}nin-gal-e KAS$_4$ uru^{ki}-ni-ta ki kúr-šè du-ù-dè
376. túg ul$_4$-ul$_4$-la-bi ba-ra-an-mú uru^{ki}-ta ba-ra-è
377. uri$_5^{ki}$-ma ^{d}a-nun-na-bi bar-ra ba-su$_8$-ge-eš
378. uri$_5^{ki}$-ma NE IM-bi KI x x x a ba-a-te
379. uri$_5^{ki}$-ma giš-bi tu-ra-àm gi-bi tu-ra-àm
380. bàd-bi en-na nigin$_2$-na-bi-da a-nir ba-da-di
381. u$_4$-šú-uš-e ^{giš}tukul-e igi-bi-šè sag ì-sìg-sìg-ge
382. uri$_5^{ki}$-ma ^{urudu}ḫa-zi-in gal-gal-e igi-bi-šè ù-sar ì-ak-e
383. ^{giš}gíd-da á mè-ke$_4$ si bí-íb-sá-sá-e-ne
384. ^{giš}ban gal-gal ^{giš}illar ^{kuš}e-íb-ùr-ra ur im-da-gu$_7$-e
385. ^{giš}ti-zú-ke$_4$ muru$_9$ šèg-gá-gin$_7$ bar-ba mi-ni-in-si
386. na$_4$ gal-gal-e ní-bi-a pu-ud-pa-ad im-mi-ni-ib-za
386a. u$_4$-šú-uš uru^{ki}-ta im ḫul-e mu-un-da-an-gi$_4$-gi$_4$
387. uri$_5^{ki}$ nè-bi-ta nir-gál ḫúb-gaz-e ba-gub

388. un-bi lú erim$_2$-e á bí-íb-gar ^{giš}tukul-e la-ba-su$_8$-ge-eš

389. uru ^{giš}tukul-e sag nu-šúm-mu-a šà-gar-e im-ús

390. šà-gar-e uru a-gin$_7$ ba-e-si gá-la nu-um-ta-dag-ge
391. šà-gar-e igi-bi im-gam-me-e sa-bi im-lu-gú-ne
392. un-bi a nigin$_2$-na ba-e-si zi ur$_5$ i-ak-e
393. lugal-bi é-gal ní-te-na-ka zi gig mu-un-pa-an-pa-an
394. nam-lú-ulu$_3$-bi ^{giš}tukul ba-e-šub ^{giš}tukul ki bí-íb-tag
395. šu-bi gú-bi-šè ba-ši-ib-ri-ri ér mu-un-še$_8$-še$_8$-ne
396. ní-bi-a ad mi-ni-ib-gi$_4$-gi$_4$ inim im-šár-šár-e-ne
397. me-li-e-a du$_{11}$-ga-me nam-mu daḫ-me nam-mu
398. èn-šè-àm ka garaš$_2$-a-ka i-im-til-le-dè-en-dè-en
399. uri$_5^{ki}$-ma šà-bi nam-ús-àm bar-bi nam-ús-àm
400. šà-bi-a níg-šà-gar-ra-ka i-im-til-le-dè-en-dè-en
401. bar-bi-a ^{giš}tukul elam^{ki}-ma-ka ga-nam-ba-[e-til-l]e-en-dè-en
402. uri$_5^{ki}$-ma lú erim$_2$-e á bí-ib-gar ga-nam-ba-til-e-dè-⟨en⟩-dè-en
403. zi-bi murgu-bi-šè ì-ak-e gù-téš-a bí-in-sì-ke-eš

404. é-gal a ba-šub-ba šu ba-e-lá-lá ^{giš}si-gar-bi bí-in-bu-bu-uš

405. elam^{ki}-e a maḫ è-a-gin$_7$ gidim im-ma-ni-íb-gar

374. Suʾen took an unfamiliar path away from his beloved Ur.
375. Ningal . . . in order to go to an alien place,
376. Quickly clothed herself (and) left the city.
377. (All) the Anunna stepped outside of Ur,
378. Ur . . . approached,
379. The trees of Ur were sick, the reeds of Ur were sick,
380. Laments sounded all along its city wall.
381. Daily there was slaughter before it.
382. Large axes were sharpened in front of Ur,
383. The spears, the arms of battle, were being launched,
384. The large bows, javelin, and siege-shield gather together to strike,
385. The barbed arrows covered its outer side like a raining cloud,
386. Large stones, one after another, fell with great thuds.
386a. Daily the evil wind returns to (attack) the city.
387. Ur, which had been confident in its own strength, stood ready for slaughter,
388. Its people, oppressed by the enemy, could not withstand (their) weapons.
389. (Those) in the city who had not been felled by weapons, died of hunger,
390. Hunger filled the city like water, it would not cease,
391. (This) hunger contorts (people's) faces, it twists their muscles.
392. Its people are (as if) surrounded by water, they gasp for breath,
393. Its king breathed heavily in his palace, all alone,
394. Its people dropped (their) weapons, (their) weapons hit the ground,
395. They struck their necks with their hands and cried.
396. They sought counsel with each other, they searched for clarification,
397. "Alas, what can we say about it, what more can we add to it?
398. How long until we are finished off by (this) catastrophe?
399. Ur—inside it there is death, outside it there is death,
400. Inside it we are being finished off by famine,
401. Outside it we are being finished off by Elamite weapons.
402. In Ur the enemy has oppressed us, oh, we are finished!"
403. They *take refuge* behind it (the city walls), they were united (in their fear).
404. The palace that was destroyed by (onrushing) waters has been defiled, its bolt was torn out,
405. Elam, like a swelling flood wave, *left only the spirits of the dead.*

406. uri$_5$^{ki}-ma ^{giš}tukul ^{dug}saḫar$_2$-gin$_7$ sag-gaz ì-ak-e
407. lú kar-ra-bi du$_{10}$ nu-um-zil-e bàd zag-ga bí-in-dab$_5$-bé-eš
407a. ku$_6$ a nigin$_2$-na lu-ga-gin$_7$ zi-bi in-tùm-tùm-mu-ne
407b. é-kiš-nu-gál ^{d}nanna-ka lú erim$_2$-e ba-e-dab$_5$
407c. sig an-gar-bi dugud gál-la A.MUŠEN im-ze-er-ze-re-ne
408. alan AN.ZAG-ge si-a-bi gú-gur$_5$ ba-an-ne-eš
409. ^{d}nin-i̯à-gara$_2$ agrig maḫ-e erim$_3$-ma šu bí-in-dag
410. ^{giš}gu-za-bi igi-bi-ta ba-e-šú saḫar-ra ba-da-an-tuš

411. áb maḫ-bi si-mùš-bi ba-ra-an-dab$_5$-bé-eš si-bi ba-ra-an-ku$_5$

412. gud du$_7$-du$_7$-bi udu ú gu$_7$-a-bi ^{giš}tukul-e ba-an-sìg-sìg
412a. [^{giš}]nimbar-gin$_7$ gú-gur$_5$-ru ba-ab-dug$_4$ ur-bi ba-ra-an-kad$_4$

413. ^{giš}nimbar urudu níg-kala-ga á nam-ur-sag-gá
414. ^{ú}numun$_2$-gin$_7$ ba-bu ^{ú}numun$_2$-gin$_7$ ba-zé úr-ba ti mi-ni-ib-bal

415. sag saḫar-ra ki ba-ni-ib-ú-ús lú zi-zi la-ba-tuku
416. ^{giš}zé-na-bi gú ba-an-gur$_5$-uš sag šu bí-in-ḫu-ḫu-uz

417. á-an su$_{11}$-lum-ma-bi pú du$_7$-du$_7$ ba-ra-an-BU.BU-dè-eš
418. gi zi NAB$^?$ kù-ge mú-a šu ba-e-lá-lá
419. gú-un gal-gal-e mi-ni-in-gar-re-eš-a kur-re ì-íl-íl

420. é-e ^{giš}búr maḫ-bi ba-šub bàd-si-bi ba-gul

421. máš-anše zi-da gùb-bu-ba gú-da lá-a-bi
422. ur-sag ur-sag-e gaz-a-gin$_7$ igi-bi-ta ba-šú
423. ušumgal ka duḫ-a ug-gá ní íl-íl-la-bi
424. am dab$_5$-ba-gin$_7$ saman-e bí-in-šub-bu-ri ki erim$_2$-e ba-ab-de$_6$

425. ki-tuš kù ^{d}nanna tir šim ^{giš}eren-na-gin$_7$ ir-si-im-bi ba-gul

425a. a-sal-bar-bi kù-sig$_{17}$ ^{na_4}za-gìn ki x x-da du$_{11}$-ga-a-bi
426. é u$_6$-di-bi i̯à du$_{10}$-ga-ri u$_6$-di-bi ba-gul

427. u$_4$-gin$_7$ kur-kur-ra im-si-a an-usan an-na-gin$_7$ ba-e-dù

428. ^{giš}ig-bi mul$^?$ an-na x-bi [*traces*] du$_{11}$-ga-ba
429. ^{urudu}bulug gal-gal-e [?] KA [. . . -g]i$_4$-gi$_4$ ba-ra-an-bu-bu-uš

406. In Ur (people) were smashed as if they were clay pots,
407. Its refugees were (unable) to flee, they were trapped inside the walls,
407a. Like fish living in a pond, they seek shelter.
407b. The enemy seized the Ekišnugal of Nanna.
407c. . . .
408. The statues that were in the treasury were cut down,
409. The great stewardess Niniagara *cut herself off from* the storehouse,
410. Its throne was cast down before it, she threw herself down into the dust.
411. Its mighty cows with shining horns were captured, their horns were cut off,
412. Its unblemished oxen and grass-fed cows were slaughtered,
412a. They were cut down as if they were date palms, and their (carcasses) were tied together.
413. The palm tree, (strong) as mighty copper, the heroic weapon,
414. Was torn out like (mere) rushes, was plucked like (mere) rushes, its trunk was turned sideways,
415a. Its top lay in the dust, there was no one to raise it,
416. The midriffs of its palm fronds were cut off and their tops were burnt off,
417. Its date clusters that used to fall on the well were torn out.
418. The fertile reeds, which grew in the sacred . . . , were defiled,
419. The great tribute that they had collected was hauled off to the mountains.
420. The great *door ornament* of the temple was felled, its parapet was destroyed,
421. The wild animals that were intertwined on its left and right
422. Lay before it like heroes smitten by heroes,
423. Its open-mouthed dragons (and) its awe-inspiring lions
424. Were pulled down with ropes like captured wild bulls and carried off to enemy territory.
425. The fragrant aroma of the sacred seat of Nanna was destroyed like that of a cedar grove,
425a. Its architrave . . . gold, silver, and lapis.
426. The admired temple that used (to receive) first class oil, its admiration was extinguished,
427. Like a storm that fills all the lands, built there like twilight in the heavens,
428. Its door . . .
429. Great bronze pins . . . were torn out.

430. ^{kuš}da/á-si-bi a-ba I[M . . .] LI-bi-šè TÚG.P[I . . .] ba-ab-dug$_4$
431. ^{giš}nu-kúš-ù-bi-da lú kar-ra-gin$_7$ ér gig ì-še$_8$-še$_8$
432. ^{giš}sag-kul ^{giš}saḫab$_2$ kù-ga ^{giš}ig gal gú bu-i nu-mu-na-ab-bé
433. ^{giš}ig gú-gíd-da za-pa-ág-bi ba-šub lú gú bu-i la-ba-an-tuku
434. [. . .]x-ba-šè ba-lá-lá sila dagal-la ní-bi ba-ab-gar
435. ki x x x KI.LUGAL.GUB-bu-na nindaba-bi ba-kúr

436. ki$^?$ kù-ba tigi$_2$ šem$_5$ ^{kuš}á-lá-e gù nun nu-mu-ni-ib-bé

437. ^{giš}tigi$_2$ maḫ-ba ér$^?$ x[. .]-si-a šìr kù nu-mu-na-ab-bé
438. dub-lá-maḫ ki nam-ku$_5$-re-dè ka-inim-ma nu-gál

439. ^{giš}gu-za ki di ku$_5$-ru-bi nu-mu-un-gub di si nu-um-sá-e

440. ^{d}alamuš-e ^{giš}gidri ba-da-an-šub šu-ni gu$_4$$^?$-ud-gu$_4$-ud
441. á-ná-da kù ^{d}nanna-ke$_4$ balag na-mu-un-tag-ge-ne

442. dub-šen kù lú igi nu-bar-re-dam erim$_2$-e igi i-ni-in-bar
443. ^{giš}ná-gi$_4$-rin-na nu-um-gub ú za-gìn nu-mu-un-bara$_3$
444. alan AN.ZAG-ge$_4$ si-a-ba gú-gur$_5$ ba-an-ne-eš
445. engiz ensi kišib$_3$-gál-bi eš-da šu li-bí-in-du$_7$-uš

446. gú ki-šè gál-la-bi ba-e-su$_8$-su$_8$-ge-eš kúr-re ba-ab-laḫ$_5$-e-eš
447. us-ga kù šu-luḫ daddag-ga šà-gada-lá-bi-e-ne
448. giš-ḫur me kù-ga ba-da-ḫa-lam-e uru kúr-šè ba-e-re$_7$-eš
449. ^{d}en.zu-e šà ḫul-la-ni a-a-ni-ir ba-ši-in-gin
450. igi a-a ugu-na ^{d}en-líl-lá-šè du$_{10}$ ki ba-ni-in-ús
451. a-a ugu-mu èn-tukum-šè níg-ka$_9$-mu igi erim$_2$ mu-e-du$_8$ èn-tukum-šè SAR

452. nam-en nam-lugal šúm-ma-za-àm x mu-e-ši-dé$^?$
453. a-a ^{d}en-líl lú á-ág-e du$_{11}$-ga zi
454. inim kù-zu kalam-m[a . . .]
455. [d]i$^?$ níg-kúr-zu š[à$^?$ . . .]
456. šà sú-mu-ug-ga i-zi-gin$_7$ ḫu-luḫ-ḫa-za igi-zi bar-mu-un-ši-ib
457. a-a ^{d}en-líl nam mu-e-tar-ra galga ba-ra-an-du$_8$-du$_8$
458. šiki PA nam-en-na suḫ kéš-da-gá
459. u$_4$ sikil maḫ luḫ-luḫ x x[. . .]x ^{túg}mu-sír-ra mi-ni-in-mu$_4$
460. ^{d}en-líl-le dumu-ni ^{d}en.zu-ra inim zi mu-un-na-ab-bé

430. . . .
431. Together with its . . . it? wept bitterly like a fugitive.
432. The bolt, the holy lock . . .
433. . . .
434. . . . was placed on the wide street.
435. . . . the food offerings of his *royal dining place* were altered (for the worse),
436. In its sacred [. . .] the *tigi*, *šem*, and *ala* instruments did not sound their splendid notes,
437. Its mighty *tigi* [. . .] did not sing its sacred song.
438. Verdicts were not given at the Dublamaḫ, the place where oaths used to be taken,
439. The throne was not set up at its place of judgment, justice was not administered.
440. Alamuš threw down his scepter, his hands *trembled*.
441. (Musicians) no longer played the *balag* instrument in the sacred bedchamber of Nanna,
442. The sacred box that no one had set eyes upon was seen by the enemy,
443. The divine bed was not set up, it was not spread with clean hay,
444. The statues that were in the treasury were cut down,
445. The temple cook, the dream interpreter, and the "seal keeper" did not prepare the ceremony,
446. They stood in submission and were carried off by the foreigners.
447. The holy *uzga*-priests of the sacred lustrations, the linen clad priests,
448. Forsake the sacred rites and decrees, they go off to a foreign city.
449. In his grief Suʾen approached his father,
450. He went down on his knee in front of Enlil, the father who begot him.
451. "O father who begot me, how long will the enemy eye be cast upon my account, how long . . . ?
452. The *en*-ship and the kingship that you bestowed [. . .] . . . ,
453. Father Enlil, the one who advises with just words,
454. The wise words of the land [. . .],
455. Your inimical judgment [. . .],
456. Look into your darkened heart, terrifying like waves!
457. O father Enlil, the fate that you have decreed cannot be explained!
458. . . . of *en*-ship, my ornament."
459. . . . he put on a mourning garment.
460. Enlil then provides a favorable response to his son:

461. dumu-mu uru nam-ḫé giri$_{17}$-zal ša-ra-da-dù-a bala-zu ba-ši-ib-tuku

462. uru gul bàd gal bàd-si-bi sì-ke ù-ur$_5$-re bala an-ga-àm

463. sá mi-ri-ib-du$_{11}$-ga bala u$_4$ kukku$_2$-ga BI.IR gál-lu ša-ra-da
464. dúr-ù-ri ki-tuš é-temen-ní-gùr-ru-za zi-dè-eš dù-dù-àm
465. uri$_5$^{ki} giri$_{17}$-zal-la ḫé-en-dù un ḫé-en-ši-gam-e
466. úr-bi-a níg ḫé-en-gál ^{d}ašnan ḫé-éb-da-tuš
467. pa-bi-a giri$_{17}$-zal ḫé-en-gál ^{d}utu ḫé-en-da-ḫúl
468. ^{giš}banšur-ba ḫé-gál ^{d}ašnan-ka gú-da ḫé-em-mi-ib-lá
469. uri$_5$^{ki} uru an-né nam tar-re ki-bi ḫa-ra-ab-gi$_4$-gi$_4$

470. ^{d}en-líl-le gù zi dé-àm gú an-šè ḫé-en-zi

471. ^{d}nanna-ra ma-da sig igi nim-ma gú ḫu-mu-na-ab-si-a
472. ^{d}en.zu-ra kaskal kur-ra-ke$_4$ si ḫé-en-na-sá-e
473. muru$_9$-gin$_7$ ki ús-sa-a-gin$_7$ šu mu-un-na-gá-gá
474. inim du$_{11}$-ga an ^{d}en-líl-lá-kam šu zi ḫé-gá-gá
475. a-a ^{d}nanna uru^{ki}-ni uri$_5$^{ki}-ma sag íl-la mu-un-gub
476. šul ^{d}en.zu é-kiš-nu-gál-la-šè im-ma-da-an-ku$_4$-ku$_4$
477. ^{d}nin-gal-e É.NUN-kù-ga-na ní mu-ni-ib-te-en-te-en
477a. uri$_5$^{ki}-ma é-kiš-nu-gál-la-na im-ma-da-an-ku$_4$-ku$_4$
478. ki-ru-gú 4-kam-ma
479. uru^{ki} líl-lá-àm šà-bi a-še-⸢ra⸣ gi ér-ra ba-an-mú
480. šà-bi a-še-ra gi ér-ra ba-an-mú
481. un-bi a-še-er-ra u$_4$ mi-ni-ib-zal-zal-e
482. giš-gi$_4$-gál-bi-im
483. u$_4$ gig-ga u$_4$ gaba-zu zi-ga-ab u$_4$ é-za gi$_4$-bi
484. u$_4$ urú gul-gul u$_4$ gaba-zu zi-ga-ab u$_4$ é-za gi$_4$-bi

485. u$_4$ é gul-gul u$_4$ gaba-zu zi-ga-ab u$_4$ é-za [g]i$_4$-[b]i

486. u$_4$ ki-en-gi-ra ba-e-zal-la kur-re ḫé-eb-zal
487. u$_4$ ma-da ba-e-zal-la kur-re ḫé-eb-zal
488. kur ti-id-nu-um^{ki}-ma-ka ḫé-eb-zal kur-re ḫé-eb-zal
489. kur gu-ti-um^{ki}-ma-ka ḫé-eb-zal kur-re ḫé-eb-zal
490. kur an-ša$_4$-an^{ki}-na-ka ḫé-eb-zal kur-re ḫé-eb-zal
491. an-ša$_4$-an^{ki}-e im ḫul dal-la-gin$_7$ kuš$_7$ ḫé-ni-ib-su-su

461. "My son, the city that was built for you in joy and prosperity, it was given to you as your reign,
462. The destroyed city, the great wall, the walls with broken battlements: all this is part of the (appointed) reign,
463. . . .
464. . . . your dwelling—the Etemenniguru—that was properly built.
465. Ur shall be rebuilt in splendor, may the people bow down (to you),
466. There is to be bounty at its base, there is to be grain,
467. There is to be splendor at its top, the Sun will rejoice there!
468. Let an abundance of grain embrace its table,
469. May Ur, the city whose fate was pronounced by An, be restored for you!"
470. Having pronounced his blessing, Enlil raised his head toward the heavens (saying):
471. "May the land, north and south, be organized for Nanna,
472. May the road(s) of the land be set in order for Suʾen!
473. Like a cloud hugging the earth, they shall submit to him,
474. By order of An and Enlil (abundance) shall be bestowed!"
475. Father Nanna stood in his city of Ur with head raised high (once again),
476. The hero Suʾen entered into the Ekišnugal.
477. Ningal refreshed herself in her sacred living quarters,
477a. In Ur she entered into her Ekišnugal.
478. *The fourth kirugu.*
479. There is lamentation in the haunted city, "mourning" reeds grew there,
480. In its midst there is lamentation, "mourning" reeds grew there.
481. Its people spend their days in moaning.
482. *—the antiphone of the kirugu.*
483. O bitter storm, retreat O storm, storm return to your home!
484. O storm that destroys cities, retreat O storm, storm return to your home!
485. O storm that destroys temples, retreat O storm, storm return to your home!
486. Indeed, the storm that blew on Sumer, blew on the foreign lands,
487. Indeed, the storm that blew on the land, blew on the foreign lands,
488. It has blown on Tidnum, it has blown on the foreign lands,
489. It has blown on Gutium, it has blown on the foreign lands,
490. It has blown on Anšan, it has blown on the foreign lands,
491. (And) it leveled Anšan like a blowing evil storm.

492. šà-gar lú níg-ḫul ḫé-en-da-dab$_5$ un ḫé-em-ši-ib-gam-e
493. me an-na giš-ḫur un gi-né an-né nam-kúr-re

494. di-kuru$_5$ ka-aš bar-re un si sá-sá-e an-né nam-kúr-re

495. kaskal kalam-ma-ke$_4$ giri$_3$ gá-gá an-né nam-kúr-re
496. an-né ^{d}en-líl-bi nam-kúr-ru-ne an-né nam-kúr-re
497. ^{d}en-ki ^{d}nin-maḫ-bi nam-kúr-ru-ne an-né nam-kúr-re
498. ^{íd}idigna ^{íd}buranun-na a-bi tùm-dè an-né nam-kúr-re

499. šeg$_x$(IM.A) an-na ki-a še gu-nu an-né nam-kúr-re

500. íd a-bi-da a-šà še-bi-da an-né nam-kúr-re

501. ambar-ambar-re ku$_6$ mušen tùm an-né ⟨nam-kúr-re⟩
502. ^{giš}gi gi sun gi ḫenbur mú-mú-dè an-né nam-kúr-re

503. an-né ^{d}en-líl-bi nam-kúr-ru-ne
504. ^{d}en-ki ^{d}nin-maḫ-bi nam-kúr-ru-ne
505. pú ^{giš}kiri$_6$ làl geštin ù-tu ⟨an-né nam-kúr-re⟩

506. an eden-na ^{giš}maš-gurum ù-[tu] ⟨an-né nam-kúr-re⟩
507. é-gal-la zi su$_{13}$-ud gál [ù-tu] ⟨an-né nam-kúr-re⟩
508. a-ab-ba ḫé-gál níg ù-tu an-[né nam-kúr-re]
509. ma-da un lu-a sig igi nim-ma an-[né nam-kúr-re]
510. an-né ^{d}en-líl-bi nam-kúr-re-ne an-né nam-kúr-re
511. ^{d}en-ki ^{d}nin-maḫ-bi nam-kúr-re-n[e an-n]é nam-kúr-re
512. uru dù-dù-a un [šár-šár$^{?}$]-ra$^{?}$

513. an-ki nigin$_2$-na un sa[g s]ì-ga

514. ^{d}nanna nam-lugal-zu du$_{10}$-ga-à[m ki-z]a gi$_4$-ni-ib
515. uri$_5^{ki}$ bala du$_{10}$ nam-ḫé u$_4$ ḫé-ib-su$_{13}$-ud-dè
516. un-bi ú sal-la ḫé-eb-ná e-ne-su$_{13}$-ud ḫé$^{!}$-em-ak$^{?}$
517. a nam-lú-ulu$_3$ ba-ḫúb KU-re egí-re mu-lu ér a-še-re
518. ^{d}nanna a uru-zu a é-zu a nam-lú-u$_{18}$-lu$_7$-zu
519. ki-ru-gú 5-kam-ma-àm

492. Famine has overwhelmed the evil doer—may (that) people submit!
493. May An not change the decrees of heaven, the plans to treat the people with justice,
494. May An not change the decisions and judgments to lead the people properly,
495. Travel on the roads of the land—may An not change it,
496. May An and Enlil not change it—may An not change it,
497. May Enki and Ninmaḫ not change it—may An not change it,
498. That the Tigris and Euphrates (again) carry water—may An not change it,
499. That there (again) be rain in the skies and good crops on the ground—may An not change it,
500. That there be water courses with water and fields with grain—may An not change it,
501. That the marshes support fish and fowl—may An not change it,
502. That fresh reeds and new shoots grow in the canebrake—may An not change it,
503. May An and Enlil not change it,
504. May Enki and Ninmaḫ not change it,
505. That the orchards bear honey-plants and grapevines—may An not change it,
506. That the high plain bear the *mašgurum* plant—may An not change it,
507. That there be long life in the palace—may An not change it,
508. That the sealand bring forth abundance—may An not change it,
509. That the land be populated from north to south—may An not change it,
510. May An and Enlil not change it—may An not change it,
511. May Enki and Ninmaḫ not change it—may An not change it,
512. That cities be rebuilt, that the people be numerous—may An not change it,
513. That in the whole universe the people be cared for—may An not change it!
514. O Nanna, your kingship is sweet, return to your place!
515. May a good abundant reign be long lasting in Ur!
516. Let its people lie down in safe pastures, let them copulate!
517. O mankind . . . *egi*$_2$*-re mu-lu a-še-re*.
518. O Nanna—oh, your city! Oh, your temple! Oh, your people!
519. *The fifth kirugu*.

Chapter 5

Philological Commentary

The following notes are intended to assist in the reading of the text and to justify certain translations. In order to help place the text in the literary canon, I have often cited other "laments." As is common with all editions of Sumerian texts, multiple interpretations of words and lines are always possible. I have not listed every possible reading for each and every line but have tried to provide a consistent translation that reflects my understanding of the entire text. In view of the fact that the *Pennsylvania Sumerian Dictionary* is now a reality it makes little sense to use text editions as pretexts for the creation of Sumerian glossaries.

1. This line is listed in three "literary catalogs": *BASOR* 88 (1942) 16, line 34; *TCL* 15 28, line 29; and *UET* 6 123, line 45. In the first it follows the Ur and Nippur laments and precedes an as yet unidentified composition that began with the line uru me zi-da, 'city of the true (divine) decrees'. In the second it follows after uru me zi-da; in the Ur catalog it follows the Ur lament and precedes a composition entitled u_4 ḫuš ki-en-gi-ra. The incipits of *LE* and *LW* are not preserved but it is possible that these are the opening lines of these two laments (Green, *Eridu* 279).

There is some difficulty in the understanding of ḫa-lam in this line, as well as in the related expressions in lines 21, 27, 356, and 448. One can take ḫa-lam = *ḫalāqu*, as did S. N. Kramer, *ANET*^{3} 612, and translate 'to destroy'. There is evidence, however, that in combination with me and giš-ḫur, this verb was understood in antiquity as *mašû* 'to forget, forsake'; see Farber-Flügge, *Inanna und Enki* 151, and Cohen, *Sumerian Hymnology* 175. In lines 68 and 230 ḫa-lam is to be understood as *ḫalāqu*.

2. For ur-bi . . . gu_7 'to strike head on, to clash together, to brawl, to press together, to fight in a pack', see M. W. Green, *JCS* 30 (1978) 153–55 and *JAOS* 104 (1984) 278. Green argues for a reading ur but téš is equally possible. Note the references cited by M. Civil, *Or*, n.s. 56 (1987) 243, N 3394:6′ (*Šulgi C*): u_4 2-šè kur-re ku_6 $dara_2$-gin_7 ur-bi g[u_7 . . .], 'For two days the foreign countries gather together like fish on a string'; and *EWO* 243: ku_6 $dara_2$-gin_7 ur-bi gu_7-ù-[. . .], said of Elam and Marḫaši. Perhaps the image is one of a pack getting together to strike in unison. See also lines 113 and 384. Alternatively, one could translate 'clash together' or 'devour all' in all three lines.

4. In this line gi_4 = *peḫû* 'to lock up', as in *SBH* 31:6 where é-a àm-gi is translated *ina* É *pe-ḫu-ú*.

5. The variation between the different uru signs is, for the most part, of little importance in the text; see, for some of the lexical evidence, M. W. Green, *JAOS* 104 (1984) 278–79. For this line it may be important to note the equivalence uru_2 = ***abūbu*** (see *CAD* A/1 77), that is, as a synonym of the mar-ru_{10} of line 2, a fact that must have appealed to some of the scribes who copied these lines.

6. A similar pattern is found in *LU* 391–92: u_4 uru_2 gul-gul-e u_4 é gul-gul-e u_4 tùr gul-gul-le u_4 amaš tab-tab-e. See also *Death of Ur-Namma* 205: ᵈinanna-ke_4 tùr im-gul-e amaš im-tab-bé, with C. Wilcke's comment in *CRRAI* 17 87 n. 2, who suggests that tab is syllabic for táb = ***ḫamāṭu***, ***ṣarāpu*** 'to burn'. In view of the parallelism it is better to accept tab = ***sapānu*** 'to destroy, devastate'.

8. The word dagal is not often used as a finite verb. *Lugale* 404 is informative for the semantic range of this verb: OB kur-[re] máš anše ḫa-ra-ab-lu-e = Late [kur-re máš] an[še] ḫa-r[a-a]b-dagal-l[a] = [*šá-d*]*i-i b*[*u-u*]*l-šu li-rap-piš-ki*. The literal translation of dagal as 'wide' when used with wildlife misses the meaning, hence I have translated the verb here as to 'multiply' and in line 78 the commonly encountered phrase eden níg-dagal-ba as 'teeming plain'. A good example for such a meaning is provided by *CA* 127: a-gàr maḫ a-eštub.ku_6 dagal-la-gin_7, 'As if for great tracts with teeming carp ponds.' For another instance of the connection between lu and dagal see, for example, *OECT* 5 25 39: $eren_2$-a-ni ú-gin_7 lu-lu-a numun-a-ni dagal-la, 'Their troops (of Šimaški) are numerous as (blades of) grass, their seed is fertile.' Other examples would support a more literal translation in this line. See, for example, *Hoe and Plough* 123: é-tùr gíd-da-me-en amaš dagal-la-me-en, 'I am the one who enlarges the cattle pen, I am the one who widens the sheep fold.'

10. The first phrase of line 10, gán-né zi-dè = *mēreštu* 'cultivated field'. For ᵘKI.KAL see M. Civil, *JAOS* 88 (1968) 10, and the lexical evidence collected in *CAD* under *lardu*, 'a plant with high alkali content, used as soap'. The two possible readings of the logogram, sas and ḫurin/ḫirin, are discussed by M. Civil, *Studies Reiner* 48.

11. Usually, ᵘa-nir is rendered as 'mourning grass'; see Cooper, *Agade* 62, line 265 (see also 274): ḫar-ra-an ᵍⁱˢgigir-ra ba-gar-ra-zu ᵘa-nir ḫé-em-mú, 'May "mourning grass" grow on your highways laid for coaches!' This etymological translation, which undoubtedly renders part of the meaning for the writing a-nir, must, in the context of laments and related texts, make allusion to the misfortune that has struck the land. It is not clear, however, what plant is actually meant here and one must note that the reading of the signs is not clear. Wilcke, *Lugalbanda* 144 n. 396 notes the variation a-rí-na / ᵘa-nir in a Šulgi hymn.

12. The phrase ki . . . kin-kin = ***ašra še'û***. Thus *Nanše Hymn* 25, si-ga-ar ki mu-na-ab-kin-kin-e, was translated by Heimpel as 'she (Nanše) seeks out a place for the weak,' or, from a Ninḫursag eršemma BM 98396 6–7: ama-gan-ra aš tar-tar ki kin-kin kur úr-ra ba-te, aš tar-tar-re ki kin-kin-e kur úr-ra ba-te,

'As for the birth-giving mother—inquiring, searching, she approached the base of the underworld, by inquiring, searching, she approached the base of the underworld' (S. N. Kramer, *Eretz Israel* 16 [1982] 142); *Bird and Fish* 107: ku_6-e ki si-ga-aš mu-un-kin-kin, with gloss *aš-ra-am ša-qum-mi-iš* in *CT* 42 42 ii 10′: 'The fish, in silence, searched for his (the bird's) place.' Note also *LU* 370: uri_5^{ki}-ma dumu sila ḫa-lam-ma-gin_7 ki mu-e-ši-kin-kin, 'Ur, like a child lost in the streets, searches for you.' There seems to be little difference between ki . . . kin and kin, although note the contrast in *CT* 15 8 rev. 7–8: lú-ù ki bí-kin-kin e-ne nam-mu-pàd-dè e-ne ⟨nam-mu-pàd-dè⟩, é-ri-a ì-kin-kin e-ne nam-mu-pàd-dè e-ne ⟨nam-mu-pàd-dè⟩. See also A. Falkenstein, *WO* 1 (1950) 381.

14. It is possible to read the beginning of the line as dam tur, dam dumu, or dam $banda_3$. The latter reading was preferred by A. Falkenstein, *WO* 1 (1950) 378, and H. Neumann, *La femme dans le Proche-Orient Antique* (Paris, 1987) 135. If one accepts this interpretation then it would follow that the reference to the 'lap' should have a sexual connotation. Similar images are used to describe the nonhuman nature of "demons" in Sumerian literature who cannot enjoy sex and snatch away the wife from the man during their revels; see the passages cited by Alster, *Dumuzi's Dream* 104–5. The reading $banda_3$ is supported by the occurrences of dam ban_3-da (*PSD* B 84) and by the parallel passage found in *Sumerian Lullaby* 35–38: dam ḫé-en-da-zé-eb du_5-mu ḫé-en-da-zé-eb dam $banda_3$ úr-ra-na ḫa-ba-ḫúl-e du_5-mu du_{10}-ub zé-ba-na ḫa-ba-$bulug_3$-e, 'May the wife be happy with him, may the son be happy with him, may the junior wife take joy in his embrace, may the son grow vigorous on her sweet knee.'

16. For the various writings of umeda 'wetnurse', see P. Steinkeller, *ASJ* 3 (1981) 88–90. Lullabies appear to be a special attribute of wetnurses in Sumerian literature; see C. Wilcke, *JNES* 27 (1968) 233 n. 13, and M. Civil, *Aula Orientalis* 1 (1983) 50.

17–19. The idea that "kingship" is a quality that can be given or taken away is a concept that is also a component of the ideology of power that is expressed in the *Sumerian King List*. See my observations in *JAOS* 103 (1983) 237–48.

18. The phrase šu . . . lá is difficult. Cooper, *Agade* 254 rendered it as *luʾû* 'to pollute, desecrate, defile'. This lexical equation is probably based on šu pe-el-lá . . . dug_4. P. Attinger, *RA* 78 (1984) 119, points out that šu . . . lá-(lá) is translated by Akkadian *eṣēlu, kasû,* and *lupputu*. I would, provisionally, separate šu . . . lá from šu . . . lá-lá and translate the first as 'to block, paralyze, immobilize', and the latter, Akkadian *lupputu*, as 'to desecrate'. Note that in line 330 the parallelism between šu . . . lá-lá and gú-$giri_{16}$ . . . gar suggests that the verb also means 'to overwhelm, run over'.

22. See the recent discussion of sag-ki . . . gíd 'to frown (as a gesture of divine displeasure)' by Cooper, *Agade* 235. It is interesting that in this passage first An shows displeasure with all countries and then Enlil, the active force in the pantheon, casts an approving glance at *foreign* lands, thus putting into play the forces that will destroy Sumer.

24. Literally, 'After Nintu had scattered all the creatures that she had created.'

28. The translation does not render properly the complex syntax of the Sumerian with the topicalization of Ur and the "decrees of kingship." Literally, urim.ak me nam-lugal.ak bala.bi su.su.e.de is 'Of Ur, of the (divine) decrees of kingship, its reign to alienate.'

29. In her discussion of šu sùḫ-a . . . dug_4 'to confuse, upset, disturb', M. W. Green, *JCS* 30 (1978) 143, noted that the construction šu NP dug_4 is rendered into Akkadian as NP-*iš malû*. In *LSUr* there are five such constructions: šu pe-el-lá . . . dug_4 (29, 99), šu sùḫ-a . . . dug_4 (67, 123), šu ki-in-dar . . . dug_4 (49), šu ḫul . . . dug_4 (115), and šu líl-lá . . . dug_4 (143, 149; see commentary on line 345). The general meaning of the construction appears to be 'to endow with, turn into NP'. The NPs are, for the most part, adjectives that are derived from verbs that form part of the standard repertoire of terms for 'destruction' in literary laments (ḫul, pe-el) or nouns such as líl (see Krecher, *Kultlyrik* 47). It is necessary to understand ḫul and pe-el as near synonyms, as is documented by Nabnitu G_1 12″–13″ (*MSL* 16, 284): ḫu[l] = *šu-ul-pu-tu*, pi-il-lá = [MIN (*šu-ul-pu-tu*)] 'to desecrate'; see also *SBH* 28 14–16: še-eb uru_2-zé-eb-ba^{ki} ba-ḫul-la-ta tin-tir^{ki} nu-um-me é ^{d}am-an-ki ba-ḫul-la-ta é-abzu nu-um-me é ^{d}asar-lú-ḫi ba-pe-el-la-ta é-sag-íl nu-um-me, 'The brickwork of Eridu has been destroyed and Babylon is no more, the temple of Enki has been destroyed—the Eabzu is no more, the temple of Marduk has been destroyed—the Esagila is no more.' It is also possible to translate šu pe-el-lá . . . dug_4 by *qullulu* 'to diminish, discredit'; see Krecher, *Kultlyrik* 185.

Usually translated as 'Princely Son', dumu nun-na is one of the standard epithets of Nanna; see Hall, *Moon God* 646–47.

30. Together with the verb si-il, igi te-en occurs in this line and in line 101 (kur-kur-re du_{10}-ús dili dab_5-ba-bi igi te-en-bi ba-si-il). Normally, igi te-en = *igitennu* 'fraction, proportion', or *itannu* 'interstice of a net'. The latter meaning certainly does not fit here nor in line 101. The contexts require that the predicate describe an act of destruction; hence I have taken it to mean 'to destroy proportions', that is to upset balance, or unity.

31–37. These lines are translated by S. N. Kramer, *Bulletin of the Asia Institute* n.s. 1 (1987) 12–13.

32–33. I have understood the pronoun -bi, affixed to ki-tuš, as referring back to un. It is also possible that it resumes Ur. In that case the lines would be translated as, 'That its people no longer dwell in their quarters, that they be given over (to live) in an inimical place, that (the soldiers of) Šimaški and Elam, the enemy, dwell in their place.'

33. Note the variant line in BB: LÚ×KÁR.SU^{ki} elam^{ki} lú ḫa-lam-ma ki-tuš-bi TUŠ-ù-dè. The writing of LÚ.SU as LÚ×KÁR.SU is a pun that works only on the graphic level: LÚ×KÁR = heš$_5$ 'captive', but it is also syllabic for še$_{29}$-mašku (for the reading of LÚ.SU as Šimaški, see P. Steinkeller, "On the Identity of the Toponym LÚ.SU(.A)," *JAOS* 108 [1988] 197–202). The expression is practically a standard one; see *Išbi-Erra* year "16": mu ^{d}iš-bi-èr-ra lugal-e ugnim LÚ.SU.A ù elam^{ki} bí-in-ra (see *BIN* 10 2). The "day date" that probably comes from the beginning of the same year names only Elam (*BIN* 10 124:3: u$_4$ elam ba-ab-ra-a). Note also *LU* 244: LÚ.SU^{ki} elam^{ki} lú ḫa-lam-ma ušu$_3$-gin$_7$ ba-an-ak-e-eš; and *LE* 4:10: LÚ.⸢SU⸣^{ki} elam^{ki} lú ḫa-l[am-ma igi i-ni]-in-bar.

35. For ^{giš}búr, see the commentary on line 420 below. The tradition that Ibbi-Sin was lead in captivity to Anšan is also reiterated in an Isin dynasty text that describes the graves of the kings of the dynasties of Ur and Isin (*PRAK* II D 41 ii and duplicates; see T. Jacobsen, *JNES* 12 [1953] 182–83; Edzard, *Zwischenzeit* 51).

36. The mountain za-bu occurs also in *Lugalbanda* 2:1–2: lugal-bàn-da kur ki sù-rá gá-la ba-ni-in-dag iši za-bu^{ki}-a nir ba-ni-in-gál. The late version of the latter line reads iši sa-a-bu-a n[ir ba-ni-in-gál] = *ina* KUR-*i sa-a-bi* [. . .]. The only other occurrence known to me is in *Lugalbanda* 1:192: akkil-bi-ta iši za-bu-e. See also Wilcke, *Lugalbanda* 68.

Wilcke, *Lugalbanda* 33–36 and Cohen, *Enmerkar* 50 have assumed that the mountain Zabu is to be identified with Sabum, well known from third-millennium administrative and monumental texts. There is in fact no good reason to make this identification and the late Akkadian version of *Lugalbanda* 2, cited above, can hardly be used to support this identification. The spelling *sa-a-bu-a* in this text is probably based on the entry in the Lipšur Litanies (E. Reiner, *JNES* 15 [1956] 132:1–2): [KUR] *sa-a-bu lip-šur*.

38. It is often difficult to distinguish gú ^{min_6}min-a-ba paleographically and thus the two different MIN signs, written almost as a ligature, can be mistaken for SI or GÚ (see, for example, Cooper, *Agade* 26, who read gú SI.A-bé in citing this line). For other instances of this writing see line 328 below, *CT* 42 30:3′, and particularly *KAR* 16 31–32: lugal-e gú ^{min_6}min-a-ni giri$_3$ mu-na-[gá]-gá = *šar-ru i-na kap-pi ki-lá-la-an* GIRI$_3$.MEŠ-*šu* [*i*]*š-kun*, 'The king stepped on both banks (of the Isinnitu canal).' Particularly interesting is W. G. Lambert, *Studies Albright* 345 rev. 5: lugal-mu kur-ra gi-min$^{[m]in_6}$-ba-gin$_7$ dili mu-un-da-bad-du = *be-lu$_4$ šá šá-da-a ki-ma qa-an šun-na-a e-di-iš tu-na-as-su-ú*, 'My lord, you who separated the mountain like a double reed.' In this passage the Sumerian min^{min_6}-(a)-ba has probably been reinterpreted as min-tab-ba.

40. This is a standard image. Compare *Lugale* 696: uru-bi du$_6$-du$_6$-da ḫa-ba-šed, 'You have razed its citie(s) to ruins'; *LW* 4:25: maš-gana$_2$ á-dam-bi mu-⸢un-gul⸣-gul-lu-uš du$_6$-du$_6$-ra mi-ni-in-si-ig-eš, 'They destroyed its settlements and villages; they razed them into rubble'; *Išbi-Erra* A i 5′: [. . .] uru^{ki} du$_6$-du$_6$-da šed-e-dè; *Inninšagura* 16: ki í[b-du$_{11}$-ga-n]i-šè uru^{ki} du$_6$-du$_6$-da é líl-lá [x] uzug é-ri-a-šè ì-gál, 'Wherever she has spoken, the cities become mounds, temples become haunted places, the shrines become waste land'; *SLTN* 128 i 5′: é-bi du$_6$-du$_6$-da ba-šid-e a-ri-a-šè mu-un-ku$_4$ (*CT* 42 23 B:13, a different version of the same composition, has é d[u$_6$-d]u$_6$-da ba-an-ku$_4$ é-ri-a ba-an-[ku_4]); *SBH* 20b (p. 41) rev. 4′: [ba]-⌜an⌝-mar [ur]u_2?-a-ni du_6-du_6-da-aš [ba-an-mar] (see Cohen, *Balag Compositions* 219). The long curse formula in Abi-sare 4 (*UET* 8 65) should be read, in lines 6.5–6.7, as uru^{ki}-bi du_6-du_6-ra ḫe-en-šed (not -ra).

41. For ^{giš}ḫaš . . . ak = *sag/kāšu* 'to murder', see Å. W. Sjöberg, *ZA* 54 (1961) 65.

42. For ki . . . tag 'to sow', see M. Civil, *Or*, n.s. 54 (1985) 32.

43. This same line occurs in *Inanna and Iddin-Dagan* 138b with a positive verbal form. The various forms of the name of the ox driver's song have been studied by M. Civil, *Kramer AV* 90.

44. There is a distinct confusion in the predicate of this line and in line 48. The one Nippur manuscript (U) has šurim ki nu-tag-⌜e⌝-dè 'that dung not be dropped on the ground'. A different ending is found in all the Ur sources and in PP, a text of unknown provenience. In the main edition the Nippur text has been chosen but one should keep in mind the variants.

There are problems in the reading of the alternate versions of 44 and 48. In the first instance BB, DD, DDa, and PP have x or x x ḫa-lam-e-dè (PP: ḫa-la-dè). Unfortunately, the signs rendered here as x and x x are not identifiable and are preserved in BB and DD only.

45. The word ^{gi}šukur = *gubru* 'shepherd's hut, corral'. As Sladek, *Descent* 216 has noted, *gubru* A and B in *CAD* are to be collapsed into one entry.

46. Note also the positive equivalent of this image in *EWO* 29–30: [gù un]u_3-dè i-lu-lam-ma-bi du_{10}-ge-eš im-mi-ib-bé, [sipa]-dè du_9-du_9 ^{dug}šakir-ra-ka-na u_4 im-di-ni-ib_2-zal-e, 'The cowherd was sweetly intoning his chant, the shepherd spent the day in churning the churn' (cited by T. Jacobsen, *JAOS* 103 [1983] 198). On this line and parallels see now M. G. Hall, *JCS* 38 (1986) 160.

50. On ḫáb 'stink', see Å. W. Sjöberg, *JCS* 25 (1973) 137. The reading til is based on BB in which the scribe began to write -le but erased it and wrote e, as in H, U, and UU. The writer of PP understood the verb as úš-ù-dè. A parallel is found in *Letter B 8* 14: $kiri_6$ a nu-du_{11}-ga-gin_7 $asila_5$-mu ḫáb-ba ba-an-til.

53. For a discussion of numun . . . è/i-(i) see, most recently, Sjöberg, *Temple Hymns* 104 and 153. There are two distinct verbs, numun . . . i/è and numun . . . i-i/è 'to engender, multiply'. There is some doubt as to the meaning of the first one and, whatever the original etymology, it would be better not to translate it as 'to make the seed come forth'. This verb is most often attested as an adjective describing temples, divinities, and cities, including Ur (*SLTN* 79 3: numun i-i suḫuš kalam-ma gi-né ḫé-gál ki ús-sa). I find it difficult to establish a meaning for this adjective. For lack of a better solution, I have tentatively accepted the cosmological connections to origins of humanity that have been noted by T. Jacobsen and J. J. A. van Dijk (see Sjöberg's discussion), hence the translation 'primeval'.

55. The variants in this line provide a good example of how difficult it is to establish manuscript traditions of Sumerian literary texts. Text Q, from Nippur, agrees with PP, of unknown provenience, providing the reading ^{d}nin-maḫ. A different Nippur text, H, reads [^{d}nin-ḫur-sag-g]á-ke$_4$, and agrees with BB, from Ur.

60. For ^{giš}ig-šu-úr = *mēdelu ša dalti* 'bolt of a door', see Å. W. Sjöberg, *Or*, n.s. 37 (1968) 233.

The meaning of ama$_5$ poses problems. Cooper, *Agade* 236 understood ama$_5$ as 'a part of a house or a special building reserved for women'. T. Jacobsen, *apud* Cooper, *Agade* 22 with n. 10, suggests the ingenious translation 'womb' for the line under discussion here and renders it as 'Nintu put door-locks on the wombs of the land,' reading PISAN×SAL as arhuš. This translation agrees well with the role of this goddess as a divine midwife and, moreover, plays upon her common epithet ama 'mother', but it is based on late lexical equations that cannot be supported by the evidence of unilingual Sumerian texts. The following selected examples are representative of the usage of ama$_5$:

> *Ḫendursanga Hymn* 256′: ki-sikil-bi ama$_5$ níg-diri-ga dúr [k]i mu-un-gá-gá, 'Its young woman will establish herself in a large woman's chamber.'
>
> *Inninšagura* 75: ki-sikil tur ama$_5$-na TÚG?.TÚG? . . . , 'She dresses? the adolescent girl in her chamber. . . .'
>
> *Inninšagura* 138: é-dù-a ama$_5$ dím-me níg-gú-na TUK.TUK numdun-dím sa$_6$ ^{d}inanna za-kam = *e-pé-iš bi-tim ba-ni-e ma-aš-ta-ki-im ra-še-e e-nu-tim ša-ap-ti še-er-ri-im na-ša-qum ku-ma eštar*, 'To build a house, to build a woman's chamber, to have implements, to kiss the lips of a small child are yours, Inanna.'
>
> *CA* 7–8: u$_4$-ba eš$_3$ a-ga-dè^{ki} kù ^{d}inanna-ke$_4$, ama$_5$ mah-a-ni-šè im-ma-an-dù-dù, 'At that time holy Inanna built the sanctuary Agade as her grand woman's domain.'
>
> *CA* 11: dumu bàn-da ama$_5$ gá-gá-gin$_7$, 'Like a young girl establishing a woman's domain.'
>
> *CA* 61: ki-sikil ama$_5$-na šub-bu-gin$_7$, 'Like a young woman abandoning her woman's domain.'
>
> *CA* 217: ki-sikil-bi ama$_5$-na giš ḫul ḫé-en-da-ab-ra, 'May its young woman be cruelly killed in her woman's domain.'
>
> *LU* 130: uri$_5^{ki}$ ama$_5$ níg si-a-mu, 'Ur, my living quarter filled with goods.'
>
> *LU* 380: dumu bàn-da-gin$_7$ ama$_5$-zu-šè nin-mu (var.: ki-sikil) é-zu-šè, 'Like a young child (return) to your women's quarters, my lady, (return) to your dwelling.'
>
> *Enlil and Sud* 78: lú tur-mu šà n[á . . . k]ù-ga-zu ama$_5$ dùg, 'My little one, sleeping indoors [. . .] your pure [. . .], the private quarters are better (for you).'

Balag 44:266: me-e ama_x(PISAN×IGI)-gá ama_5-mu nu-mèn a-gin_7 ⟨in-na-a-dé⟩, 'How was I to say to my dwelling, "You are not my dwelling?"' [spoken by Inanna].

Inanna and Bilulu 40: ⌜ama_5? ama⌝ u-gù-na-ka mu-un-DU.DU, 'In the chamber of her mother who bore her (Inanna) was pacing (to and fro).'

Message of Ludingira 4–5: ama-mu mud-àm ù nu-mu-ni-i[b-ku-ku] ama_5-a-ni ka-gìr al-gi_{16}-ba-⌜ab⌝, 'My mother is *troubled*, she cannot sleep. . . .' (This follows primarily the Nippur text Ni. 2759 [S. N. Kramer, *Belleten* 40 (1976) 415]. The two texts of unknown provenience have major variants for line 5: *TLB* 2 5: ama_5-a-ni ka-gìr al-gi-ba-ab; *TCL* 15 39:5: ama_5 sag gi_4-a ka-gìr x x [. . .].)

Inanna and Bilulu 47: dumu ama u-gù-ni kin-gi_4-a-gin_7 ⌜ama_5?⌝-ta im?-ma-ta-è?, 'Like a child sent on an errand by its mother she went out from the chamber.'

Udug ḫul (OB) 774–75: guruš ki mè-ta mu-ni-i[n]-ra-aš ki-sikil ama_5-ni-ta mu-ni-⌜in⌝-ra-aš = *ina maš-ta-ki-šá*, 'They struck down the soldier on the battlefield, they struck down the young woman in her chambers.' Compare the contrast in *Nanâ Hymn* 7–8: *qa-diš-tum na-šat par-si i-leq-qi eṭ-lu ina tu-ub la-li-šú ù* KI.SIKIL *ṣe-ḫer-tum ina maš-ta-ki-šá ú-šel-li ana-ku-ma* MIN (=^{d}*na-na-a*), 'Holy one who holds the ordinances; she takes away the young man in his prime, she removes the young girl from her bedchamber—still I am Nanâ.'

Dialog 2 181–82: šeš-mu-ne aga_3-uš lugal-la ugula 50-meš nin_9-mu-ne ama_5 gi-na ^{giš}ig-gin_7 ab-gub-gub-bu-ne.

Šuruppak's Instructions 129–30: ibila-zu é-zu-šè im-me dumu-munus-zu ama_5-ni-šè im-me, 'Your successor is for your house, your daughter is for her woman's house.'

Inanna and Iddin-Dagan 113–14a: ama_5 kalam-ma ú du_{10} gar-ra-ba kur-kur sag gi_6 un gú diri-ba ama_5 kalam-ma-ka du_8-du_8 gar-ra-ba, 'When good food has been placed in the storehouse of the land, when all the lands, the black-headed fold, the people, have assembled, when abundance has been placed in the storehouse of the land.'

Inanna and Iddin-Dagan 139: ama_5 kalam-ma-ka níg mu-un-da-lu-lu, 'Everything is made abundant in the storehouse of the land.'

LU 240: ama_5 kalam-ma šár-šár-ra-ba izi im-ma-an-bar_7-bar_7, 'Fire blazed in all abounding storehouses of the land.'

Nanše Hymn 12: ama_5 kalam-ma-ka dugud mu-un-dè-gal (var.: [mu-un-d]a-lu-lu), 'The storehouses of the land prosper in her presence.'

Lahar and Ašnan 57–58: $erim_3$ kalam-ma-ka níg mu-ni-ib-lu-lu-un, ama_5 kalam-ma-ka dugud mu-un-dè-gál, 'The storerooms of the land they fill abundantly, the storehouse of the land are bulging with them.'

STT 179 15–16 = *CT* 17 33 8: ama_5 kalam-ma-šè ab-igi-in-bar ama_5 (var.: ama) kalam-(ma) im-sù = *ana maš-tak ma-a-tu₄ ip-pa-lis-ma maš-tak ma-a-ti ú-riq*, '(The demon) looked at the storehouse(s) of the land and emptied the storehouse(s) of the land.'

The divergent translations of the Sumerian word ama_5 and the Akkadian *maštaku* result from the fact that, in the first millennium at least, the Akkadian word had a wider semantic range than did ama_5. It is clear from the references cited above that in OB Sumerian literary texts this lexeme refers to the private quarters of women and young children; thus note that it is used to contrast the proper place of a young woman and a young man. With few exceptions this usage is still found in late bilingual texts, as can be seen from the entries in the dictionaries. In general, *maštaku* means 'living quarters'. In some examples by metonymic extension the word acquired the meaning of 'storehouse'. The original logogram, É×MUNUS, suggests the primary meaning of the word although sometimes it becomes confused with É×MI = itima 'dwelling place' (e.g., *CA* 209). In a few instances the word must be translated as 'storehouse' already in OB texts, but that meaning, it would appear from the evidence adduced above, was primarily restricted to the expression ama_5 kalam-ma, which should be translated as 'storehouse / dwelling quarters of the land', and not as the 'women's quarters of the land'.

65. The syllabic spelling of ga-ba-ra-ḫum 'rebellion' indicates that the lexeme is treated in this text as a loan word from Akkadian. Other syllabic writings are attested in a hymn to Inanna (ga-ba-ra-ḫum/ḫu-um [*Inninšagura* 22]) and *Proto-Izi* (gaba-ra-aḫ [II 536]); see Å. W. Sjöberg, *ZA* 65 (1976) 214. It is usually assumed that Akkadian *k/gabaraḫḫum* was originally borrowed from Sumerian *gaba-ra-aḫ (*CAD* G 1–2; S. J. Lieberman, *SLOB* 1 240). This is one more instance of a Sumerian loan word in Akkadian being borrowed back into Sumerian.

68. Note that the Ur sources BB and DDa have variant lines that contain the standard expression for divine abandonment in Mesopotamian literature, 'to stand aside' (bar-ta gub), rendered here as 'to step aside'. A similar line is found in *LW* 2:23′: uru dingir-bi ba-da-gur sipa-bi ba-da-a[n-. . .]. M. W. Green, *JAOS* 104 (1984) 268, restored [$tak_4^?$]. The variant in BB that begins uru^{ki}-ba dingir uru^{ki}-bi-e-ne must ultimately derive from a misreading of the verb gur as uru. PP, of unknown origin, probably agreed with A, also of unknown provenience, and with the Nippur text N. RR, also from Nippur, omits the line altogether.

69. For zi . . . pa-an/ág 'to breathe, to exhale', see M. Civil, *JNES* 23 (1964) 8.

70. The meaning of šu . . . dù is not entirely clear here. I have accepted šu . . . dù = *kamû* 'to bind', for which see Å. W. Sjöberg, ZA 54 (1961) 65. See also the difficult line in *LW* 3:25: ⌜e-ne⌝ šu-ne-ne ba-dù-dù šà múš ì-ak-ne, 'As for them, they shall be immobilized, they shall lose all courage.' For a different interpretation see M. W. Green, *JAOS* 104 (1984) 271.

71. Perhaps dab_5-bé-šè is to be read KU-bi-šè. This difficult word is discussed by Alster, *Instructions* 105. M. Civil, *JNES* 43 (1984) 286 reads dúr-bi-šè and translates the phrase as 'at the bottom, at the back, in last place'.

72–78. These lines are translated by S. N. Kramer, *Bulletin of the Asia Institute*, n.s. 1 (1987) 13.

73. The image of a 'faithful' (zi) man building a house or temple is found in a variety of contexts; see Sjöberg, *Temple Hymns* 111. As a verb, tur 'to diminish', has been discussed by M. Sigrist, *RA* 73 (1979) 96.

79. Compare *LU* 193: šika bar_7-bar_7-da sahar im-da-tab-tab un-e še àm-sa_4. See also *Inanna and Ebiḫ* 138: im-ḫul zi-ga šika im-bar-re; and *Inanna and the Fire-Plant* 3=36: šika bar_7-bar_7-ra ba-šèg-gá-ba. Bibliography for discussions of šika bar_7-bar_7 can be found in P. Attinger, *RA* 78 (1984) 117; note also the expressions collected by Hallo and van Dijk, *Exaltation* 79–80 (*sub* izi-ne-ne(r), to be read izi bar_7-bar_7; see S. N. Kramer, *The Bible World: Essays in Honor of Cyrus H. Gordon* (New York, 1980) 95 n. 10. Note also *Lugale* 274: ní me-lám saḫar ì-ur_4-ur_4 šika im-e-eš ì-šèg.

80. As noted by C. Wilcke, *Sumerological Studies Jacobsen* 302 there is a question whether one should identify MI.EDEN.NA with gi_6 eden-na 'deep shade', which is preceded by the word it qualifies (usually $kiri_6$ or sila; see M. Civil, *OA* 22 [1983] 4 n. 9; F. Carroué, *ASJ* 8 [1986] 55). The word also occurs in *LU* 188: u_4 mir-mir-da NE.MI.EDEN.NA bar ba-da-an-tab-(tab). A late bilingual text provides an equation with *anqullu* 'an atmospheric phenomenon' (according to *CAD*). The normal logogram for the latter word is IZI.AN.BAR_7, which, as the Akkadian contexts show, must have denoted a fiery effect in the sky, or a shadow cast by such a phenomenon. I have chosen the variant from the Nippur source RR; the verb appears to be different, however, in all extant manuscripts.

80α. This line, which together with the following one are attested only in manuscripts from outside of Nippur, has a direct parallel in *CA* 188–89: KA ba-dub-dub sag ba dab_5-dab_5, KA ba-dub sag numun-e-eš ba-ab-gar, '*Mouths* were crushed, heads were crashed, *mouths* were crushed, heads were sown as seeds.'

Å. W. Sjöberg, *AfO* 24 (1973) 36, considers u_4-mud to be a word for 'evening' and thus translates it in the *Nungal Hymn* line 3 as 'dusk'; Cooper, *Agade* 25 translated u_4-mud as 'bloody day'. The differences in translation arise from the problems inherent in the lexical texts, which provide the Akkadian equivalent *ūmu daʾmu* 'dark day' for u_4 mud, and the homophonous word *damu* 'blood' for Sumerian mud. Cooper has pointed out to me that mud = *daʾmu* only in late texts, as a result of the homonymy of Akkadian *damu* and *daʾmu*, hence his interpretation is preferred here.

80β. The differant verbs used to describe the action of the hoe are listed in M. Civil, *Kramer AV* 94. Note the similar use of al ra in *LU* 258: ^{d}mu-ul-líl-e é-mu šu ḫé-bí-in-bal ^{giš}al-e ḫa-ba-ra.

81. Literally, 'the storm never slept', taking igi . . . lim as a variant of igi . . . lib = *dalāpu* (based on a suggestion of M. Civil). See now the syllabic spelling i-gi-li-ib-bi in *Inninšagura* 162 (Harmal manuscript R). For examples of an dúb and ki sìg, see Cohen, *Balag Compositions* 76–77.

82. For the first part of the line, see *Gilgameš and Ḫuwawa* 77: kur ba-sùḫ-sùḫ gissu ba-an-lá, 'The mountains were darkened, they were covered by shadow.' Perhaps sùḫ-sùḫ should be read as $siḫ_5$-$siḫ_5$ in light of the loanword *seḫseḫī* 'at twilight'; see A. Falkenstein, *ZA* 53 (1959) 100 n. 18. M. Civil, *JCS* 20 (1966) 120–21, proposes a reading sùḫ-$saḫ_4$ in the compound sùḫ-$saḫ_4$ . . . za. See also M. G. Hall, *JCS* 38 (1986) 159.

87. This line occurs in almost identical fashion in *Lugale* 87. Properly speaking, giš tir-ra are not trees in a forest, but the growth in 'riverain thickets and copses'; see P. Steinkeller, *AOS* 68 75.

88–89. There can be no doubt about the rendering of su in 89 since the first part of the line is a stock expression and the verb is translated by *ṭubbû* 'to drown' in bilingual texts (see the references cited in *PSD* B 217 and 219). It is not certain, however, how to understand su_{13} in line 88. Only witness UU preserves the beginning for both lines, and thus one is reluctant to interpret su and su_{13} as writings of the same verb. There is some confusion in the lexical texts concerning this use of su; see *CAD* A/2 317 (*arû* C and D).

The reading ligima for GIŠ.IGI.TUR.TUR is based on equations in lexical texts (*ligimû* 'offshoot, bud'). See also *MSL* 12 140 4 (and possibly 8) where the Akkadian equivalent is *pīʾu*.

93. For zur-re-eš . . . dug_8 / zar-re-eš . . . sal see, most recently, Volk, *Die Balağ-Komposition* 281. It is quite possible that nothing is to be restored in the second break. The line could then be restored as un / kur-kur zur-re-eš mu-un-dug_8-dug_8 zar-re-eš mu-un-sal-e-eš, 'They piled up the lands / people into heaps, they spread them out like sheaves.'

94. The restoration of this line is uncertain. See, perhaps, *LU* 185: ^{giš}tukul uru-ke_4 (var.: uru^{ki}-a ^{giš}tukul-e) sag-gaz ì-ak-e ur-bi ì-gu_7-e, 'The weapons of the city (var.: in the city, weapons) attack, they consume all / gather together for attack.' Note that the second sign is not má, as in *AS* 12 36 and in all other translations. An audacious restoration would perhaps read, [^{íd}idigna ^{í}]^{d}buranun-na ad_6 ì-me-a [kaskal ḫar-ra-an-na sag]-gaz ì-ak-e, 'There were corpses floating down the Tigris and Euphrates, there was murder on the roads and highways.'

101. References for du_{10}-ús dili dab_5 'to keep on one track' as a metaphor for obedience have been collected by Sjöberg, *Temple Hymns* 77.

102. The uncertain restoration of the end of the line is based on line 435 below and on *LU* 322: nu-nuz-mèn (var.: ^{d}nanna) èš uri_5^{ki} nindaba-bi ba-kúr-ra-àm (var.: im-ma-an-ku_5-da-mu). The root of the final verb is preserved only in V, in which it is the only sign of the line left. Texts A and N contain the beginning of a verbal chain that must be reconstructed as ba-d[a$^{?}$-. . .]. The logical restoration is kúr but one must then posit that V had a different predicate.

103. The use of the verb šu bal . . . ak in this line harkens back to the first and third lines of the text. The meaning appears to be sightly different, however, for here the predicate refers, metaphorically, to trade and market exchange. See M. Civil, *JCS* 28 (1976) 80.

104. For zi . . . gi_4 see the comments of M. Civil, *Sumerological Studies Jacobsen* 132. Note that here, as in other passages of the text, ní-te-na may mean 'in fear', rather than 'alone'.

106. A number of buildings were named Enamtila, including a part of the temple of Enlil in Nippur (e.g., Cohen, *Sumerian Hymnology* 113:18) and a temple, possibly of Dingirmaḫ, in Malgium (C. Wilcke, *ZA* 68 [1978] 127:12; see also *IRSA* 254 and 300). In the current line it is obviously the name of the royal residence in Ur. The palace of Ur-Namma was named é-gal-gibil 'New Palace' (*Death of Ur-Namma* 148; *UET* 3 76 6–7: é-gal-gibil ki-a-nag ur-^{d}namma-šè). Šulgi's palace was the é-ḫur-sag (references in Castellino, *Two Šulgi Hymns* 240; H. Limet, *CRRAI* 20 81; Sjöberg, *Temple Hymns* 3 78). Note that the Nanna hymn published by Å. W. Sjöberg in *JCS* 29 (1977) 9–10 contains the following lines (18′–19′): é-ḫur-sag é lugal-la-šè ⟨in-gá-e-re_7-en-dè-en⟩, é-nam-ti-la nun šul-gi-šè in-gá-e-re_7-en-dè-en, 'To the Eḫursag, the house of the king ⟨we go⟩, to the Enamtila of prince Šulgi we go!' It can be established that a structure by the name of Enamtila existed in Ur at the time of Ibbi-Sin on the basis of an economic text from the reign of the last king of Ur (*UET* 3 1495 rev. 5: x aga_3-uš é-nam-ti tuš-a; the Eḫursag is also attested in *UET* 3 915). Note also that this structure is named as the residence of the king in association with Ibbi-Sin in *Winter and Summer* 234: é-nam-ti-la ki-tuš kù nam-lugal-la an-né gar-ra-na (Ibbi-Sin is mentioned by name in line 230). The same composition, however, refers to the Enamtila as the residence of Enlil (*Winter and Summer* 105: é-nam-ti-la é ^{d}en-líl-la-šè). One therefore suspects that Enamtila is simply another name for Eḫursag. Particularly important here is the occurrence of é-nam-ti-la in the Inanna—Dumuzi text Ni 9602 (S. N. Kramer, *PAPS* 107 [1963] 505–7) line iii 12–15: é-nam-ti-la é lugal-la-ka nitadam-a-ni ul-la mu-un-da-an-tuš é-nam-ti-la é ^{d}dumu-zi-da-ka ^{d}inanna ul-la mu-un-da-an-tuš ^{d}inanna é-a-ni húl-la-e, 'In the Enamtila, the house of the king, his wife dwelt with him in joy, in the Enamtila, the house of the king, Inanna dwelt with him in joy. Inanna, rejoicing in his house. . . .' Further in the same text the palace of the king is called by this name. Is this a general description of a royal palace, or is it possible that the text contains references to the "sacred marriage"?

107. The beginning of this line is problematical. I have emended ki to du_6 in the two sources of this line even though collation shows that in both cases the scribes wrote ki. Thus I have read $du_6^!$ al-ak-e, as in *LW* 3:3: a-ma-ru du_6 al-ak-e gù im-ma-ab-zi, 'A devastating flood shall be invoked'; and *LW* 4:4: a-ma-ru du_6 (written ki$^!$) al-ak-e x [. . .]. The similarity of ki and du_6, as well as the existence of al . . . ak 'to hoe', may have been the source of this confusion. It is, of course, possible that one should emend the *LW* line and translate 107 as, 'The storm hacks away, it levels (everything).' For šu . . . ùr-ùr see Å. W. Sjöberg, *OrSuec* 19–20 (1970–71) 159–60.

110–11. Compare *CA* 190–92: sag zi sag lul-la šu-bal ba-ni-ib-ak mèš-mèš-e an-ta i-im-ná úš lú lul-e ús lú zi-da-ke$_4$ an-ta na-mu-un-DU, 'Loyal men were confounded with traitors, young men lay upon young men, the blood of traitors ran upon the blood of loyal men'; and *LW* 3:21: numun zi sag lul-la sag zi-da šu-bal mi-ni-ib-ak-a-a-aš, 'They confounded good offspring, traitors and loyal people' (see Cooper, *Agade* 25–26).

118. The refrain, a uru gul-la é gul-la-mu gig-ga-bi im-me, will now be found after many of the sections concerning shrines, cities, and divinities throughout the second ***kirugu***. With one exception, ***Lugalbanda*** 220, this refrain is always uttered by goddesses. There is a problem, however, with the rendering of this line in a composite text. Some sources use the first person pronoun -mu and in these texts the refrain must be translated as, '"Alas, the destroyed city, my destroyed temple!" bitterly he/she cries.' In other sources the pronoun is third person -na, and the lines must be understood as, '"Alas!" he/she cries out bitterly over the destroyed city, his/her destroyed temple.' The majority of sources follow the first-person version, but in some lines the only surviving witness contains the alternative third-person line. The composite text requires consistency. In this case I have chosen to utilize the first-person refrain in all lines in the composite text. The same variant has been selected for the main text in the score, except in cases where the third-person alternative is the only preserved version. This discrepancy between the composite text and the surviving witnesses is found in lines 135, 138, 142, and 154.

This refrain is related to similar lines in other laments. In the *Eridu Lament* similar expressions are encountered in the giš-gi$_4$-gál sections at the end of the first two *kirugus*: *LE* 1:28: a uru$_2$ gul-la é gul-la-ri gig-ga-bi im-me, '"Alas!" (Eridu) cries out bitterly over the destroyed city, over that destroyed temple'; and *LE* 2:20: eridu^{ki} gul-la-ri gul-la-bi gig-ga-àm, 'Oh, the destruction of Eridu, its destruction was grievous!' In the *Ur Lament*, there is a couplet that provides another variation on this theme: *LU* 255–56: lú nu-nuz-e ér é ḫul-a-na uru ḫul-a-na gig-ga-bi im-me egi$_2$-re èš uri$_5$^{ki} ḫul-a-na gig-ga-bi im-me, 'The mistress bitterly cries out a lament over her destroyed temple, the princess cries out bitterly over her destroyed shrine of Ur.' (There are numerous variants to this line: na-ám-uru for ér é, mi-ni-íb-bé for im-me, na-ám-é for èš uri$_5$^{ki}, and gal-la-bi for gig-ga-bi.)

123. On the translation of ní-ba lu-a as 'teeming multitudes', see Cohen, *Enmerkar* 178–79. For a slightly different rendering see Falkenstein, *Götterlieder* 63.

128. The verb úš = *sekēru* 'to block up' is often used in connection with watercourses, particularly in Ur III administrative documents. See the discussion by B. Lafont, *RA* 74 (1980) 38–39.

129 (also **499**). Usually, še gu-nu is translated as 'mottled/speckled barley'. M. Powell, *Bulletin on Sumerian Agriculture* 1 (1984) 67, questions that interpretation and suggests that še is here a general term for corn and gu-nu / gùn-nu = *banû* 'fine, beautiful, of good quality'. The verbal form nu-gál is not actually attested in either preserved manuscript: F has the complete line with ⟨nu⟩-gál and LL has only [. . .] nu-un-gál [. . .].

130. Compare *LU* 274: eden kiri$_4$-zal-bi dù-dù-a-mu gir$_4$-gin$_7$ ḫa-ba-ḫu-ḫur, 'My steppe, established for joy, was scorched like an oven.'

131. On a suggestion of M. Civil, I take bu = *našarbuṭu, našarbuṣu* 'to flit, to chase about'. In *PSD* B 170 this verb is entered as bú, but this line is not quoted (see also M. Roth, *JAOS* 103 [1983] 277). Note that the verb is written bú and bu$_5$ primarily in post-OB sources. The earlier texts prefer bu.

134. For the writings of the name ^{d}nin-zu-an-na, see D. R. Frayne, *CRRAI* 28 31.

136. It is difficult to render nu-me-a in this clause into English. With the postposition -da the verbal form means 'without', Akkadian *balu* (see G. Gragg, in J. W. M. Verhaar, ed., *The Verb "Be" and Its Synonyms* [Dordrecht, 1968], 3:100). Without -da this negative version of the copula functions as the opposite of al-me-a and must be rendered into English as 'is not, although not'. See, for example, *CA* 170: uru^{ki} šà eden bar dagal nu-me-a mú-sar mu-un-dè-gál, 'In the cities' midst, though not the widespread exterior plains, they planted gardens'; or *Udug ḫul* (OB) 284: ^{d}n[in]-⌜geštin dub⌝-[sar-ma]ḫ a-ra-li nu-me-a, 'without Ningeština, the great scribe of the Netherworld'. Note that even without -da, nu-me-a is sometimes translated into Akkadian as *balu*, as in *MSL SS1* 80 75–80 (MB grammatical text); see also, for example, *Letter B 11* 13–14: eren$_2$ daḫ-ḫu-um engar šà-gud lú.^{giš}apin nu-me-a gud-didli-ta a-šà giš bí-ùr, 'Although there are not (enough) replacement workers, oxdrivers (and) plowmen, the field has been harrowed with each (available) ox.' Thus, in the present context, the meaning is ambiguous. One could also translate the line as, 'Isin, although it is a sanctuary without a harbor, was split by (onrushing) waters.'

140. Note the alternative line in N: ^{d}en-líl-le uru^{ki}-ni èš nibru^{ki} kur-re ba-ab-gar, 'Enlil handed over his city, the shrine Nippur, to the highlanders.'

143, 145–46. These lines have been cited by G. Gragg, *TCS* 3 162; lines 143–46 were translated by S. N. Kramer, *Bulletin of the Asia Institute*, n.s. 1 (1987) 13. It is tempting to understand the 'mountain snakes' of line 145 as an anticipatory designation of the Gutians in the following line, keeping in mind the fact that in the Utu-ḫegal inscription the Gutians are described as muš-ul$_4$ ḫur-sag-gá (*RA* 9 [1912] 112:2). On the identity of the Gutians in line 146 see, most recently, Klein, *Three Šulgi Hymns* 59 n. 145.

In line 143 Gragg read an eden-na-aš; the reading an eden-na dili follows C. Wilcke, *ZA* 62 (1972) 55.

In line 146, šà . . . bal is not commonly encountered as a verb. Compare, however, *Lugale* 34: OB kur-ra šà i-ni-bal numun-bi ba-tál-tál = Late kur-ra šà i-ni-in-u$_5$ numun ba-tál-tál = *šá-da-a uš-tar-kib ze-ra ur-tap-pi-iš*, '(The Asakku demon) bred in the highlands, he multiplied his progeny.'

Klein, *Three Šulgi Hymns* 116 connects this line and *Šulgi D* 346: numun gu-ti-um-ma še saḫar-ra-gin$_7$ mu-bi-bi-re-a-ta, 'After he dispersed the seed of the Gutians like seed-grain.'

144. For lines 144–45 I have chosen to follow F. Sources N and V have a slightly different line here: adab^{ki}-bu é íd-dè lá-a-ri ki bala-šè ba-ab-dug$_4$, 'Adab, which stretches out along the river, was treated as a rebellious land.' The end of this line is identical with the predicate of 145 in F, however this line does not exist in both of these sources. It appears likely that the two lines were conflated in N and V but it is equally possible that F is secondary, having two lines instead of one.

The writing of the verbal root with bu (in the phrase a-e bu) in line 196 confirms that PI in 144 must be read bu$_x$ (as in bu$_x$-ba . . . za). Note that in Ur III texts from Umma the verb is written bù (*PSD* B 164).

147. Compare *Flood Story* 140: u$_4$-bi-a ^{d}nin-t[u níg-dím]-dím-a-[ni-šè ì-še$_8$-še$_8$]. This was T. Jacobsen's restoration but it is rejected by S. N. Kramer, *AnSt* 33 (1983) 119 n. 23.

150. This line is related to the refrain en-bi gi$_6$-par$_4$-ta ba-da-an-kar ki erim$_2$-e ba-ab-dug$_4$/DU in lines 153, 184, 192, 205, and 250. The reading and interpretation of the last verb in these lines is difficult to ascertain. The variants for the root (DU/dug$_4$) are distributed in a bewildering manner. The one Ur source that covers five of these lines (text EE, lines 150, 153, 184, 192, 205) has dug$_4$ in all cases. The majority of the Nippur sources have DU. Two Nippur tablets, however, complicate the matter. F has dug$_4$ in 150, but DU in 153; B has dug$_4$ in 184 and DU in 192. One solution to this problem is to accept the variant ba-ab-dug$_4$ and to translate the line as, 'Inanna abandoned Uruk, it became an enemy place.' The variation in B and F, however, suggests that the alternation dug$_4$/DU is phonetic and that DU is the better reading. We must then decide whether to read de$_6$/túm or gin/du, that is 'to carry' or 'to go'. The prefix -b- makes it difficult to accept this as an intransitive verb, but it is possible that one may have to consider such an interpretation. The matter is further complicated by the occurrence of the same predicate in two lines further in the text. In these lines all sources have the same verbal root, DU:

331. áb.šilam-ma amar-bi ba-da-ab-dab$_5$ ki erim$_2$-e ba-ab-DU

424. am dab$_5$-ba-gin$_7$ saman-e bí-in-šub-bu-ri ki erim$_2$-e ba-ab-DU

In these two lines it makes sense to take -e as a locative rather than as an ergative and to read the verbal root as de$_6$ 'to carry'. One assumes, of course, that the interpretation of these two lines bears on the analysis of the refrain. Thus while it is possible that the scribes were playing on the various possibilities provided by the auxiliary verb -dug$_4$, in this edition I have chosen to understand the verb as de$_6$ in all cases except for line 150. This means that in line 150, for which no variant DU is preserved, I have had to provide a reading in the composite text that is not justified by any source. A distribution of the variants reveals the following pattern:

	150	*153*	*184*	*192*	*205*	*250*	*331*	*424*
B			dug$_4$	DU				
C						DU		
E								DU
F	dug$_4$	DU						
H							DU	
I			DU	DU	DU			
N		DU		DU				
T								DU
X						DU		
EE		dug$_4$	dug$_4$	dug$_4$	dug$_4$			
JJ								DU
MM								DU

Likewise, the verbal form ba-da-an-kar can mean either 'was snatched' or 'abandoned'. In Mesopotamian literature gods abandon (kar = *ezēbu*, *ekēmu*) their shrines in such moments, they are not usually removed. Therefore, I have chosen to translate this pattern in two different ways, mindful of the problems that remain unresolved. Inanna abandons Uruk and thus it can be taken by the enemy. Then, the Gipar is plundered and the main priest taken away. One should add that šu . . . lá-(lá) (line 152) could be translated here as 'overrun', which would provide an even stronger image.

155–56. It is usually maintained that the Sigkuršaga was the temple of Šara in Umma; for references see Å. W. Sjöberg, *JCS* 34 (1982) 69, and Sladek, *Descent* 219, with previous literature. If this were indeed the case then one would be at a loss to explain the relationship between the Sigkuršaga and the Emaḫ, which must obviously be restored in line 156. The latter is the normal name of Šara's temple (Sjöberg, *Temple Hymns* 111); it is attested in royal inscriptions and in the Umma field name a-šà igi-é-maḫ-šè (Pettinato, *Untersuchungen* 1/2 7). It is possible to interpret sig$_4$-kur-šà-ba as an epithet of Umma ('brickwork of the midst of the highlands'), but that would be difficult in *Inanna's Descent* where the parallelism with a following sequence suggests that it is indeed the name of a temple of Šara:

328. ga-an-ši-re$_7$-dè-en umma^{ki}-a sig$_4$-kur-šà-ga-šè (var.: še-ZU-eb-kur-šà-ba-šè) ga-an-ši-re$_7$-dè-en

329. um[ma^{ki}-a] sig$_4$-kur-šà-ga-ta

330. ^{d}šara$_2$ uru-ni-a giri$_3$-ni-šè ba-an-šub

338. ga-e-re$_7$-en-dè-en bàd-tibira^{ki}-a é-muš-kalam-ma-šè ga-an-ši-re$_7$-en-dè-en

339. bàd-tibira^{ki}-a é-muš-kalam-ma-ma-ta

340. ^{d}lú-làl-e uru-ni-a giri$_3$-ni-šè ba-an-šub

328. "Let us go on, let us go to Sigkuršaga, the temple in Umma!"

329. At the Sigkuršaga in Umma

330. Šara, in his own city, threw himself at her (Inanna's) feet.

338. "Let us go on, let us go to Emuškalama, the temple in Badtibira!"

339. At the Emuškalama in Badtibira

340. Lulal, in his own city, threw himself at her (Inanna's) feet.

The Emuškalama was the temple of Inanna in Badtibira, most probably distinct from the Emuš, which was the temple of Dumuzi. The messengers of Inanna are visiting her children, hence Lulal is found in the Emuškalama. This evidence is not conclusive, however. In the twelfth *kirugu* of the *Nippur Lament* cities are enumerated with a following epithet—in no case is there a name of temple mentioned:

236. é-bi umma^{ki}-a sig$_4$-kur-šà-ga-(ke$_4$) (var.: sig$_4$ ki uru unu^{ki}-KU-ka) ḫul-bi ba-ab-ak-e

237. ugu-bi-ta tidnum nu-gar-ra íb-ta-zi-ge-eš

The final reference, encountered in a hymn to Ninisina (Å. W. Sjöberg, *JCS* 34 [1982] 68 iii 8′) must be read [é]-bi umma^{ki}-a [s]ig$_4$-kur-šà-ga-ka; all the cities in this text are followed by descriptive phrases, as in the *Nippur Lament*. On this basis I have chosen to take 'brickwork in the midst of the highlands' as a phrase describing Umma, rather than the name of a distinct temple in that city (note, however, that in line 207 below a similar phrase includes the name of a temple: ^{d}nin-ḫur-sag é-nu-tur-ra-ke$_4$ u$_4$ hul ba-an-da-dal). The kur, 'highland', is not to be taken literally here but is a cosmic metaphor. See, for example, the description of Nippur in *Temple Hymns* 42: šà-zu kur hé-gál-la nam-hé-a dù-a, 'Your interior is a "mountain" of abundance, built in plenitude.' I admit that the translation of this epithet makes little sense and it is possible that it has other meanings. Perhaps relevant is the personal name from ED Lagaš, sig$_4$-kur (*DP* 135:5, 593:3).

157. We expect here the spouse of Šara to be Ninura (^{d}nin-ur$_4$-ra), and not Ninmul, who, together with her consort Enmul, belongs to the "ancestor gods" found at the beginning of certain god lists (e.g., AO 5376 i 4 [*RA* 20 (1923) 98]).

158. At the beginning of the line one should perhaps restore simply uru or é. For la-la . . . gi$_4$, compare *LU* 323: É.NUN-kù é gibil-gibil-la-mu la-la-bi nu-gi$_4$-a-mu, 'O E., *my all-new house*, whose bounty is no longer satisfying'; and *CA* 56: dumu gi$_7$-gin$_7$ é ki-gar di-da la-la-bi nu-um-gi$_4$, 'Like an aristocrat, talking about founding a house, she (Inanna) could not get enough of those luxuries' (thus Cooper, *Agade* 53). P. Attinger, *RA* 78 (1984) 101, renders this line as, 'Ce n'est pas que, tel un "aristocrate," elle se fût dégoûtée *du temple bien fondé qu'elle ordonait* (*de construire*).' For la-la . . . gi$_4$-(gi$_4$) see, most recently, Kutscher, *Oh Angry Sea* 143 and *CAD* L 50 for the Akkadian equivalent *lalâ šebû*. The most direct parallel to this line is found in *LE* 5:7–8: uru$_2$ munus-zu nu-ti[l-la la-]a-zu nu-gi$_4$-a-mu me-a ér-zu ba-gig uru$_2$-zé-eb.k[i u]ru$_2$ munus-zu nu-til-la la-la-zu nu-gi$_4$-a-mu ⌜me-a⌝ ér-zu ba-šéš?, 'You, my city, whose woman does not dwell (there), whose charms do not satisfy (her)—where is a lament uttered bitterly for you? Uruzeb! You, my city, whose woman does not dwell (there), whose charms do not satisfy (her)—where are tears wept for you?'

159. The translation 'lightning storm' is but a guess for the difficult im-gír. Note im-gír for im-mir as an equivalent of *ištānu* 'north wind' in *MDP* 18 254 rev. ii 13 (see Sjöberg, *Temple Hymns* 103 n. 58).

163–72. These lines are translated by S. N. Kramer, *Bulletin of the Asia Institute*, n.s. 1 (1987) 13.

167. The divine epithet dumu gi_7 is usually translated into English as 'princely son'; see Hall, *Moon God* 646–47. The epithet has been discussed often, most recently by Cooper, *Agade* 240, who translates the word as 'aristocrat', following C. Wilcke. In *LSUr* this epithet is applied to Nanna in lines 362a, 363, 371, and 372. To distinguish this epithet from dumu nun, often rendered in the same manner, I have translated dumu gi_7 as 'Noble Son', although in line 179, for syntactic reasons, I have translated nam-dumu gi_7 as 'noble youth'. See the commentary to that line.

168. Guabba was the cult city of ^{d}nin-mar^{ki}; see Neumann, *Handwerk* 99 n. 532, with previous literature. The reading of the name of this deity has been the subject of dispute; for the latest opinion, with a summary of previous discussions, see R. M. Whiting, *ZA* 75 (1986) 1–3. Whiting is of the opinion that "Mar was a pre- or proto-historic geographical name that did not survive except in the name of this deity" (p. 1). Such an interpretation is plausible but one must take into consideration the deity ^{d}nin-mar-gi_4 who is attested in the god list from Abu Salabikh (*OIP* 99 83 iv 4′ = 84 ii 2′). In view of the fact that this list, as opposed to Fara writings, consistently writes the determinative ki in divine names, it is difficult to view gi_4 here as a syllabic writing of ki. There is no apparent etymology of mar-gi_4 but that should not be a major obstacle since there are numerous Mesopotamian divinities whose names cannot be readily translated. In view of this I would propose a modification of Whiting's analysis: early mar-gi_4 was reinterpreted as mar^{ki} already in ED III times and was later the subject of some confusion. One line of analysis viewed mar^{ki} as an old geographical name and another parallel interpretation saw in it an old writing for an element ki-mar, hence the OB toponym é-ki-mar (*SLTN* 103 7′, 8′).

I have taken te to mean 'approach'. It is also possible that one should consider understanding te as te(n) = *balû* 'to become extinguished', although that is usually written te-en. In that case the translation would read, 'As for Ninmar, the (sacred) fire was extinguished in the shrine Guabba.'

170. On this line see Wilcke, *Lugalbanda* 140. The same author discusses lines 170 and 171 in *Sumerological Studies Jacobsen* 209.

171. I cannot translate this line. Perhaps relevant is Antagal VIII 112 (*MSL* 17 173): KA$^{ka\text{-}i\text{-}zi}$IZI = MIN (= *ḫa-ma-ṭu*) *šá* IZI.

172. M. Yoshikawa, "Lagaš and Ki-Lagaš, Unug and Ki-Unug," *ASJ* 7 (1985) 157–64, has argued that ki-lagaša is a term that encompassed the whole district that included the cities of Lagaš, Nina, and Sirara.

The verb šu-(a) . . . gi_4 in this line and in lines 175–76 is understood as 'to hand over'; see Å. W. Sjöberg, *JCS* 26 (1974) 174. For šu-a . . . gi_4 = *šunnû* 'to repeat', see Hallo and van Dijk, *Exaltation* 90.

173. Note that text EE has nin-gá for the simple nin of source B. In a recent book review M. Cooper (*JCS* 38 [1986] 124–26) discussed the term nin-gá in Ur III texts from the reign of Šulgi. Following A. L. Oppenheim (*AOS* 32 93), he suggested that nin-gá is not a personal name. He concluded that this is in fact a designation of the queen of the Ur III state, in all likelihood Šulgi-simti. Cooper proposed that nin-gá is to be understood as the Sumerian equivalent of *bēlet bītim* 'Lady of the House'. This would imply that gá = *bītum*, an equivalence found only in lexical texts explaining the element gá in compounds, always in initial position. Another explanation is required, one already hinted at in *CAD* B 190a (where nin-gá is interpreted as 'referring to the queen, the wife of the king'), namely that nin-gá means literally, 'My Lady', that is, 'Her Majesty'.

This interpretation of nin-gá (and nin-mu in line 278) as 'Her Majesty', in turn, leads us to analyze a parallel term found in limited distribution in Ur III documents: lugal-mu. Limet, *Anthroponymie* 175 took lugal-mu as an abbreviated personal name and there is reason to believe that in a few case this may in fact be the best interpretation. The majority of references, however, strongly suggest that lugal-mu means 'Milord', hence 'His Majesty'.

The most common usage of the term is found in the expression u_4 lugal-mu é PN kas ì-nag-gá-a, 'When His Majesty drank beer in the house of PN.' This phrase is used in a group of texts that record the disbursement of silver rings. Various high officials of the Ur III state are involved and all the extant texts date from the time of Amar-Suena (references in my article in *Syro-Mesopotamian Studies* 2 [1978] 1–16, and in M. Sigrist, *Or*, n.s. 48 [1979] 45). It is of course possible that the same individual, an otherwise unknown high official named lugal-mu, was involved in all of these texts. Proof that this is not the case is found in the largest of all of these texts, an unpublished tablet that records many different metal items that were disbursed 'when His Majesty drank beer in the house of Šarrum-bani', undoubtedly the high ranking military official who was governor of Abiak and then built the Muriq-Tidnim fortifications (this tablet, from Phillips University, was kindly made available to me by R. David Freedman). The first series of entries lists no less than 39 lines of metal items, followed by the entry lugal-mu. This is followed by an comparable list of items involving Šulgi-simti, Simat-Ea, and other royal women and other high officials of the state. The only person who could precede the queen in such a list would have to be the ruler of the state, hence lugal-mu must designate the king. As with nin-gá, an interesting instance of such usage is found in line 371 below: u_4-ba lugal-mu dumu gi_7-ra ur_5-ra-ni ba-an-BAD, 'Then, (upon hearing this), His Majesty, the Noble Son, became distraught.'

It should be noted that the use of a frozen form consisting of a noun followed by a possessive pronoun is not unique to these two terms in Sumerian. Already in the Sumerian logograms used in the ED Ebla administrative texts and found in the lexical lists from Tell Mardikh one encounters this in kinship terms, hence ŠEŠ.MU 'my brother' for 'brother', AMA.MU 'my mother' for 'mother', etc. (see Pettinato, *MEE* 2 55–56). Long after the fall of the Ur III dynasty a similar usage is found in Akkadian texts from Mesopotamia and the West; ^{d}*šamši*^{ši} 'My Sun' is a well-known term for 'His Majesty' (discussed most recently by S. Dalley, *Iraq* 48 [1986] 98–99).

178–79. Note that the scribe of text B wrote the name of the city Kiniršа with ša in line 178 and with šà in 179.

179. There are difficulties in this line. C. Wilcke, *CRRAI* 19 222 translated this line as, '(Dumuziabzu) lieferte$^{?}$ [Ki]nirša, ihre Stadt des . . . tums, zur Plündurung$^{?}$ aus.' The problem is the proper rendering of the unique occurrence of uru nam-dumu gi$_7$-ra. The question here is whether one should take nam-dumu gi$_7$ as an abstract formation of dumu-gi$_7$ or whether one should interpret it as nam-dumu followed by an adjective. Note that there is evidence that nam-dumu-(ni) was a term for the crown prince in OB texts. The best example for this is found in an inscription of Išme-Dagan of Isin in which he refers to the city of Dūrum as uru^{ki} nam-šakkana nam-dumu-na-ka-ni, 'the city in which he was military governor of his *dauphinage*' (see my remarks in *Mesopotamia* 12 [1977] 90–91). This terminology is also attested in OB Proto-Lu (*MSL* 12 33–73) but does not carry over into the canonical series Lú = *ša*. Thus lines 2 and 3 have lugal followed by nam-dumu-na (two texts add dumu lugal between these lines), sukkal šà é-a followed (in some manuscripts) by either sukkal lugal or sukkal nam-dumu-na (6–6b, see also text B$_3$ 5–6 [p. 67]), and the sequences uku-uš lugal, uku-uš nam-dumu-na (110–11), and sagi-a lugal, sagi-a é-gal, sagi-a nam-dumu-na (121–23). In the present context both interpretations may apply and uru nam-dumu gi$_7$-ra-ka-ni may be 'the city of her *dauphinage*', if such an epithet can be applied to a female deity. See also the commentary to line 167.

180. There has been a long debate on the reading and identification of the city written AB×ḪA^{ki} (modern Zurghul) and its relationship to the temple or temple-district Sirara. The latest extensive discussion can be found in W. Heimpel, *JCS* 33 (1981) 100–101. Recently, J. A. Black, "A Note on Zurghul," *Sumer*, in press, has provided a brief overview of older views on the subject and provided a catalog of inscriptions found at the site.

186. The Edana-Nanna appears to have been a specific geographical place and not simply a general designation like Edana, which refers to way stations on highways, particularly those that Šulgi claims to have constructed. For a specific place named Edana see Ali, *Sumerian Letters* 73 n. 2, and *RGTC* 2 49; note also é-da[na] in broken context in *ISET* I 188 (Ni 9821) 3′. Of particular interest is the entry in Kagal Bogh. I F 20: [é-dana] = [e]-ti-an-na = *bi-it si-i-in* (*MSL* 13 152). The reading dana rather than danna is based on the Ur III spellings é-da-na and é-te-na, which are, most probably, different writings for the same locality (most recently M. Yoshikawa, *ASJ* 8 [1986] 301–2). See also Edzard, *Zwischenzeit* 55 n. 250.

187. I do not understand the verb. A similar image may perhaps be found in *LW* 4:23: maš kar-ra-gin$_7$ ur x [. . .] un ad$_6$-bi mu-un-si-il-le-eš, 'They . . . like stampeding goats . . . ; they dissevered the people's corpses.'

192. Gaeš was sacred to Nanna and therefore I have assumed that the en in this city was female.

193. I have understood bara$_2$ an-na as a noun and an adjective, and thus different from bara$_2$ an-na-ka 'heavenly dais' (genitive construction), which occurs, for example, in *EWO* 74: an lugal-da bara$_2$ an-na-ka di si sá-e-me-en, 'I am the one who renders justice together with King An on the heavenly dais'; and *EWO* 199: en-zu en idim an lugal-da bara$_2$ an-na-ka i-im-tuš, 'Your lord, the important lord, sits with King An on the heavenly dais.'

195. For the reading ^{giš}nimbar, rather than ^{giš}gišimmar 'date palm', see M. Civil, *Aula Orientalis* 5 (1987) 28–29.

196–97. The city of Aššu is otherwise unknown. Note that it is written aš-šu^{ki} in N and aš-šú in EE. It is possible that níg-erim$_2$ nu-dib ^{d}nanna-ka is the proper name of a holy site in that city. Note, perhaps, as a parallel, *UET* 9 111 ii' 8′: bara$_2$ si-ga níg-erim$_2$ nu-dib. It is difficult to believe that this literary text would contain place names that are not attested in any of the thousands of Ur III administrative documents, but that is apparently the case. There is a city IŠ.SU^{ki} (*YOS* 4 66:3) but there is little probability that there is any connection between this locality and Aššu.

199. The Epuḫruma 'House of the Assembly' is not attested elsewhere.

200. The reading of the name of the city KI.ABRIG$_2$^{ki} is not certain; see B. Groneberg, *RGTC* 3 2 (to be read *āl-abraqqim*?). The location of the city is also disputed and since it is so rarely mentioned it is difficult to pinpoint this place on a map. The few ED references suggest that the city lay in the Lagash region (Å. W. Sjöberg, *MNS* 146; *RGTC* 1 85). No Ur III references are extant. Note also that in the tablet of ED riddles found at Lagash, Ningublaga is associated with a canal named AB×ḪA-gar (R. D. Biggs, *JCS* 32 (1973) 30 ix 2′).

(E)-Gabura in line 201 is the name of the temple of Ningublaga in KI.ABRIG$_2$^{ki}. Charpin, *Ur* 222 notes that in OB times Ningublaga was worshiped in a temple called the (E)-Gabura in Ur. He speculates that after the destruction described in *LSUr*, KI.ABRIG was not occupied again and the cult of Ningublaba and her spouse was moved to Ur. There are, indeed, no references to this city after the Ur III period, or during that time, for that matter, although Edzard, *Zwischenzeit* 55 n. 251 has suggested that the locality ÁB.NUN.ME.DU^{ki} attested three times in OB texts from Ur, may be KI.ABRIG$_2$^{ki}. In the present text, however, Niniagara, the spouse of Ningublaga, is already present as a deity in Ur, as is evidenced by line 409 (^{d}nin-ìà-gara$_2$ agrig maḫ-e erim$_3$-ma šu bí-in-dag; the connection between the agrig and Ningublaga has already been noted; see Charpin, *Ur* 378). There is, therefore, a distinct possibility that the cult of these deities were already worshiped in Ur before the fall of the Ur III state. Note, for example, the references to the cult of these deities in the Ur III texts from Ur (*UET* 3, indexes), as well as in Drehem documents such as *BIN* 3 198 and Sigrist, *Account Texts* 315, which mention the šabras of Enki, Nanna, Ningublaga, Utu, and Ningal. Although the city of Ur is not directly mentioned, the order of deities clearly indicates the place that is involved, and the analogy with the badly preserved Ur text *UET* 9 44, which mentions the šabras of Ningal and Ningublaga, further strengthens the case. Note also the offerings to Ningublaga in Ur in Legrain, *TRU* 320:2. Charpin's hypothesis is an attractive one, but it is based primarily on the evidence of *LSUr*, which cannot be taken at face value, and the fact that the (E)-Gabura is the name of the Ningublaga temple in two cities, a phenomenon that is otherwise well attested.

202. On Nin(e)i̯agara, who also occurs in line 409, the wife of Ningublaga, see T. Jacobsen, *JAOS* 103 (1983) 198. Ur III and OB sources seem to favor the fuller spelling. The name ^{d}nin-é-i̯à-gara$_2$ occurs in *UET* 3 149, 161, 164, and 822; the same spelling is attested in the OB god list published by W. G. Lambert, *Mélanges Birot* 183:98, in the god list *TCL* 15 10:159, as well as in *Lipit-Ishtar* 4:19. In *An-Anum* III 36 the name is written ^{d}nin-garaš$_3$, glossed in one source by ni/i̯à-ga-ra; see Litke, *An = Anum* 141. In *LSUr* the Nippur texts contain the shorter spelling, without é; the full writing is only attested in an Ur source of line 409 (II).

206. Egida is the name of the temple of Ninazu in Enigi; see the hymn to this temple in Sjöberg, *Temple Hymns* 27:181. Note the occurrence of é-gíd-da (*UET* 3 877 1′) and kišib é-gíd-da-bi-me-éš (*UET* 9 349 3′), which may be a type of building rather than a reference to the temple of Ninazu. In view of the -ke$_4$ at the end of Egida, it may perhaps be preferable to translate as, 'Ninazu of Egida deposited his weapon in the corner.'

To put something in the corner is to immobilize it, as is evidenced by *Eršemma* 106 18–19: me gal-gal-bi é àm-gi$_4$ me-bi al-ur$_4$-ur$_4$ ub ba-ra-an-gub, 'Her (Ištar's) divine ordinances have been locked up in the temple, her divine ordinances have been collected and deposited in the corner.' (Translation differs from the one offered by Cohen, *Sumerian Hymnology* 70 and is based on the later bilingual version of these lines in *SBH* 31 rev. 7–8, where ub-ba ba-da-gub is translated by Akkadian *ina tupqi šuzzuzu*.)

207. A temple by the name of Enutura is otherwise unattested.

210. Note that the hymn to the temple of Ningizzida in Gišbanda follows upon the hymn to the Egida in Sjöberg, *Temple Hymns* 28–29. For gi ér-ra mú (also in lines 361 and 479), compare the eršemma incipit gi ér-ra bí-in-mú in the literary catalog published by S. N. Kramer, *StOr* 46 (1975).

216. The divine name ^{d}nin-é-ḫa-ma occurs in the OB god list AO 5376 v 37 (*RA* 20 [1923] 99) and in *An-Anum* IV 42 (Litke, *An = Anum* 171). In the lists it is a name of Ištar but in *LSUr* she is obviously the spouse of Asaluḫi, who occurs below in line 218. The latter deity was worshiped in Kuʾara during the Ur III period, as is documented in four texts: *(a) TCL* 2 5482, *(b) TCL* 2 5514, *(c)* Sigrist, *Account Texts* 488, and *(d) TAD* 49. In none of these texts does the spouse of Asaluḫi appear. The order of deities in these texts is interesting. In *(a)* offerings were made to Asaluḫi and Šulgi in the temple of Asaluḫi, followed by Ḫaia, Nindamgalnuna, Mardu, Nindamana, Ningizzida, and Lugal-URU.SAG. In *(b)* the deities are Asaluḫi, Šulgi, Nindamana, Ensimaḫ, Ḫaia, Ningizzida, and Lugal-URU.[SAG]. In *(c)* only Asaluḫi and Šulgi are mentioned, and in *(d)* Asaluḫi is followed by Ninsun and a-šà ^{d}ASAL. Of these deities only Nindamgalnuna and Nindamana are possible candidates for the role of wife of Asaluḫi. In OB texts when Asaluḫi was identified with Marduk, his wife was Ṣarpanitum, Sumerian ^{d}pa$_{4}$-nun-an-ki (Green, *Eridu* 93), and, as a result, a god list identifies Nin-é-ḪA-ma with the name of this goddess (K 29 [*CT* 25 pl. 36] + unpublished Ki. 1902.5-10.28 [courtesy W. G. Lambert] obv. 8: ^{d}nin-é-ḪA-ma = MIN (= ^{d}*ṣar-pa-ni-tum*)).

218. LUL.KU . . . DU is most probably related to the enigmatic LUL.GU . . . ak of pre-Ur III text discussed, most recently, by F. Pomponio, *WO* 13 (1982) 95-96; M. Civil, *JNES* 32 (1973) 60 n. 10; and P. Steinkeller, *SEL* 1 (1984) 14 n. 10. None of the proposed translations of the verb fit this line.

220. This is the only time that this refrain is uttered by a male deity. Is it possible that a line mentioning Ninsun has been omitted? There are only three sources for this line: C (Nippur), AA (Nippur), and EE (Ur). C and EE have this line after 219. AA is broken at this point so that in lines 218 and 219 only the first two signs are preserved. When I recollated this text in December 1987, I decided that text AA preserved the faint traces of a sign in the line following 219, possibly ⌈DINGIR⌉. I would now suggest that at least one source had a line concerning ⌈d⌉[nin-sún. . .] before 220. This possibility is not strong enough, however, to warrant a renumbering of the entire text. For the present, line 219′ has been added to the composite text.

221. For parallels to the first part of the line, see M. W. Green, *JCS* 30 (1978) 159.

224. The faint signs of C undoubtedly preserve the names of two deities, Igiḫegala and Kaḫegala, in that order; the Ur source FF has only three signs preserved at the beginning of the line: ^{d}KA-x-[. . .]. My own collations of the third sign do not point to ⌈ḫé⌉ and a further recollation by I. Finkel confirms this. And yet, one expects ^{d}KA-ḫé-[gál-la] as the first in the pair, in accordance with the standard order of these deities, who are variously described as the doorkeepers (ì-du$_{8}$) of Enki or the Laḫama's of Eridu (references in M. J. Geller, *Iraq* 42 [1980] 38; M. W. Green, *JCS* 30 [1978] 149; and W. G. Lambert, *Or*, n.s. 54 [1985] 201).

232–34. In the present context there is a clear allusion to the standard formula found in certain types of incantations, the "Asaluḫi/Marduk—Ea dialog," in which Ea answers his son in the following words: dumu-mu nu-e-zu a-na a-ra-ab-daḫ-e-en ^{d}asar-lú-ḫi a-na nu-e-zu a-na a-ra-ab-daḫ-e-en, 'My son, what is it that you do not know, what more can I add for you, Asarluḫi, what is it that you do not know, what can I add for you?'; see Falkenstein, *Haupttypen* 54. See also line 397.

251–64. These lines are translated by S. N. Kramer, *Bulletin of the Asia Institute*, n.s. 1 (1987) 13. Lines 251–53 present particular problems. First, line 251 is identical with 293 but there is a possibility that the lines may have to be read differently. The problem lies with the reading of the verb GIN/GUB. On the basis of 252 and 253 one could suppose that gub is the preferred reading (gub-bé). The use of the postpositions -šè and -ta would suggest a verb of movement, however, hence -gin/du. The matter is further complicated by the occurrence of the Akkadian interpretation of the phrase ú-šè gin-na-mu as *ša ana iṣi illiku* ('who went to fetch kindling for me') invoked by Falkenstein, *Gerichtsurkunden* II 2 (see also Limet, *Anthroponymie* 247). If one accepted a reading gub of the first verb in 252–53, one could translate as, 'In Ur no one went to fetch food (or: firewood), no one went to fetch water. The ones doing duty at the food (or: firewood) went away from the food (or: firewood) and thus will not return, the ones doing duty at the water (sources) went away from the water (sources) and thus will not return.'

255. S. N. Kramer understood ḫa-al-ma as a geographical or ethnic name. There is no other evidence for such a name and one must therefore wonder if this is not a writing of lú ḫa-lam-ma 'vandal'. The latter occurs as a description of the Šimaškians and the Elamites in the laments; see *LU* 244: LÚ.SU^{ki} elam^{ki} lú ḫa-lam-ma eše gín ba-an-ak, 'Šimaškians and the Elamites, the vandals, treated (the temple) as if it were (a mere) thirty shekels (worth)'; *LE* 4:9–10: dub-šen kù lú igi nu-b[ar-r]e-da, LÚ.⌜SU⌝^{ki} elam^{ki} lú ḫa-l[am-ma igi in-ni]-in-bar; *LE* 8:4: [lú] ḫa-lam ak-a-gin$_7$ sag nu-mu-u[n-šub. . .]; above 230: [gu]-ti-um^{ki} lú ḫa-lam-ma-ke$_4$ me-zé-er-zé-re-ne. Note also the Šu-Sin inscription published by M. Civil, *JCS* 21 (1969) 31:25: mar-dú lú ḫa-lam-m[a] 'the Amorites, the vandals'; and *OECT* 5 28:11 and duplicates (long version of letter from Išbi-Erra to Ibbi-Sin): elam^{ki} ur idim lú ḫa-lam-ma-ke$_4$ 'the Elamites, howling dog(s), vandal(s)'. Green, *Eridu* 303 n. 1 suggested, ingeniously, that ḫa-al-ma could be a writing for Ḫaltamti or Ḫa(l)tammati, the native name of Elam. This was based on A. L. Oppenheim's proposal (*RA* 63 [1969] 95) that such a reading was attested in an Akkadian text from Mari. Unfortunately, this reading is no longer tenable; see J.-M. Durand, *MARI* 3 (1984) 277–78.

257. Perhaps the end of the line contained the phrase KU-bi-šè (gál), for which see the commentary to line 71.

263. There has been much confusion concerning the city Kisiga (BÀD×KÙ) and Dūrum (BÀD×AN); see most recently W. Röllig, *RlA* 5 (1980) 620–22, and my article in *Mesopotamia* 12 (1977) 83–96. This line concerns the city that was sacred to Inanna and Dumuzi, most probably modern Tell el-Lahm. The restoration is based on the standard literary sequence 5–10 (Alster, *Dumuzi's Dream* 87), although one must admit that here the sequence would have to be reversed. An early example of the use of this pattern is found in *IAS* 282 iii 3′–4′: lú 5 nu-me-a lú 10 nu-me-a.

267. Compare, for example, *SBH* 19 20: zi-ga u$_5$-e-a zi-ga u$_5$-e-a en zi-ga u$_5$-e-a = *ti-bi ri-kab ti-bi ri-kab be-lu$_4$ ti-bi ri-kab*, 'Arise! Mount up! Lord, arise! Mount up!'

271–76. These are probably stock lines from the lament literature. K. Volk has been kind enough to send me his preliminary transliteration of BM 38593, most probably a part of tablet 17 of the late edition of the balag composition uru$_2$ àm-ma-ir-ra-bi, which contains lines that are closely parallel to those found in *LSUr*. The relevant lines are quoted here by his permission (BM 38593: 42–48):

42. egi-mèn nu-un-ga-mu-da ba-an-da-u$_5$ kur ⌜gi$_4$⌝-[in-bi$^?$] dè-mèn
ru-ba-ku it-ti ⌜*ma*⌝*-ak-k*[*u-ri-ia*] *lu-ur-k*[*ab*] ⌜*lu*⌝*-ú a-mat* KUR*-i ana-ku*
43. kù nu-zu-a-⌜mu⌝-da [ba-an]-da-u$_5$ kur ⟨ ⟩
44. ⌜na$_4$ gú nu⌝-zu-a-mu-da ⌜ba⌝-an-da-⌜u$_5$⌝ kur ⟨ ⟩
45. gašan x x x-DU bí-in-du$_{11}$-ga-ra ⌜kur⌝-ra na-ám-gi$_4$-in-e
be-⌜*el*$^?$*-tu*$^?$⌝ *šá x-lu* UR*-x-ku aq-bu-ú ina* ⌜KUR⌝*-i a x x*
46. kur-ra x x gi$_4$-in kur-ra na-ám-gi$_4$-in-e sag nu-mu-e-da-ús-e *ina* ⌜KUR*-i*⌝
[. . .] *x x x x dul-la* ⌜*ul*⌝ *e-*⌜*le-*ʾ⌝*-i*
47. ⌜kur$^?$-ra$^?$⌝ x [. . .] x x x x sag ⟨ ⟩
48. ⌜kur-ra$^?$⌝ x [. . .] x x x x sag ⟨ ⟩

272. Following Sjöberg, *Nanna-Suen* 125 I take kiš-nu-gál as a variant of giš-nu$_{(11)}$-gal 'great light'. Perhaps the light on the mountains signifies that they are very high, and thus close to the heavens.

292. W. Heimpel, *JCS* 38 (1986) 136 n. 29, argues that the phrase ^{giš}ig gub in *CA* 168 refers to doors standing open and his translation has been accepted here. The same interpretation was suggested independently by B. Alster, *WO* 16 (1985) 162. Thus note *LE* 2:4: [abul-la-bi ^{giš}s]i-gar bí-in-ku$_5$ ^{giš}ig-bi u$_4$-dè im-ma-gub, 'It cut the lock from the main gate, its door stood open to the weather'; and *CA* 168: abul kalam-ma-ka ^{giš}ig im-ma ba-e-gub, 'In the city-gates of the land the doors stood open to the wind.' Previously it had been assumed that this phrase referred to the dislodging of doors; see Cooper, *Agade* 50, with older literature. The interpretation offered by Heimpel and Alster is undoubtedly correct in light of the Ur version of line 404. The two Nippur sources of that line, E and QQ, provide a reading of é-gal a ba-šub-ba ba-e-lá-lá ^{giš}si-gar bí-in-bu-bu-uš. In II (from Ur) line 404 reads abul-la-bi ^{giš}si-gar bí-in-du$_8$-du$_8$-uš ^{giš}ig-bi u$_4$-dè gub-bu.

293. This is a repeat of line 251. See the commentary above.

294. If the reading of the root of the verb is correct then one must connect the predicate with šu . . . nigin = *ṣâdu* 'to prowl', usually written nigin. This equation is established on the basis of an unpublished lexical text

(UM 29-15-79 rev. ii 13) by Klein, *Three Šulgi Hymns* 215. His translation, 'traversed', appears to be correct, but the contexts he cites suggest 'to run, rush toward a goal'. Thus see *Enki Letter* 51: ki nam-tag dugud-da šu-nigin-zu ár ga-à[m-i-i], 'As you rush toward the place of heavy sin, I will surely [sing your] praises'; *Death of Ur-Namma* 74=75: ^{giš}gigir ba-da-šú ḫar-ra-an im-ma-da-sùh šu nu-um-ma-nigin; 164: [me-l]i-e-a sig_4 uri_5^{ki}-ma-šè šu nu-um-ma-nigin, 'Woe, I cannot proceed to the brickwork of Ur!' There are semantic problems with this interpretation. I assume that lines 293–95 are a description of a famine and its consequences and thus one would expect an image of inactivity in line 294.

299. For igi $nigin_2$ and related expressions, see M. W. Green, *JCS* 30 (1978) 143.

300. On this line, and parallel usages of gi dili dù-a-gin_7 sag . . . sìg, see Alster, *Dumuzi's Dream* 91–92. The occurrences of sag . . . sìg have been collected by Alster, *Dumuzi's Dream* 91–92, with further comment by Klein, *Three Šulgi Hymns* 159. All the parallel passages (with solitary reeds) describe an action that represents a gesture of fear. The use of sag . . . sìg in the current line with the auxiliary verb gar cannot have such a meaning and hence I have attempted to reconcile the two by translating the verb transitively, 'to inspire fear'. I interpret the phrase as an image of total paralysis; the city was incapable even of shivering in fear. Compare also *Eršemma* 163.1:9: kur $erim_2$-šè gi dili dù-a-gin_7 sag ì-sìg-sìg-ge, 'You make the enemy land shiver in fear like a solitary reed.' Note, unfortunately in broken context, *LW* 2:9′: [. . .] KA mu-un-ak-e sag sìg-ge nu-gá-gá.

301 and **407a.** Note the variants to this line. The verb lug has been studied by P. Steinkeller, *SEL* 1 (1984) 5–17, and P. Michalowski, *SEL* 1 (1984) 19–22, with a discussion of these lines (see already M. Civil, *Studies Oppenheim* 88). The differences between the readings cited there and those in the score are a result of collation. It is now clear that there was a major confusion in line 301; šu . . . dab_5 in GG makes sense but šu $nigin_2$-na lu-ga in X does not, nor does šu lu-ga in HH unless one emends the signs to read pú lu-ga 'living in a pond'. Confusion between a-$nigin_2$ = *amirānu* 'standing water' and the verbs šu . . . $nigin_2$ 'to move around' and šu . . . dab_5 probably resulted in the variants found in these texts.

302–7. These lines were treated by S. Cohen, *Kramer AV* 108 and Berlin, *Enmerkar* 84 with different readings in line 306. For reading lunga is somewhat arbitrary in view of the variety of syllabic spellings of the word provided in lexical texts; see the references cited in Civil, *Studies Oppenheim* 88 and in *MSL* 9 152–53. Although the reading is not certain, it seems clear that the word ends with -n. In view of the following line, however, I have taken -na to be the third person possessive pronoun. Epigraphically, $munu_3$ is uncertain, but if it is correct, then it is 'the cereal which, after germination, will become greenmalt'; that is, one of the basic ingredients for making beer (Civil, *Studies Oppenheim* 76).

303. LUGAL.BI.GUB is unclear. I have, for lack of a better interpretation, translated it as 'royal station'. Note that in view of the context, one could connect GUB with zú . . . gub 'to eat'; see the commentary on line 435.

309. For this image see the references collected by W. W. Hallo, *CRRAI* 17 132. Note the citation from an unpublished bilingual duplicate from Ur of *Nisaba Hymn* 55: gur_7-du_6 gur_7-maš-a = [*k*]*a-re-e ti-li* [*k*]*a-re-e ma-a-ši*, '(from) grain piles (as large as) a mound (to) grain piles as small as a *mašu* measure'; cited in *CAD* M/1 401.

312. See Gudea Cyl. A XXVIII 7–8: gír-pa-na-bi gud gu_7 udu gu_7, 'its butcher knife, which consumes oxen, consumes sheep'. As Cooper, *Agade* 255 has noted, úšim . . . ná 'to lie in the grass' contrasts here, and in *CA* 248–49, with 'eating good food', and must be translated as 'to lie hungry'.

314. W. Heimpel, *JCS* 33 (1981) 106, has argued that the bur-sag was "a structure which was specifically used for the storage of regular offerings. . . ." For further references see *PSD* B 187–88, which does not define the purpose of the building. References to the difficult á sikil, which occurs primarily with beer and less often with barley, have been collected by Hall, *Moon-God* 772–73. It is possible that there is no connection between that word and á sikil in the present context and it may simply have to be rendered as, 'In the bursag, the pure "arm" of Nanna. . . .' For za-pa-ág in laments see M. W. Green, *JCS* 30 (1978) 142.

316. The translation of this line is very provisional; mu-un-DU = *šūrubtu*.

317. For this interpretation of dúr see Alster, *Dumuzi's Dream* 97.

318. It is difficult do discern whether kar-za-gìn is a proper name or not, nor is it clear whether Nanna is part of the name. This term is used of quays in Nippur, Lagash, and Ur; see, most recently, Ferrara, *Nanna's Journey* 128. In literary texts it is often difficult to decide if this is a proper name or not. For a place named Karzagina in Ur, see Sjöberg, *Mondgott* 103. In ritual contexts, however, za-gìn is clearly an adjective; see *UET* 6 67:50: kar za-gìn kar maḫ kar kù-ga, and *YOS* 11 42:10–11: a-tu_5-a 7 a-rá 7 li kur-ra 7 kar za-gìn-na. This makes it difficult to interpret the references in Ur III texts from Ur that mention offerings to the alan ^{d}amar-^{d}en.zu kar-za-gìn; see *UET* 3 105:7, 111:6, 139:6, and 142:6. All these texts date from the reign of Ibbi-Sin and document expenditures for a ceremony in the temple of Nanna in the middle of the month. Another similar text, also from the time of Ibbi-Sin (*UET* 3 147:6), provides and interesting variant: ki-a-nag ^{d}amar-^{d}en.zu [kar$^{?}$]-za-gìn. This would suggest that these rituals were connected with the funerary cult of Amar-Sin.

320. M. Civil, *Or*, n.s. 54 (1983) 36, has discussed saḫar . . . dub 'to pile up sand'. It is not possible to define what an unu_2-RI-bàn-da was. The only other occurrences known to me are in *Temple Hymns* line 305: ḫi-nun ab šà-ga unu_2-RI-bà[n-da], and in *Enki and Ninmaḫ* 41: [./././] dím-zu unu_2-RI-zu ga-a-à[m].

321. Following a suggestion of M. Civil, I have taken gir-re-e to be a writing for gi ér-ra.

325–26. These lines refer to a yearly ceremony that is known from two other sources: *Šulgi F* 13–16: i̯à du$_{10}$-a-bi gara$_2$ du$_{10}$-a-bi ^{d}nanna-a níg-mu-a a-a-ni ^{d}en-líl-ra tùr kù-ta mu-na-ni-in-ku$_4$-ku$_4$ má nisag-g[á-k]e$_4$ si um-sá ^{d}en-líl-ra nibru^{ki} tùm-dè, 'Nanna took the first quality butter and cheese from the pen, the yearly produce, for his father Enlil, he loaded it on the ship of first-fruit offerings in order to bring (them) to Enlil (in) Nippur . . .' (see C. Wilcke, *CRRAI* 19 201), and Sin-iddinam 13:212–15: ^{d}nanna lugal uri$_5$^{ki}-ma nibru^{ki} uru a-a-ugu-na-šè [n]isag-gá šà-ba asila$_2$ ḫu-mu-ni-in-de$_6$, 'Nanna, the lord of Ur, joyfully brought the firstfruit offerings to Nippur, the city of the father who begot him.' Note that an Ur III text from the Inanna temple in Nippur (6N-T 254, M. Civil, *JCS* 32 [1980] 230, date broken) documents a local version of these obligations (lines 9′–11′): u$_4$ 12 zal-la [z]ì-munu$_4$ dug$_8$-dam ù nindaba nisag ⌜é⌝ ^{d}en-líl-lá-šè gíd-dam, 'The twelfth day: to bake the brewing ingredients, and to bring the early offerings to Enlil's temple.'

329. That (gi)-dub-ba-an = *dappu* is a type of reed fence was argued by Alster, *Dumuzi's Dream* 95–96; Green, *Eridu* 214; as well as B. Alster and H. Vanstiphout, *ASJ* 9 (1987) 37. All references point to a fence made from bundled reeds. Note that this is followed in the next line by gi-sig = *kikkišu*, another type of reed fence or a reed hut.

330. For this translation of šu . . . lá-lá see the commentary to line 18.

331. One can analyze áb.šilam-ma amar-bi as two nouns and a conjunction or as an "anticipatory genitive," that is, 'the cow's young'. The first solution is followed here; see *Lugalbanda* 2:307, where áb šilam amar-bi has a variant áb šilam-ma amar-bi (see Wilcke, *Lugalbanda* 206). I understand the -da- in the first verb as a reflex of the conjunction. For the end of the line see the commentary to line 150. Note that the cows in lines 331–32 are part of the sacred attributes of Nanna. See the Nanna hymn, *UET* 6 68 and duplicates, now edited in Hall, *Moon God* 830–45, that describes these sacred herds in mythological terms. For (áb) šilam, a poetic word for 'cow', see B. Landsberger, *MSL* 8/1 62.

332. For ^{ú}munzer see M. Civil, *Studies Reiner* 46. As Civil notes, there is a deity named ^{d}áb-^{ú}munzer-ki-ág in the circle of Nanna in *An-Anum* III.

333. Gai̯au is called the 'shepherd of Sin' (sipa ^{d}en.zu-na-ke$_4$) in *An-Anum* III 86. The following line indicates that ^{d}šurim/ganam$_4$ is another name of this deity (see Litke, *An = Anum* 146). For the end of the line, compare *LU* 305: ^{d}ga-ša-an-gal-mèn na-gada pe-el-lá-gin$_7$ ^{giš}tukul šurim-ma bí-(in)-šub, 'I, Ningal, like an unworthy shepherd I have dropped (my) weapon into the dung!'

As T. Jacobsen, *JAOS* 103 (1983) 199, has pointed out, Šunidug is listed as a child of Gai̯au in An-Anum and is therefore one of the 'herdsmen of Sin' (utul maḫ ^{d}en.zu-na-ke$_4$). In his discussion he rendered this line as, 'Shunidu, who wraps up butter for (cottage) cheese, wrapped not up the butter for (cottage) cheese,' interpreting du_6-ul as *pussumu* 'to veil'. The translation offered here is based on du_6-ul-du_6-ul = *puḫḫuru* 'to gather, store', following a suggestion of M. Civil.

338. For ne-mur 'coal' see Hallo and van Dijk, *Exaltation* 80 (*sub* izi-ur_5), and Alster, *Dumuzi's Dream* 93. Perhaps the word refers not to burning itself but to the burning substances, hence it is often used together with the verb dub 'to heap'. Note also the reading ni-mu-ur KI.NE = *id-ra-nu* 'alkali, potash' in Diri IV 288 (cited in *CAD* I/J 9).

343–44. These lines repeat, almost verbatim, lines 325–26. The problem lies, however, with the pronoun in line 344. From the second person pronoun in the following line, it would appear that these lines are still part of Suʾen's address to Enlil. The scribes of the two Ur texts HH and NN repeated the third person pronoun -na- from line 325 (the only Nippur witness for this line, text K, breaks off before the pronoun).

345. I have understood $laḫ_5$ (DU.DU) as the plural stem of de_6 'to bring' in order to account for the transitive grammatical marking. Other interpretations are also possible. Note *4R* 20 no. 1 3–4: e_4-ri-a mu-un-DU.DU = *ú-šá-li-ka na-mu-iš*, 'He turned (the country) into a desert'; see *CAD* A/1 320. S. N. Kramer, *ANET*^{3} 617 translated this line as, 'The *en*'s (who lived) outside the city, the *en*'s (who lived) inside the city have been carried off by the wind (of desolation).' He interpreted the verb in the same manner but rendered líl as 'wind', as is often done in translations of lamentations. As noted in *CAD* Z 60, however, líl = *zaqīqu* means 'phantom, ghost, haunted place', never 'wind'. This word also occurs in lines 222, 347, 361, and 479. In light of this, the phrase šu líl-lá . . . dug_4 in lines 143 and 149, discussed in the commentary to line 29, has been translated here as 'to become haunted'.

347. Compare the first part of *LU* 347: uri_5^{ki} èš líl-e im-ma-an-gar.

350. For si-im-si-im . . . ak = *eṣēnu* 'to sniff', see M. Civil, *Iraq* 23 (1961) 168, and Å. W. Sjöberg, *JCS* 25 (1973) 139.

351. Of the three witnesses for this line, the two Nippur manuscripts G and K have TUR as the first sign; the Ur source HH has túl. As M. Civil (review of *PSD* B, *Or*, in press) recognized, the literary parallels favor a reading pú-sag = *šatpu* 'water hole' (see, most recently, Å. W. Sjöberg, *JCS* 25 [1973] 141). Did the phonetic similarity between túl and tur result in a reinterpretation of the beginning of the line as dumu sag?

361–62. It is usually stated that a-še-er is the Emesal form of a-nir = *tānīḫu* 'lament' (Krecher, *Kultlyrik* 91–92; J. A. Black, *ASJ* 7 [1985] 46), with the regular change of main dialect n to Emesal š. Often, however, as in the present context, the words are used together in parallel constructions. There is a possibility that a-nir was at one time read a-$šer_7$, although Proto-Kagal lists the words one after another as separate entries (lines 480–81 [*MSL* 13 80: a-še-er$^{ta\text{-}ni\text{-}ḫu}$, a-nir$^{ta\text{-}ni\text{-}ḫu}$]; for the value $šer_7$ of NIR already in Old Akkadian, see I. J. Gelb, *Kraus AV* 74). The reading nir is based on the evidence of Izi C ii 3′: ki ^{a}a-nir$^{ni\text{-}ir}$-ra = MIN (= *a-šar*) *ta-ni-ḫi* (*MSL* 13 176), already cited by F. Delitzsch, *Sumerisches Glossar* 202.

Note that lines 361 and 361a are identical with 479 and 480 (with the variant a-še-ra for a-nir-ra). This may be the reason why the Ur source added line 361a.

362a–63. These lines were briefly discussed by C. Wilcke, *CRRAI* 19 222 n. 41 in connection with a rendering of lines 362a–80 (old 364–77), as well as by Alster, *Instructions* 104 and 135. They both convincingly cite *Gilgameš and Ḫuwawa* 20 as a parallel: guruš dumu gi_7 ní-za ḫé-me-en kur-ra a-na-bi-me-en. If one were to reconstruct the present passage in harmony with that line, it would be necessary to follow Wilcke and Alster and amend the Ur text II, reading BI as ḫé and to interpret ér-ra-na-bi-me-en as a sandhi writing for ér-ra ⟨a⟩-na-bi-me-en. Collation shows that II (from Ur) has been copied correctly and the end of line 363 is broken in the only other duplicate to this line, the Nippur source G.

367. On zag = *adi*, compare *Šulgi B* 333: numun ba-i-(i)-ta zag un lu-a-šè, 'From days of yore to the time that the people had multiplied.'

368. For references to the difficult sag-bi-šè . . . è see A. Falkenstein, *AnOr* 28 30. Note the use of this phrase in *Šulgi A* 26: ^{d}šul-gi me-en lugal-kala-ga sag-bi-šè è-a-me-en, which Klein, *Three Šulgi Hymns* 191 translated as, 'I, Šulgi, the mighty king, superior to all.' Recently, Jacobsen, *The Harps* 392 and 427 provided the felicitous English translation 'take precedence'. Thus Gudea Cyl. A IV 10–11: ^{d}nanše mu du_{11}-ga-zu zi-dam sag-bi-šè è-a-àm, 'My Nanše—being that your word is true, and being that it does take precedence'; and Gudea Cyl. B II 18: en du_{11}-ga-ni sag-biš è-a, '(Ningirsu), lord whose word takes precedence.'

379. For this line see *Balag* 44:220: uru_2 mu-bi tu-ra gi-bi tu-ra. J. A. Black, *ASJ* 7 (1985) 48–49, cites parallels, including Newell 688:33 (unpublished): uru_2 mu-bi dur_5-ru gi-bi dur_5-ru-bi, and proposes that one should perhaps translate 'the town whose trees are fresh, whose reeds are fresh'; but the context clearly requires a negative image and thus it is better to interpret the predicate as t/du(r) '(to be) sick'.

382–86. These lines were treated by B. Eichler, *JAOS* 103 (1983) 97 who argues that ^{kuš}é-íb-ùr was a siege-shield. In the same article Eichler defines ^{giš}illar as javelin. I have followed his translation even though F. Groneberg, *RA* 81 (1987) 115–24, has presented good evidence that in many contexts this word designates a bow. That $u_{3/4}$-sar . . . ak means 'to sharpen' has been demonstrated beyond any doubt by Cooper, *Agade* 245–46.

386. The phrase pu-ud-pa-ad . . . za belongs to the group of expressions formed on the pattern $C_1u(C_2)$–$C_1a(C_2)$ . . . za, denoting noises, discussed by M. Civil, *JCS* 20 (1966) 119–21. *PSD* B 169 entered bu-ud ba-ad . . . za as a separate verb with one example, *Šulgi A* 68–69: na_4 di_4-di_4-bi na_4 gal-gal-bi murgu-gá bu-[u]d-ba-ad ḫi-⌜x⌝-íb-za-àm (vars.: dub dab_5, dub-dab_x(DUB),

dub-dab, dub-dáb, dab_5-dáb), 'Their small hailstones and large hailstones were thudding on my back' (see Klein, *Three Šulgi Hymns* 197). This is undoubtedly the same verb and they should be considered together. Note also bu_x(PI)-ba . . . za (*PSD* B 171).

388. M. Civil, *Mélanges Birot* 78 discusses á . . . gar.

389. S. N. Kramer, *Kraus AV* 141 (with additional information from T. Jacobsen on p. 144) cites this line, choosing a different set of variants (uru ^{giš}tukul-e sag nu-sì-ma-sì-ma-âm šà-gar-e ba-e-dib) to restore, by analogy, two lines in a Lisina lament (BM 29633 3–4): [^{kuš}A.EDIN].Á-da-na a nu-un-nag-nag enmen ì-[ni-dib nin_9-ni] ^{kuš}lu-úb-na ninda nu-un-ma-al šà-gar-re [ì-ni-dib], 'From out of her waterskin she drinks no water, she is overcome by thirst, his sister puts no bread in her bread-bag, she is overcome by hunger.' Some of these restorations are problematical.

390–407a. These lines are translated by S. N. Kramer, *Bulletin of the Asia Institute*, n.s. 1 (1987) 14.

391. Compare *CT* 17 25:24 (and unpublished duplicate) cited, with collations, in *MSL* 9 23 and by M. T. Roth, *JCS* 32/33 (1980) 133: [igi$^?$ ši/bí-in]-gam-ma sa ši/bí-in-lug-e = [. . . *ú*]-*kan-na-an šír-a-nu i-za-ar*, '(The demon) contorts [the face$^?$], he twists the sinews.' The previous citation of this passage contained the readings [sa ši-in-]-gam-ma and *šír*-[*a-nu*] at the beginning of the line. M. Civil informs me, however, that this is wrong; evidently the unpublished duplicate does not provide these readings. The present line helps to clarify the reading of LU = *zâru* 'to twist' as lug, and thus this rare word must be added to the values of lug studied by P. Steinkeller, *SEL* 1 (1984) 5–17.

397. For nam-mu = *minsu* 'what is it that?' see *MSL* 4 42 and *CAD* M/2 89. Compare *ELA* 178: lugal-za du_{11}-ga-ni nam-mu daḫ-a-ni nam-mu, 'What is it that your king has said (to me), what is it that he has added?'

398. This line is cited with brief discussion of ka $garaš_2$-ka = *pî karašîm* 'annihilation, catastrophe' in Å. W. Sjöberg, *Or*, n.s. 37 (1968) 233. If one accepts that til could be a writing of ti-l, which has a plural se_{11} in early texts, then it would be possible to translate this line as, 'How long can we continue to dwell at the brink of catastrophe?'

404. This follows the Nippur sources E and QQ. For the Ur variant (II) see the commentary to line 292.

405. The image is a common one, compare *LU* 184: im-ḫul-e a maḫ è-a-gin_7 gú-bi nu-gá-gá; *LW* 4:22: su-bir_4^{ki}-e a maḫ è-a-gin_7 a x [(. . .)] x-gin_7 ki-en-gi-ra ba-an-dá; *LW* 5:20: su-bir_4^{ki}-e a maḫ è-a-gin_7 z[i-ga . . .]; and *Inanna and Ebih* 179: a maḫ è-a-gin_7 a ù bí-dé.

406. More literally the line should be translated as, 'In Ur weapons ravished (people) as if they were pots.' The image is an old one; see already SAG.KI *ki* DUG *da-sa-bi-ir*, 'Your forehead you shall smash like a pot,' in an Old

Akkadian incantation (Westenholz, *OSP* 1 no. 7 i 3′–5′), and *Death of Ur-Namma* 50: ⌜ki?⌝ lul-la ur-^{d}namma dug-gin$_7$ ⟪a⟫ ba-ni-in-tak$_4$-aš, 'They left Ur-Namma (lying on) the *battlefield* like a (broken) pot.'

407. Heimpel, *Tierbilder* 458 read nu-um-gá and translated it as 'vulture'. The context requires a compound verb 'to run, flee' with the first element du$_{10}$. Unfortunately I am unable to identify the root in any of the extant manuscripts. The signs look like NUN/ZIL but I cannot identify any of the known compounds with du$_{10}$ (gar, ak, dug$_4$). Note that S. N. Kramer, *Bulletin of the Asia Institute*, n.s. 1 (1987) 14, must have also come to this conclusion and now translates the line as, 'Its refugees cannot run fast, they are pressed to the sides of the walls.' In *ANET* 3 618 he rendered the line, 'Its refugees cannot hasten (to escape), they are pressed tight to the side of the wall.'

The present translation is based on the following reasoning. The phrase zag-ga . . . dab$_5$ must mean 'to be surrounded', as demonstrated by Römer, *Bilgameš und Akka* 67–68, and so I interpret the end of the line to mean that the citizens of Ur were 'surrounded', that is trapped, inside the city walls. Perhaps zil may have to be interpreted in light of the lexical entry NUN$^{za\text{-}al}$ = *na-ʾa-bu-tú* 'to flee' (Erimhuš V 212 [*MSL* 17, 76]). This does not account for du$_{10}$/šár before the verbal complex, however. Provisionally, I have taken du$_{10}$ . . . zil to be a synonym of du$_{10}$ . . . bad 'to run' (note that late lexical texts equate both bad and zil with *nesû* and *petû* [*CAD* N/2 186]).

407a. See commentary on line 301.

408/444. On the word AN.ZAG and its possible readings uzug, usug 'treasure room(s)', attested only in late lexical texts, see M. Civil, *Or*, n.s. 52 (1983) 236.

409. The phrase šu . . . dag has been discussed by Wilcke, *Lugalbanda* 207, and Cohen, *Enmerkar* 296–97. Following Cohen, I interpret this verb to mean 'to cut oneself off'. It may be simpler to accept šu . . . dag as *rapādu* and translate 'ran away from the storehouse'.

410. The phrase saḫar-ra -n.tuš describes a willful act of despair; see my remarks in *JCS* 32 (1980) 95.

412. Note the variant udu gi$_4$-a-bi for udu ú gu$_7$-a-bi in text O. This may be a simple dictation error but note that Klein, *Three Šulgi Hymns* 118 cautiously suggests that gi$_4$ = *lipû* 'fat' may be involved here.

412a. Note that this line, attested only in an Ur source (II), is identical with line 195.

413. An extensive discussion of urudu níg-kala-ga is found in Cooper, *Angin* 150–53. For á nam-ur-sag-gá 'valorous arm/strength', see ibid., 116–17.

415. For the writing of ús with -ú-ús see, for example, *CA* 158 and 164, and *Angin* 203.

417. For á-an su$_{11}$-lum-ma 'spandix with ripe dates', see Landsberger, *Date Palm* 37. I understand pú du$_7$-du$_7$ as an image of ripe dates falling on wells.

419. The different variants to this line require different translations. The present version follows the Nippur sources E and SS. The Ur texts JJ and MM agree on the reading kúr for kur but they differ in syntax: 'They gathered the great tribute and the enemy carried it away' (JJ); 'The enemy carried away the great tribute that they had collected (MM).'

420. M. W. Green, *JCS* 30 (1978) 147, argues that ^{giš}búr = *gišburru* is a 'conjurer's wand'. The context, as well as the parallels cited there suggest that this is an architectural feature connected with the facade or gate of a building, a fact further substantiated by the parallelism between the first and second parts of the present line. Note *giš-bur-rum* = *ta-ri-mu* in *CT* 18 3 rev ii 28. *CAD* G 100 sub *gišburru* connects this word with ^{giš}búr 'trap'. The word with the meaning 'trap' has been discussed by Sjöberg, *Temple Hymns* 129–30; he maintains that translation in his note in *OrSuec* 23–24 (1974–75) 175. Until other evidence is forthcoming it would be better to keep separate two different words written ^{giš}búr 'trap' and 'door ornament'. (See now also Charpin, *Ur*, 290–91.)

For bàd-si = *sītu, samītu* 'battlement' (*CAD* S 117, 336: 'battlemented parapet'), see Krecher, *Kultlyrik* 169–70. Note that the passage that is the subject of that discussion, with its many parallels, demonstrates that it the part of the wall that is most often inhabited by birds.

421–24. The description of intertwined animals on the right and left of the door, "dragons" and lions, undoubtedly refers to the architectural ornamentation of the facade of the temple. See, for example, *Nungal* 22–24: ^{giš}sag-kul-bi pirig huš nam-šul-ba gú-da lá-a ^{giš}šu-di-eš-bi muš-sag-KAL eme-e-dè e-ne-pàr si-il-le-dè ^{giš}si-gar-bi muš-šà-tùr ki šúr-ra ní-bi ùr-ùr-ru-dam, 'Its bolt (has/is) raging lions, intertwined in their *power*, its bar (has/is) a . . . -snake who hisses, sticks out his tongue, its lock (has/is) a poisonous snake, *slithering* in an awe-inspiring place.' For animal ornaments on parts of doors see also W. Heimpel, *RlA* 7 (1987) 82.

425a. For a-sal-bar 'architrave', see Cohen, *Enmerkar* 288, with previous literature, and Å. W. Sjöberg, *AfO* 24 (1973) 38.

429. *PSD* B 174 cites the beginning of this line, reading $bulug_4$ with a variant bulug. This results from the confusion of signs introduced by the change from Labat, *Manuel* to Borger, *Zeichenliste*. According to the latter $bulug_4$ is NAGAR but Labat's $bulug_2$ (BÚR) is not listed. All the sources have bulug with the exception of KK, which has $bulug_2$ (BÚR) not $bulug_4$ (NAGAR).

431. The first word of line 431, ^{giš}nu-kúš-ù, Akkadian *nukuššû*, is a part of a door. This passage is reconstructed primarily on the basis of the Ur text JJ, which is extremely difficult to read in this section. The only other duplicate for the first part of the line, QQ (Nippur), has nam-lú-ulu_3-[bi]-da.

435. Usually, KI.LUGAL.GUB has been etymologized as 'the place where the king does service (to the gods)' (Steible, *Rīmsîn* 49) or as 'royal stand' (Klein, *Three Šulgi Hymns* 162). Note, however, that KI.LUGAL.GUB is frequently mentioned with food; see for example, *TCL* 15 12:12–13: é-kiš-nu-gál ^{giš}banšur [sikil]-la ki-ág ^{d}en.zu-na lugal KI.LUGAL.GUB-ba ḫé-du$_7$-bi kisal-maḫ-e si-a, 'The Ekišnugal is the beloved holy table of Suen, the king, the ornament of the l., occupies the Kisalmaḫ'; and *LN* 24–25: KI.LUGAL.GUB ku$_3$ kin-sig$_7$ unu$_2$ gal-ba kurun$_2$ làl bal-bal-e nam-šè bí-in-tar-ra, 'At the holy k., at the evening feast of its (Nippur's) banquet hall, where libation of wine and syrup has been decreed.' Perhaps one should understand KI.LUGAL.GUB as an abbreviation from *ki lugal zú-gub 'where the king eats', that is, the place where the ruler shares a cultic meal with the gods. Compare the logogram NÍG.GUB (LUGAL) = *naptan* (*šarrim*), often encountered in the Mari texts. Another solution has been proposed by Frayne, *Historical Correlations* 440–43, who would read KI.LUGAL.GUB as šiten$_x$ and interpret it as a type of votive vessel for liquids.

438. The dub-lá-maḫ is called 'the place where justice is rendered' in royal inscriptions (see Amar-Sin 12:19–21 and Šu-ilišu 1:12–13), as well as in literary compositions (for example, *VS* II 68:16). It is not certain that nam . . . ku$_5$ should not be rendered as nam . . . tar in these passages. Note that in an Ur III court protocol (*UET* 3 45) an oath is taken (nam-erim$_2$ . . . ku$_5$) at the Dublamaḫ, although that by no means signifies that court proceedings took place there. A broken OB text from Ur (*UET* 5 257) probably also refers to similar activities. See now also W. G. Lambert, *Or*, n.s. 54 (1985) 193, and P. Steinkeller, *ZA* 75 (1985) 39 n. 1.

440. Alamuš was the sukkal of Nanna; see Hall, *Moon God* 745–46.

441. I read balag on the basis of collation, although the only two tablets that preserve this part of the line are not well preserved. For music in the á-ná-da, see *Išme-Dagan* Z c rev. ii 11′: á-ná-da nar ka-silim-ma á-ná-da-ka ḫé-a. Charpin, *Ur* 196–97 provides references for á-ná-da and argues for a meaning 'couche contigue', and although he notes the fact that á-ná-da and é-ná both occur in Gudea there can be little doubt that in temples this word designates the sleeping chambers of the gods.

There is still some question as to the identity of the balag instrument; see most recently Cooper, *Agade* 252. The term most commonly used for playing a stringed musical instrument is šu . . . tag = *lupputu*. In this line tag is either an abbreviation of this verb, or simply the word for striking a percussion instrument. There is general agreement that in Sumerian literary texts balag is indeed a drum and therefore the latter interpretation is followed here.

442. Usually misread as ^{urudu}šen, dub-šen has been studied by P. Steinkeller, *OA* 20 (1981) 243–49 and *OA* 23 (1984) 39–41. Further additions, including occurrences of almost identical parallels to this line in literary texts, can be found in J. Bauer, *Altorientalische Notizen (21–30)* (Hochberg, 1985) 20–22, and M. Civil, *Aula Orientalis* 5 (1987) 20–21.

443. Compare *Temple Hymns* 210: é ú za-gìn ^{giš}ná-gi-rin-na bara$_2$-ga á-ná-da kù ^{d}inanna-ke$_4$, 'House with shining hay strewn and upon the lustrous bedchamber of Inanna.' For a discussion of the words found in this line see

Sjöberg, *Temple Hymns* 93–94, and for numerous similar phrases see *PSD* B 146.

444. See commentary on line 408.

447. In economic texts us-ga is most commonly translated as 'fattening shed'. It has been suggested that in literary texts this word denotes a part of the temple complex; see van Dijk, *Götterlieder* 125. One suspects that occurrences in Ur III administrative texts should be reexamined; the traditional rendering 'fattening shed' is based on an equivalence of é us-ga with *bīt marî* in Hh. 13 2a (see B. Landsberger, *MSL* 8/1 15 n. 92), but the identification is highly unlikely. For the latest discussion and bibliography see Cooper, *Agade* 256; M. W. Green, *JCS* 30 (1978) 149; and Ferwerda, *Early Isin* 39. As Cooper notes: "No one has as yet adequately explained the contradiction between the us-ga as a fattening pen for animals on one hand, and a place frequented by linen-clad priests performing purification ceremonies on the other." This contradiction may not, in fact, exist as the translation 'fattening shed' for the é-us-ga of Ur III administrative texts can hardly be correct (on the latter see Jones-Snyder 227–32). The reading é-us-ga also occurs in Proto-Kagal 94 (*MSL* 13 69). A survey of the examples cited by Jones and Snyder, as well as a random investigation of a few hundred occurrences in subsequently published Drehem documents, reveals that only a few animals at a time are ever sent to this place, which is often connected with the shrines of Nippur. Note also a text in which hides are bound for the é-us-ga (*MVN* 13 6:1–2, from Umma). Moreover, it is clear from the following passage that us-ga cannot be a place, for the verb indicates that the noun must be animate: *LU* 350: us-ga lú šu-luḫ-e ki-ág-e šu-luḫ nu-mu-ra-an-gá-gá, 'The u., who loves lustrations, does not prepare the lustrations.' The animate nature of us-ga is also suggested by Old Akkadian references such as lú us-ga (A. Pohl, *TMH* 5 210:3′), us-ga-me (D. D. Luckenbill, *OIP* 14 113:2), and us-ga-ne (T. Donald, *MCS* 9 [1964] 247:30′, courtesy P. Steinkeller). Note also A. Westenholz, *OSP* 1 33 iv:1 7: sagi us-ga, preceded by 13 muḫaldim sagi. The latter reference could, of course, be used to interpret us-ga as a place or a ritual.

As M. W. Green, *JCS* 30 (1978) 149, points out, the earliest attestation is the one in A. Falkenstein, *ATU* 618, where a person is an us-ga of Nanna. All the evidence points to the fact that the us-ga must be a type of priest and if that is not so, then one would probably expect that the word designates a type of ritual, but it certainly has nothing to do with animal husbandry. Note that already A. Goetze, *JCS* 17 (1963) 36 n. 30, drew attention to uzug 'shrine' as a possible explanation of the word. The spelling and the structure of the word suggest that it is a loan in Sumerian. Instructive is the use of the word in *CA* 256–57: ki us-ga šu-luḫ-ha gar-ra-zu ka_5 du_6 gul-gul-la-ke_4 kun ḫé-ni-ib-ùr-ùr-re, 'In the place where the u. prepared your lustrations may foxes that frequent ruined mounds sweep with their tails!'

The most common usage of the word is found with èš gar, as in *Temple Hymns* 372: us-ga kù-ga èš gá-gá-zu, 'The holy u. who maintains your shrine.'

Other similar occurrences are found in Gudea Cyl. A XX 14, XXVIII 9, *EWO* 153, and *ZAnf* 5 (1930) 265 11–12. Note also *LE* 3:5: ká us-ga UŠ nidba gal-gal g[ul-la . . .] x, 'At the gate of the . . . the great offerings.' (The emendation of UŠ to kurušda, in the primary edition, must now be rejected, as it is based on the assumption that the us-ga is a place where young animals were fattened.) There are more problematical passages, however, such as *Ḫaia Hymn* 9: ^{d}ḫa-ia šà-gada-lá é-u$_8$-nir-ra us-ga kù lu-lu. One rendition could be 'Haia, the linen-clad one, who multiplies pure u.-priests for/in the Eunir.' Another possibility is 'Ḫaia, the linen-clad one, made the u. dwell in the Eunir,' with lu for lug. This is not so simple, however, for lug should have an inanimate patient, hence us-ga has to be interpreted as inanimate (for ti(l)/lu(g) 'to settle, dwell'; see P. Steinkeller, *SEL* 1 [1984] 5–17). Recently Charpin, *Ur* 346 translated the line as, 'Haya, le prêtre-vêtu-de-lin-fin de l'Eunir, fait prospérer (les animaux) à l'engrais.'

456. The spelling sú-mu-ug is a variant for su-mu-ug = *a/idirtu* 'fear, apprehension, unhappiness'.

461. The rare prefix ša- occurs only this one time in *LSUr*. Despite attempts by A. Falkenstein, ZA 48 (1944) 69–118, and T. Jacobsen, *Studies Landsberger* 73, there has been little progress in the analysis of this prefix. There is a distinct possibility that this rare grammatical element is in reality a misunderstood reinterpretation of the "affirmative" na-. One could posit that the ED prefix šè- (e.g., in Urn. 49 iii 7 and Ukg. 15 i 5) is to be read nám-, so common in many ED literary texts. This demonstrates that already by that time the distinct šè and nám signs were beginning to be confused. Later, as a result of the misunderstanding of nám, and of the fact that ša is the Emesal equivalent of na, there emerged a new "affirmative" prefix ša-, which was really only a byform of na-. This is quite hypothetical, however, and does not explain the few instances of the ED prefix ši-. See also now Thomsen, *The Sumerian Language* 206–8.

470. Compare *LN* 254: u$_4$ nibru^{ki} gú an-šè zi-zi-i ì-ne-éš im-mi-in-du$_{11}$-ga.

476. Reading é-kiš-nu-gál-la-šè with KK; see examples such as *VAS* 10 199 iii 25: é-kur-ra é ^{d}mu-ul-líl-lá-šè ku$_4$-ku$_4$-da-mu-dè, and many parallel passages. The variant with locative -a in JJ, é-kiš-nu-gál-la-⌜na⌝, is also acceptable.

477. Charpin, *Ur* 212 read É.NUN, correcting Kramer's translation in *ANET*^{3}, but the first sign is clearly gá in the two Ur manuscripts (JJ, KK). In both texts the scribes write gá and é differently. Only the one Nippur source O has é. Charpin, following R. Caplice, *Or*, n.s. 42 (1973) 300, notes that the É.NUN, probably to be read agrun, is a general designation for the temple of Ningal in Ur. This is probably the same location as é-^{d}nin-gal in the Ur III economic texts from Ur, just as é-^{d}nanna designates the Ekišnugal, which is not attested in any such document.

Note the occurrences of É.NUN-kù in *LU*, the first two in parallelism with the Ekišnugal:

LU 16: ga-ša-an-gal-e É.NUN-kù-ga-na mùš mi-ni-in-ga amaš-a-na líl-e, 'The Great lady (Ningal) has abandoned her holy E., her sheepfold has become a haunted (place).'

LU 49–50: é-kiš-nu-gál a-še-er gig-ga-àm a-še-er-zu gar-ra èš É.NUN-kù a-še-er gig-ga-àm a-še-er-zu gar-ra, 'O Ekišnugal, it is a bitter lament, the lament that has been set up for you, O E., it is a bitter lament, the lament that has been set up for you.'

LU 113: nu-nuz-mèn É.NUN-kù é na-ám-ga-ša-an-na-mu, 'I am a woman, the E., the temple of my queenship. . . .'

LU 323: É.NUN-kù é gibil-gibil-la-mu la-la-bi nu-gi$_4$-a-mu, 'O E., *my all-new house*, whose bounty is no longer satisfying.'

In administrative texts É.NUN is attested but not É.NUN-kù, which seems to be standard in literary and monumental sources. If, indeed, É.NUN is the same place then it may an abbreviation and É.NUN-kù was the full name of the temple complex of Ningal. It is interesting, however, that the two Ur sources have gá-nun rather than É.NUN, particularly as a complex by that name was standing in the city in OB times; perhaps confusion with the gá-nun-maḫ was involved. Whatever the source of the confusion, it is interesting to note that an Ur copy contains textual difficulties on a matter of local topography. One should also point out that the addition of line 477a in the two Ur manuscripts is poetically awkward since the subject of that line is not in 477, but in lines 475 and 476.

483–92. These lines are translated by S. N. Kramer, *Bulletin of the Asia Institute*, n.s. 1 (1987) 14.

483. For gaba . . . zi with the meaning 'to depart' in this line see Å. W. Sjöberg, *AfO* 24 (1973) 39. Compare the cry of Ningal in *LU* 111–12: gù ḫu-mu-dúb eden-na u$_4$ gi$_4$-a me-e ḫé-em-ma-dug$_4$ u$_4$-da gaba-bi ba-ra-mu-da-zi, 'I screamed: "Return, O storm, into the steppe!" Oh, how I cried out, but the storm did not depart.'

486. I have interpreted ḫé-eb-zal in this line, and the ḫé- prefixed verb forms in the lines that follow, as an affirmative (ḫé- + *ḫamṭu*); see already C. Wilcke, *CRRAI* 19 221 with n. 40.

491. For kuš$_7$ . . . su-su see J. S. Cooper, *Angin* 113 and Å. W. Sjöberg, *Kramer AV* 423.

493. I have interpreted nam-kúr-re here as a "prohibitative" (na- + *marû*).

498–507. These lines are a variation on a standardized list of fertility elements that is attested in various texts, most often in connection with Nanna. This *topos* has been most recently discussed by Ferrara, *Nanna's Journey* 150, with previous literature. The following comparison demonstrates the relationship between the *LSUr* passage and the standard list, conveniently numbered according to the occurrence in *Nanna's Journey to Nippur* 332–39 (the list is repeated in 341–48).

LSUr	*Nanna's Journey to Nippur*
498. ^{íd}idigna ^{íd}buranun-na	332. i$_7$-da a-eštub
499. šeg$_x$ an-na ki-a še gu-nu	333. a-šà-ga še gu-nu
500. íd a-bi-da a-šà še-bi-da	
501. ambar-ambar-re ku$_6$ mušen	334. ambar-ra ku$_6$-da suḫur.ku$_6$
502. ^{giš}gi gi sun gi ḫenbur	335. ^{giš}gi gi sun gi ḫenbur
	336. ^{giš}tir-^{giš}tir-ra šeg$_9$ šeg$_9$-bar
505. pú ^{giš}kiri$_6$ làl geštin	337. an eden-na ^{giš}maš-gurum
506. an eden-na ^{giš}maš-gurum	338. pú ^{giš}kiri$_6$ làl geštin
507. é-gal-la zi su$_{13}$-ud gál	339. é-gal-la zi su$_{13}$-ud gál

It is not possible to establish when the standard list originated. It is interesting, however, that according to C. Wilcke, *CRRAI* 19 180, *Nanna's Journey to Nippur* was originally composed during the time of Ur-Namma. Should this be the case, we would be able to prove that the *LSUr* passage contains direct allusions to these literary motifs. Note also that the royal inscription Rin-Sin 27:19–23 contains an abbreviated version of this motif.

499. See commentary on line 129.

501–11. The reconstruction of lines 501–7 is dependent solely on the Nippur source D. Because lines 493–500, 502, and 508–11 contain a repeated phrase at the end of the line (an-né nam-kúr-re, as well as plural forms in 503 and 504) one must wonder whether 501 and 505–7 did not also contain this refrain in other manuscripts.

506. The ^{giš}maš-gurum plant appears to have symbolic value as a mark of prosperity; see *CA* 175: IM.UD sír-da la-ba-šèg ^{giš}maš-gurum la-ba-mú, 'The gathered clouds did not reign, the mašgurum plant did not grow.' The word is now attested in the ED word list D from Ebla where *MEE* 3 172:54: DÍM×MAŠ / maš-gur$_x$(DÍM) = *ARET* 5 23:5: me-si-gú-⌜ru$_{12}$⌝-um, as interpreted by M. Civil, *ZA* 74 (1984) 161–62. See also A. Falkenstein, *AfO* 16 (1952/53) 63.

512–14. Once again we are dependent entirely on D for the reconstruction of these lines. The restoration of 513 is fairly certain, but much depends on this since the syntax of the previous two lines makes little sense if the reconstruction of this line is correct. Once again one must assume that unless 513 has been read wrong, the ends of 512 and 513 must have contained the refrain an-né nam-kúr-re.

513. This phrase is a cliché, see *ELA* 145 and Å. W. Sjöberg, *JCS* 21 (1969) 33. It is already attested in two Ur III sources: an inscription of Šu-Sin (M. Civil, *JCS* 21 [1967] 33 x 17–18, as read by Cohen, *Enmerkar* 202), and an unpublished Ur III hymn to Nisaba, 6 N-T 80 (NBC 1107) 23: [a]n ki nigin$_2$-na [un sag sì-ga]. See also *LN* 325: un sag gi_6-ga u_8-gin_7 lu-a sag sì-ga (UM 55-21-304 + 3 N-T 315 iv 33), with variant: sag gi_6 u_8-gin_7 lu-⸢a un⸣ sag sì-ga-ba (*TMH* 4 16 vi 17, collations in Wilcke, *Kollationen* 56), 'the black-headed multitudes, the people who are protected'; and *Šulgi B* 223: unken gar-ra-mu un sag sì-ga-da-gin_7, 'the gathered assembly, protected people'. See also Klein, *Three Šulgi Hymns* 216. P. Attinger, *RA* 78 (1984) 109 n. 50, has now questioned the translation 'protected people' and suggests that sag . . . sì means 'baisser la tête (en signe de deuil)'.

516. The end of the line is preserved only on the left edge of KK and the lack of space clearly posed problems for the scribe. The emendation of the bi sign to ḫé is based on a suggestion of J. Cooper. This makes perfect sense in the context; bi, in this case, is an unfinished ḫé.

517. The phrase ba-ḫúb KU-re is very uncertain. The second sign is definitely ḫúb in both extant manuscripts. C. Wilcke, *CRRAI* 19 223 read 517–18 as [dumu] gi_7-re mu-lu ér a-še-re ^{d}nanna a uru-zu a é-zu a nam-lú-ulu_3 uru-DA.

The emesal phrase egi_2-re (var.: nin/egi_2-bi) mu-lu ér a-še-re is difficult to explain here. Two possible explanations may be offered. The passage could be interpreted antiphonally and the emesal exclamation would then be the words of a gala priest or, as Green, *Eridu* 289 has suggested, of Ningal. The phrase appears to be incomplete, however, and thus another interpretation may be offered. There is a possibility that these words constitute the incipit of a text that was meant to be recited at this point, a balag or even an eršemma that began, 'The princess, who (was overcome) by lamentation and crying. . . .' Compare, for example, the incipit egi_2-re a-še-er-re in the catalog BM 23612:1 (S. N. Kramer, *Diakonoff AV* 206 line 1). The 'princess' is undoubtedly Ningal, the spouse of Nanna; see *LU* 254–56: ama ^{d}nin-gal uru-ni lú $erim_2$-gin_7 bar-ta ba-da-gub lú.nu-nuz-e ér é ḫul-la-na gig-ga-bi im-me egi_2-re (var.: ^{d}nin-gal-e) èš uri_5^{ki} ḫul-a-na gig-ga-bi im-me, 'Mother Ningal, as if she were an enemy, stood aside from her city, the mistress cries bitterly over her destroyed city, the princess cries bitterly over her destroyed shrine of Ur.'

518. For parallels in the laments see M. W. Green, *JCS* 30 (1978) 161.

Chapter 6

Score

In the score, a dash (-) represents a sign identical with the one in the composite text, an asterisk (*) is used when a particular sign is not present, and a slash (/) represents an indented line. Half brackets are used in the score (but not in the composite text) to symbolize a partially preserved grapheme. Unless otherwise indicated, signs that are attested in hand copies but are no longer extant on the original are still transliterated in the score. (See above, p. 27, for a more detailed explanation of the score.)

1. u4 šu-bal aka-dè giš-ḫur ḫa-lam-e-dè

	u4	šu-	bal	aka-	dè	giš-	ḫur	ḫa-	lam-	e-	dè
H	[					]	-	-	-	-	-
U	-	-	-	-	-	-	-	-	-	-	-
BB	⌞-⌟	-	-	-	⌞-⌟	[			la]m	-	-
CC	[				]	-	-	-	-	me[	]
DD	[ ]	-	-	-	⌞ ⌟	gi[š					]
DDb	-	-	-	-	-	-	-	-	l[am		]

2. u4-dè mar-ru10-gin7 ur-bi ì-gu7-e

	u4-	dè	mar-	ru10-	gin7	ur-	bi	ì-	gu7-	e
H	[					u]r	-	-	-	-
U	-	-	-	-	-	-	-	-	-	-
BB	-	-	-	-	-	[		]	-	-
CC	[					]	-	-	-	⌞ ⌟
DD	[	d]è	-	-	-	-	b[i			]
DDb	-	-	-	-	-	-	-	-	[	]

3. me ki-en-gi-ra šu-bal aka-dè

	me	ki-	en-	gi-	ra	šu-	bal	aka-	dè
H	[					š]u	-	-	-
U	-	-	-	-	-	-	-	-	-
BB	-	-	-	-	r[a	š]u	⌞ ⌟	-	-
CC	[			]	-	-	-	-	-
DD	-	-	-	-	-	š[u			]
DDb	-	-	-	-	-	-	b[al		]

4. bala sa$_6$-ga é-ba gi$_4$-gi$_4$-dè

	bala	sa$_6$	ga	é	ba	gi$_4$	gi$_4$	dè
H	[			]	–	–	–	–
U	–	–	–	–	–	–	–	–
BB	–	–	–	⸢–	–⸣	–	–	–
CC	[	]	–	–	–	–	–	–
DD	–	s[a$_6$]	–	–	–	g[i$_4$		]
DDb	–	–	–	–	–	–	g[i$_4$	]

5. uru$_2$ gul-gul-lu-dè é gul-gul-lu-dè

	uru$_2$	gul	gul	lu	dè	é	gul	gul	lu	dè
H	[					]	–	–	–	–
U	–	–	–	–	–	–	⸢–⸣	–	–	–
BB	⸢–⸣	[gu]l	–	ù	–	–	–	–	ù	–
CC	[	gu]l	–	–	–	–	–	–	⸢–⸣	–
DD	uru	–	–	–	–	–	–	–	–	[ ]
DDb	u[ru	gu]l	–	–	–	–	[			]

6. tùr gul-gul-lu-dè amaš tab-tab-e-dè

	tùr	gul	gul	lu	dè	amaš	tab	tab	e	dè
H	[					ama]š	–	–	–	–
U	–	–	–	–	–	–	⸢–	–	–⸣	–
BB	–	–	–	ù	–	–	–	–	bé	–
CC	[	g]ul	–	–	–	–	–	t[ab	]	–
DD	–	–	–	–	–	–	–	–	–	[ ]
DDb	[	]	–	°	–	am[aš				]

7. gud-bi tùr-bi-a nu-gub-bu-dè

	gud	bi	tùr	bi	a	nu	gub	bu	dè
H	[						gu]b	–	–
U	–	–	–	–	–	–	⸢–	–	–⸣
BB	–	–	–	–	–	–	–	–	d[è]
CC	[	b]i	–	–	–	–	–	–	–
DD	⸢–⸣	–	–	–	–	–	–	–	d[è]
DDb	g[ud		tù]r	–	–	–	[		]

8. udu-bi amaš-bi-a nu-dagal-e-dè

H [daga]l – –
U – – – – – – – ⌜⌝ [d]è
BB – – – ° – – – – d[è]
CC [b]i – ° – – – – ⌜⌝
DD ⌜⌝ – – – – – – – d[è]
DDb ud[u b]i – [ ]

9. íd-bi a mun$_4$-na tùm-ù-dè

H [ ] ⌜⌝ –
U – – – – – – ⌜⌝ [d]è
BB – – – – – – – d[è]
CC [d]è – – – túm – d[è]
DD – dè – – – – e [ ]
DDb í[d]

10. gán-né zi-dè ᵘKI.KAL mú-mú-dè

H [ ] – – –
U – – – – – – – m[ú d]è
BB – – – – – – – – – d[è]
CC [z]i – – – – – – d[è]
DD Omits line

11. eden-né ᵘa-nir mú-mú-dè

H [ ] – –
U – – – – – m[ú-m]ú –
BB – e – – – – – –
CC [ ] – – – ⌞ ⌟ [ ]
DD Omits line

12. ama dumu-ni-ir ki nu-kin-kin-dè

H [ki]n –
U – – – ° – – – – –
BB – – – – – – – – –
CC [ ] ⌞ – – ⌟ [ ]
DD – – – ° – – – – [ ]

13. ad-da a dam-mu nu-di-dè

H [ ] – ⸢⸣
U – – – – – – – –
BB – – – – – – – –
DD – – – – – – – [ ]

14. dam banda$_3$ úr-ra nu-ḫ̮úl-le-dè

U – – – – – – – –
BB – – [ú]r – – – – –
DD [d]am – – – – – – [ ]

15. tur-tur du$_{10}$-ba nu-bulug$_3$-gá-e-dè

U – – – – – – * ⸢⸣ –
BB – – – – – – – ⸢⸣ –
DD [tu]r – – – – g[á]

16. umeda-e u$_5$-a nu-di-dè

U – – – – – ⸢⸣ –
BB – – – – – – –
DD [ume]da-⸢e⸣ [ ]

17. nam-lugal-la ki-tuš-bi kúr-ru-dè

U – – – – – [b]i – – ⸢⸣
BB – – – – – – ⸢⸣ – –

18. eš-bar kin-gá šu lá-e-dè

U – – – ⸢e⸣ – – ⸢ ⸣
BB – ⸢ ⸣ – [ ] – ⸢⸣

19. nam-lugal kalam-ma kar-kar-re-dè

U ⸢⸣ – la ⸢⸣ – – ⸢ ⸣ –
BB – – – – [ ] ⸢e⸣ [ ]
DDa [luga]l – – ⸢⸣ [ ]

20. igi-bi ki šár-ra gá-gá-dè

U	–	–	–	kúr-šè		–	–	–		
BB	⌜ ⌝	–	–	–	–	–	[	]		
DD	⌜–	–	–⌝	–	–	[		]		
DDa	[b]i	–		–	–	–	–	[ ]		

21. inim du$_{11}$-ga an ^{d}en-líl-lá-ta giš-ḫur ḫa-lam-e-dè

U	–	–	–	–	– –	–	–	–	–	–	–	–	[	]		
BB	–	–	–	–	⌜– –⌝	–	°	–	–	–	–	–	–	[ ]		
DD	–	–	–	–	–[									]		
DDa	–	–	–	–	– –	–	–	–	–	–	–	–	–	d[è]		

22. u$_{4}$ an-né kur-kur-ra sag-ki ba-da-an-gíd-da-ba

U	–	–	–	–	–	–	–	–	–	–	°	–	d[a]	
BB	–	–	⌜ ⌝	–	–	–	–	–	–	–	–	–	–⌜a⌝[ ]	
DD	⌜ ⌝	–	–	–	–	ta	sa[g						]	
DDa	–	–	–	–	–	ta	–	°	–	–	–	–	– – –	

23. ^{d}en-líl-le igi-ni ki kúr-ra ba-an-gar-ra-a-ba

U	–	–	–	–	–	–	–	–	–	–	–	g[ar				]	
BB	–	–	–	–	–	–	–	–	–	–	–	–	–	–	–	⌜ ⌝	
DD	–	–	–	–	–	–	k[i									]	
DDa	–	–	–	–	–	–	–	–	–	–	ra	–	–	–	–		

24. ^{d}nin-tu-re níg-dím-dím-ma-ni zag bí-in-tag-ga-a-ba

U	–	–	–	–	–	–	–	–	–	–	–	i[n				]	
BB	–	–	–	–	–	–	–	–	–	–	–	–	–	–	–	–	–
DD	–	–	–	e	–	–	[									]	
DDa	–	–	–	e	–	–	–	–	–	–	–	–	–	–	°	–	–

25. ^{d}en-ki-ke$_{4}$ ^{íd}idigna ^{íd}buranun-na šu bí-in-bal-a-ba

U	⌜– –⌝	–	–	–	–	–	–	[/]	–	–	–	–b[a]			
BB	–	–	–	–	–	–	–	–	–	–	–	–	–	–	–
DD	⌜– –⌝	–	–	–	–	í[^{d}						]			
DDa	–	–	–	–	–	^{íd}KIB.NUN.NA	–	–	–	–	°	–			

26. ^{d}utu ḫar-ra-an kaskal-e nam ba-an-kud-a-ba

U [ ] ⸢– – –⸣ – – ⸢⸣ k[ud]
BB Omits line
DD – – – – ⸢⸣ k[askal]
DDa – – – – – – – – – – – – – –

27. ki-en-gi-ra me-bi ḫa-lam-e-dè giš-ḫur-bi kúr-ru-dè

BB – – – – – – – – – – – – – – – – – –
DD ⸢– –⸣ g[i]
DDa – – – – – – – – – – – – – – – x –?

28. uri$_5$^{ki}-ma me nam-lugal-la bala-bi sù-sù-ud-dè

N [d]è
BB – – – – – – – – – – – – –
DDa – – ° – – – na – – su$_{13}$-su$_{13}$-⸢ud⸣-[ ]

29. dumu nun-na é-kiš-nu-gál-la-na šu pe-el-lá di-dè

N [d]è
BB [d]umu – – – – – – – – – – – – – – –
DDa – – – – – – – – ° ° – – – – – d[è]

30. ^{d}nanna un u$_8$-gin$_7$ lu-a-na igi te-en-bi si-il-le-dè

N [ ]x-la-ka
BB [ ] – – – – – – – – – – – – – – –
DDa – – – – ⸢– –⸣ – – – ta ° – – l[e]

31. uri$_5$^{ki} èš nindaba gal-gal-la nindaba-bi kúr-ru-dè

N [kú]r – –
BB – – – – – – – – – – – –
DDa – – ⸢– –⸣ – – – nindab[a]
U Traces

32.	un-bi ki-tuš-ba nu-tuš-ù-dè ki erim$_2$-e šúm-mu-dè
N	[tu]š – – / [er]im$_2$ – – – –
U	[ ]⸢ba⸣ – – – – – – – k[i]
BB	– – – – bi – – – – – – – – – –
DDa	– ° – – – – – – – lú – ° šú[m]

33.	LÚ.SU^{ki} elam^{ki} lú kúr-ra ki-tuš-bi tuš-ù-dè
N	[l]ú kur – – – ba – – –
U	[L]Ú – – – – – – – – t[uš]
BB	LÚ×KÁR.SU^{ki} elam^{ki} lú ḫa-lam-ma ki-tuš-bi tuš-ù-dè
DDa	– – ° – – – – – – – – – ° –

34.	sipa-bi é-gal ní-te-na lú erim$_2$-e dab$_5$-bé-dè
N	[t]e – – – – – – –
U	lugal-bi – – – – – zi ⸢gig?⸣ [mu-un-pa-an-pa-an]
BB	– – – – la – – – – – – – – –
DDa	⌞⌟ – – ° – – – – – – – – –

35.	^{d}i-bí-^{d}en.zu kur elam^{ki}-ma-šè ^{giš}búr-ra túm-mu-dè
N	[ ] – – – – ° – / [bú]r – – – –
U	– – – – – – – – – – – – – – x[ ]
BB	– – – – – – – – – – – – – – bur re – ù –
DD	x[ ]
DDa	– – – – – – – – – ° – – – – – – – m[u]

36.	iši za-bu gaba a-ab-ba-ka-ta zag an-ša$_4$-an^{ki}-šè
N	[ ] – – – – – – / [a]n-ša$_4$-an^{ki}-na-šè
U	– – – ki – ḫur-sag-gá – – – – a[n]
BB	– – – – – – – – – – – – – – – –
DD	– ⌞ – – [ ]
DDa	– – [gab]a ° – – ° – – – – – x[ ]

37.	buru$_5$^{mušen} é-bi ba-ra-an-dal-a-gin$_7$ uru-ni-šè nu-gur-re-dè
N	[ ] ⸢– la –⸣/ [ ]
U	– – – – – – ° – – – – – – [ ]
BB	– – – – a – – – – – – – – – – – – – – °
DD	– ° – – – [ ]
DDa	b[uru$_5$ b]a – – – ° – – – – – – – –

38.	^{íd}idigna ^{íd}buranun-na gú $^{\text{min}_6}$min-a-ba ú ḫul mú-mú-dè
U	– – – – ° – – – – [ ] / – – – – ⸢⸣
BB	– – – – – – – – – bi – – – – –
DD	– – ^{íd}KIB.NUN-n[a]
DDa	[KI]B.NUN^{ki} – – – – – – – – ⟨ ⟩

39.	kaskal-la giri$_3$ nu-gá-gá-dè ḫar-ra-an nu-kin-kin-dè
U	– – – – – – – – – – – – – [ ]
BB	– ré – – – – ⸢⸣ – – – – – – –
DD	[ ] – – – – – d[è]
DDa	[d]è – – – – – – [?]

40.	uru á-dam ki gar-gar-ra-ba du$_6$-du$_6$-ra šid-dè
U	– ⸢– – –⸣ – – – bi – – – – d[è]
BB	– – – – – – – – – – – – – –
DD	– – – – – – a – d[u$_6$]
DDa	[d]u$_6$ – da ⸢– –⸣

41.	un sag-gi$_6$ lu-lu-a-ba ^{giš}ḫaš-šè aka-dè
U	– – – ⸢– –⸣ – – – – – – –
BB	– – – – – – – – ⸢⸣ e – –
DD	° – – – – – – – ḫa[š]
DDa	[^{gi}]^{š} – a – ⸢⸣

42. gán-né zi-dè ^{giš}al nu-ru-gú-dè numun ki nu-tag-dè

U – – – – – – – – – – – – – – ge
BB – – x – – – – – ⌜– –⌝ – – – – – –
DD – – – – – – – – – – [ ]
DDa [d]è – – – – –
PP ⌜ ⌝ – – – – a[l] ⌜– –⌝ [ ]

x in BB is an erased gana$_2$.

43. e-el-lu šìr gud su$_8$-su$_8$-ba eden-na nu-di-dè

U ⌜– –⌝ – – – – – – – – – – –
BB – – – – – – – – – ⌜ ⌝ – – –
DD e-lu – – – – – – – – ⌜– –⌝
DDa [ ] – – –
PP è-lú – – – – b[a n]u – –

44. é-tùr-ra ià gara$_2$ nu-aka-dè šurim ki nu-tag-e-dè

U – ⌜ ⌝ – – – – – – – – – – ⌜ ⌝ –
BB – – – – ga-ar$_5$-ra – – – x ḫa-lam-e-dè
DD – – – – – – – – / x x ḫa-lam-e-dè
DDa [ ] ḫa-la[m]
PP – – – – – – – – x[ ] ⌜ḫa⌝-la-dè

45. sipa-dè ^{gi}šukur-ra amaš kù-ga šu nu-nigin-dè

U [ ] ⌜ ⌝ – – – – – – – – ⌜– –⌝
BB – – – – – – – – – – – –
DD Omits line
DDa Probably omits line
PP – – – – – – – – – ° – –

46. i-lu-lam-ma du$_9$-du$_9$ ^{dug}šakir$_3$-ra amaš-a nu-di-dè

U ⌜– –⌝ – – – – – – – – – – – –
BB – – – – – – – – – – – – – – –
DD e – – – – – ° – ° – ° – – –
DDa [ ] x [ ]
PP – – – – – – – – – – – – – – –
UU [d]u$_9$ – – – a / [ ] ⌜ ⌝ – – –

47. eden-na máš-anše tur-re-dè níg-zi-gál til-le-dè

	eden	na	máš	anše	tur	re	dè	níg	zi	gál	til	le	dè
U	–	–	–	–	⸢⸣	–	–	–	–	–	–	e	–
CC	–	–	–	–	–	–	–	–	–	–	–	–	–
DD	[	n]a	–	–	–	–	–	–	–	–	–	–	–
PP	–	–	–	–	–	zi!	–	–	–	–	*	–	–
UU	[					r]e	–	–	–	–	–	–	⸢⸣

48. níg-úr limmu$_2$ ^{d}šakan$_2$-na-ke$_4$ šurim ki-a nu-tag-ge-dè

	níg	úr	limmu$_2$	d	šakan$_2$	na	ke$_4$	šurim	ki	a	nu	tag	ge	dè
U	–	–	–	–	–	–	–	im	*	*	–	–	⸢⸣	–
BB	–	–	–	–	–	*	–	–	–	*	–	–	–	–
DD	[				š]akan$_2$	–	–	DÚR	–	–	–	–	–	–
PP	–	–	–	–	–	–	–	–	–	–	nu-di-tuk-ge-dè			
UU	[							]	–	*	–	–	–	–

49. ambar-ra šu ki-in-dar di-dè numun nu-tuk-tuk-dè

	ambar	ra	šu	ki	in	dar	di	dè	numun	nu	tuk	tuk	dè
H	[										tu]k	⸢⸣	d[è]
U	–	–	su	–	–	–	–	–	–[1]	–	–	–	–
BB	–	re	–	–	–	–	–	–	–	–	–	–	–
DD	[			]	⸢	–⸣	–	⸢	⸣	–	–	–	–
PP	–	–	–	–	–	–	–	–	–	–	–	–	–
UU	[							d]è	–[1]	–	–	–	–

1. In U and UU the sign is clearly mu.

50. ^{giš}gi gi sag-ḫul mú-mú-dè ḫáb-ba til-e-dè

	giš	gi	gi	sag	ḫul	mú	mú	dè	ḫáb	ba	til	e	dè
H	[									b]a	–	–	–
U	–	–	–	–	–	–	–	–	–	–	–	–	–
BB	–	–	–	–	–	–	–	–	–	–	–	–[1]	–
PP	–	–	–	–	–	–	–	–	–	–	–	ù	–
UU	[								ḫá]b	–	–	–	–

1. e written after erased beginning of LI.

51.	pú	^{giš}kiri$_6$	ú	gibil-lá	nu-me-a	ní-ba	šú-šú-dè
H	[					]	- - -
Q	[			]	- -	⌜- -⌝	[ ]
U	-	- -	-	- -	- - -	- -	- - -
BB	-	- -	-	- -	- - -	- -	- -ù-
PP	-	- -	-	- -	- - -	- -	- - -
UU	[					]	⌜⌝ - -

52.	uri$_5$^{ki}	am	gal	ù-na-gub-ba	ní-bi-ta	nir-gál
J	[					ni]r-⌜gál⌝
H	[				n]í - ⌜⌝	- -
Q	[u]ri$_5$^{ki}	⌜⌝	[ ]	⌜⌝ - ⌜⌝ [		]
BB	- -	-	-	- - - -	- - -	- -
PP	uri$_2$^{ki}	-	-	- - - -	- - -	- -
UU	[				]	⌜⌝ [gá]l

53.	uru	numun	i-i	nam-en	nam-lugal-la	ki	sikil-la	dù-a
H	[						sik]il -	- -
Q	[ ]	-	-°	- -	⌜⌝ -	°	- [	]
BB	-	-	°°	- -	- - -	-	- - -	- -
PP	-	-	--	- -	- - -	-	- - -	- -
TT	[							] x

54.	gud-gin$_7$	saman	ul$_4$-la-bi	šub-bu-dè	gú	ki-šè	lá-e-dè
H	[		b]i	- - -	-	- -	- - -
Q	[ ] -	⌜⌝	- - -	š[ub			]
BB	- -	-	- - -	- - -	-	- -	- - -
PP	- -	-	- - -	- - -	-	- -	- ° -
TT	[						] -

55.	an	^{d}en-líl	^{d}en-ki	^{d}nin-maḫ-bi	nam-bi	ḫa-ba-an-tar-re-eš
H	[			-g]á-ke$_4$	- -	- - - - - -
Q	[	e]n -	- - -	⌜- -⌝ - -	na[m	]
BB	-	-e[n]	⌜⌝- -	^{d}nin-ḫur-sag-gá-ke$_4$	- -	° - - - - -
PP	-	- - -	- - -	- - - -	- -	- - ° x[1] - -
TT	[					] - - - - -

1. Looks like tag, probably an attempt to write an+tar.

56. nam-tar-ra-bi níg nu-kúr-ru-dam a-ba šu mi-ni-íb-bal-e

H [ ] ⸢ ⸣ - a - - - ib - -
Q [ ] - - - - - - - - - ⸢ ⸣ š[u]
BB - - [n]u - - - - - - - - - - - -
PP - - - - - - - - - da - - a - - - - - - -
TT [ ] - - -

57. inim du$_{11}$-ga an ^{d}en-líl-lá-ka sag a-ba mu-un-gá-gá

H [ ] - - - a - - - - -
Q [du$_{11}$-g]a - - - - - - - - - s[ag]
BB - - [e]n - ° kam - - - - - - -
PP - - - - - - - - - ta - - - - - - -
TT [u]n - -

58. an-né ki-en-gi ki-tuš-ba bí-in-ḫu-luḫ un-e ní bí-in-te

H [b]í-ib - - - - / - - - -
Q [e]n - - - - - ⸢ib⸣ ḫ[u]
BB - - k[i tu]š - - - - - - - - - - -
CC [k]i - - - ⸢ ⸣ l[uḫ]
PP - e - - - - - - ° - - - - - - - - -
TT [ ] - - - -

59. ^{d}en-líl-le u$_{4}$ gig-ga mu-un-zal uru-a me bí-íb-gar

H [m]u - - - - - - ib -
Q [ ] ⸢ ⸣ - - u[n]
BB - - - [ ] - - - - ⸢ - ⸣ - ib -
CC [ ] ⸢ ⸣ - - - - - ki [ ]
PP [lí]l - - - - - - - - - - - - -
TT [ ] - -

60. ^{d}nin-tu-re ama$_{5}$ kalam-ma-ka ^{giš}ig-šu-úr im-mi-in-DU

H [m]a - - - - - / [i]m - - -
N [ ] ⸢ ⸣
Q [ ] ⸢ ⸣ g[^{iš}]
BB - - - ⸢ ⸣ - - ke$_{4}$ - - - - - - - -
CC [ ] - - - - - - - - - [ ]
PP ⸢ ⸣ - t[u-r]é-e - - - ke$_{4}$ - - - - ba-da-an-gi$_{4}$
TT [ ] x

61. ^{d}en-ki-ke$_4$ ^{íd}idigna ^{íd}buranun-na a im-ma-da-an-kéš

N [ ]⌜NUN⌝ e / [ ] -
BB - - - - - - - - - - - - - - -
CC [í]^{d} - - - - - [ ]
PP - - - - í[^{d} KI]B.NUN.NA - - - ° - -
TT [e]n - - í[^{d}] í[^{d}] - - ° - -

62. ^{d}utu níg-si-sá inim gi-na ka-ta ba-da-an-kar

N [a]n -
BB - - - - - - - - - - - d[a-a]n -
PP - - - - s[á] - -
RR [k]a-t[a]
TT ⌜- -⌝ - - - - - - - - x x ?

63. ^{d}inanna-ke$_4$ mè šen-šen-na ki bal-e ba-an-šúm

N [še]n-še[n b]a - -
BB - - - - - - - - - - ⌜⌝ - -
PP - - - m[è b]a - ⌜⌝
RR [k]i - a ⌜- -⌝ [ ]
TT - - - - - - - - - - - - -

64. ^{d}nin-gír-su-ke$_4$ ki-en-gi ga-gin$_7$ ur-e ba-an-dé

N [gí]r ⌜⌝ - - e[n g]a - / - - b[a-ni-i]n-dé
BB - - - - - - - - - - - - m[i]-ni-in-dé
PP - - ⌜- -⌝ - [ ] ⌜⌝
RR [g]i - - - - - - -
TT - - - - - - - - - - - - ba-ni-in-dé

65. kalam-ma ga-ba-ra-ḫum im-ma-an-šub níg lú nu-zu-a

A - - - - - ⌜⌝ - - - š[ub] - - - - ⌜àm⌝
N - - - - - - - - a[n] - - ⌜- àm?⌝
BB - - - - - - - - - - - - - - - -
PP - ° g[a]x -
RR [m]a - - - - - - -
TT - - - - - - - - - - - - - - - -

66.	níg	igi	nu-gál-la	inim	nu-gál-la	níg	šu	nu-te-gá-dam
A	–	–	– – °	–	– – e	–	–	– – – –
N	–	–	– – °	–	– – –àm	–	–	⌜– – –⌝ –
BB	–	–	– – –	–	– – –	–	–	– – – –
DDa	[ ]	–	– – [					]
PP	⌜⌝	i[gi						]
RR	[					]	–	– – – e –
TT	–	–	– – °	–	– – e	–	–	– – – –

67.	kur-kur-re	ní-te-a-bi-a	šu	sùḫ-a	ba-ab-dug$_4$
A	– – –	– – – – –	–	– –	– – –
N	– – –	– – – – ta	–	– –	– – –
BB	– – –ke$_4$–	ta ° – –	–	– –	– – –
DDa	– – –	– ta ° ⌜– –⌝	[		]
PP	k[ur				]
RR	Omits line				
TT	– – –	– – – – ta	–	– –	– – –

68.	uru^{ki}	dingir-bi	ba-da-gur	sipa-bi	ba-da-ḫa-lam
A	– °	– –	– – –	– –	– – – –
N	– –	– –	– – –	– –	– – – –
BB	uru^{ki}-ba	dingir uru^{ki}-bi-e-ne bar-ta ba-DU-ge-eš			
DDa	uru-ba	dingir-bi-ne bar-ta ba-[			]
PP	[			]	⌜– – –⌝la[m]
RR	Omits line				
TT	?				

69.	nam-lú-u$_{18}$-lu	ní-te-bi-a	zi	gig	mu-un-pa-an-pa-an
A	– – – °	– –a– –	–	–	– – – – – °
N	– – – °	– – – –	–	–	– – – – ⌜⌝ °
BB	– – – ⌜⌝	– – – –	–	–	– – – – – –
DDa	– – – –	– – – [			]
PP	[			m]u	– – – ⌜⌝ °
RR	[		z]i	–	– – – – – –
TT	– – – –	– – na-ka	–	–	– – – – – °

70.	u$_4$-dè	šu-ne-ne	ba-dù-dù	u$_4$	nu-mu-un-ne-gi$_4$-gi$_4$
A	– –	– – –	– – – –	–	– – – – – – –
N	– –	– – –	– – – –	–	– – – – – / –
BB	– –	– – –	– – – –	–	nu-m[u-u]n-ši-íb-gur-re
PP	[				-g]i$_4$-[g]i$_4$
RR	[	]	x [		] mu-e-da-an-gi$_4$-⸢gi$_4$⸣
TT	– –	– – –	– – – –	–	– – – – – – –

71.	u$_4$	gi$_4$-a		mu-un-ne-tuk-àm	u$_4$	dab$_5$-bé-šè	nu-DU
A	–	– –		– – – – – –	–	– – – –	– –
N	–	– –		– – – – [à]m	–	– – – –	– –
BB	–	– –		– – na – –	–	– – [	n]u-um-DU
PP	–	– –	mu-gi$_4$-a	mu-un-tuk-a	u$_4$	dab$_5$-bé-šè	n[u]
RR	[	g]i$_4$ –		m[u		b]é –	– –
TT	–	– –		– – – – – –	–	– – – –	– –

72.	^{d}en-líl	sipa	sag	gi$_6$-ga-ke$_4$	a-na	bí-in-ak-a-bi
A	– – –	–	–	– – – –	– –	– – – – – –
N	– – –	–	–	– – – –	– –	– – – – – –
BB	– – –	–	–	– – – –	– –	– ⸢ ⸣ – – –
PP	– – –	–	–	– – na	– – àm	– ⸢– – – ba⸣
RR	[ ] – –	si[pa				b]í – a[k]
TT	– – –	–	–	– – – –	– –	– – – – – –

73.	^{d}en-líl-le	é	zi	gul-gul-lu-dè	lú	zi	tur-re-dè
A	– – – – –	–	–	– – – – –	–	–	– – –
N	– – – – –	–	–	– – ⸢ ⸣ –	–	–	– – –
BB	⸢– –⸣ – – –	–	–	– – – – –	–	–	– – –
PP	– – – – –	–	–	– – – – –	–	–	– – d[è]
RR	⸢ ⸣ – – l[e						] ⸢ ⸣ [ ]
TT	– – – – –	–	–	– – – – –	–	–	– – –

74. dumu lú zi-da-ke$_4$ dumu sag-e igi ḫul dím-me-dè

	dumu	lú	zi	da	ke$_4$	dumu	sag	e	igi	ḫul	dím	me	dè
A	–	–	⌜⌝	–	–	–	–	–	–	–	–	–	–
N	–	–	–	–	–	–	–	–	–	–	–	–	–
BB	–	[ ]	⌜	–	⌝	[dum]u	–	–	–	⌜⌝ bi	–	–	–
PP	–	–	–	–	–	–	maḫ	–	–	–	–	e	–
RR	–	–	–	d[a						]	⌜⌝	e	⌜⌝
TT	–	–	–	–	–	–	–	–	–	– bi	–	e$^?$	–

75. u$_4$-ba ^{d}en-líl-le gu-ti-um^{ki} kur-ta im-ta-an-è

	u$_4$	ba	^{d}	en	líl	le	gu	ti	um	^{ki}	kur	ta	im	ta	an	è
A	–	–	–	–	–	–	–	–	–	–	–	–	⌜⌝	–	–	e$_{11}$
N	–	–	–	–	–	–	–	–	⌜	⌝	–	–	–	–	–	e$_{11}$
BB	⌜	⌝	[				g]u	–	–	–	–	–	–	–	–	⌜e$_{11}$⌝
PP	–	–	–	–	–	lá	–	–	–	∘	–	–	–	–	∘	–
RR	–	–	–e[n								k]ur	–	–	–	–	–
TT	[	b]a	–	–	–	–	–	–	–	–	–	–	–	–	–	–

76. DU-bi a-ma-ru ^{d}en-líl-lá gaba-gi$_4$ nu-tuku-àm

	DU	bi	a	ma	ru	^{d}	en	líl	lá	gaba	gi$_4$	nu	tuku	àm
A	[D]U	–	–	–	–	–	–	–	–	–	–	–	–	–
N	⌜	⌝	–	–	–	–	–	–	–	–	–	–	–	–
PP	–	–	–	–	–	–	–	–	–	–	ri	–	tu[ku	]
RR	–	–	–	–	r[u				l]á	–	–	–	–	–
TT	[	b]i	–	–	–	–	–	–	–	–	–	–	–	–

77. im gal eden-na eden-e im-si igi-šè mu-un-ne-DU

	im	gal	eden	na	eden	e	im	si	igi	šè	mu	un	ne	DU
A	[i]m	–	–	–	–	–	–	–	–	–	–	–	–	–
N	[			]	⌜	–	–	–	⌝	–	–	–	⌜	⌝
PP	⌜⌝	–	–	–	–	na	–	–	–	–	⌜mu-ri-DU⌝			
RR	⌜⌝	–	–	–	[		i]m	–	–	–	–	–	na	–
TT	[		ede]n	–	–	–	–	–	–	–	–	–	–	–

78. eden níg-dagal-ba sìg ba-ab-dug$_4$ lú nu-mu-ni-in-dib-bé

	eden	níg	dagal	ba	sìg	ba	ab	dug$_4$	lú	nu	mu	ni	in	dib	bé
A	⌜	⌝	–	la –	si-[ig	b]a	–	⌜⌝	[	n]u	–	–	–	–	–
PP	[ed]en	–	–	–	–	–	–	–	–	–	–	un	–	–	–
RR	–	–	–	b[a		]	–	–	⌜⌝	–	–	–	∘	–	–
TT	[			]x –	–	–	–	–	–	–	–	–	–	–	–

79. u$_4$ kukku$_2$-ga šika bar$_7$-bar$_7$-ra sa-šè ba-ab-DU

A – – – – – – ⸢⸣ sa$_4$ ⸢⸣ – – ak

PP [ ] – – sík – – – – – – – – –

RR – GÍG.G[ÍG b]ar$_7$ – re – – ak-x-a (x=erasure)

TT [ba]r$_7$ – – – – ba-ab-è-a

80. u$_4$ babbar-re izi gi$_6$ eden-na ba-da-an-tab-tab

A – – – – – – – ní-⸢ba⸣ ba-an-su$_{13}$-su$_{13}$

PP – – – NE.NE – – – ba-an-da-tag-tag

RR – – – ⸢ ⸣ – – – – – – – –

TT [ed]en-na ní-ba ba-ni-zal$^?$

80α. u$_4$ mud-e KA ì-dub-dub sag ì-dab$_5$-dab$_5$

PP – – – – – – – – – – – –

TT [ ] – bé – – – –

80β. u$_4$ ^{giš}gana$_2$-ùr an-ta è-dè uru ^{giš}al-e ba-ab-ra-aḫ

PP – – – – – – – – – ° – – – – – –

TT [ ]x da – – – – – e – –

81. u$_4$-ba an ba-dúb ki ba-sìg igi u$_4$-da ba-lim

A – – – – – – – – – – – dè – –

RR ⸢⸣ – a[n] – ⸢⸣ – – – – – – – –

TT [ ] – – – – –

82. an ba-sùḫ-sùḫ gissu ba-an-lá kur-re ur$_5$ mi-ni-ib-ša$_4$

A – ⸢⸣ – – – – – – – – – – – – –

RR – – ⸢⸣ [ ] – – – – – ra – – – – –

TT [ ] – – – – – – –

83. ^{d}utu an úr-ra i-in-ná saḫar kur-ra zal-àm

A – – – – ⸢⸣ – – ⸢⸣ [ ] – – – –

RR – – – ú[r-t]a ì ° – – – – – –

TT [saḫ]ar – – – –

84. ^{d}nanna an-[pa]-a i-in-ná un-e ní bí-in-te

A ⸢– –⸣ – [ ] – – – n[á]x – – – –
RR – – a[n] ⸢ì⸣ ° – – – – – – –
TT [u]n – – [ ]

85. uru^{ki} ba-an-d[ug$_4$$^?$ k]i-tuš ba-ab-bé-dè bar-ta ba-da-gub

A [x]x x [k]i$^?$-bi bí-x[s]u$_8$-ge-eš
RR – – – – d[ug$_4$$^?$ k]i-⸢tuš⸣ – – – – – – – – –

86. kur-kur-re uru^{ki} lú-bi nu-til-la i-im-sar-sar-re-ne

A [b]i nu-mu-un-[ ]x r[e]
RR – – – ° ° – b[i n]u – – – – – – – –
UU – – ° – – – – – [ ] / – – – s[ar]

87. giš maḫ úr-bi-a mu-un-bal-e giš tir-ra guruš$_5$-i

A [ ] – – – b[al]
RR – – – – [u]n – – – – – – –
UU – – – – – ⸢–⸣ – ⸢– –⸣ / ° – e ⸢–⸣ ì

88. pú ^{giš}kiri$_6$ gurun-ba mu-un-su$_{13}$-su$_{13}$ ligima ì-bu-re

A [ ] ⸢–⸣ – – u[n]
RR ⸢– – –⸣ – – m[u s]u$_{13}$ – – – – –
UU – – – – – – – – – / – – – –

89. buru$_{14}$ išin-bi-a mu-un-su-su ^{d}ašnan ì-tur-re

RR [iš]in-ba mu-u[n] – – – – –
UU – – – – – – – – / – – – – –

90. [. . .]-la sag [. . .-i]n-bal-bal-e

N [ ] –$^?$ – [ ] x x –
RR [ ] – s[ag i]n – – –

91. [... ba-da]-kar-ra-bi [... ba-a]b-DU

N [ ] ⌞ - ⌟ / [a]b -
RR [ ]-⌜an⌝-DU

Note: RR was joined and copied from a combination of casts and originals and it was difficult to determine the exact number of lines missing between 90 and 91 in this text. It is possible that one or two lines may have to be reconstructed before 91.

92. [... ^{ú}]numun$_2$ x ba-da-kar-ra-bi [^{ú}]numun$_2$ x ba-ab-DU

N [ ] - - ⌞ ⌟ - - - / [ ] ⌞⌟ - - - -
RR [-d]a-an-DU

93. [... zur-r]e-eš mu-un-du$_8$-du$_8$ [...za]r-re-eš mu-un-sal-sal-e-eš

N [r]e - - - - - / [za]r - - - - - - - - -
RR [ ] ⌞⌟ - - ° °

94. [... ^{í}]^{d}buranun-na ad$_6$ ì-me-a [...sag]-gaz ì-ak-e

N [^{í}]^{d} - - - - - - [ ] - - - -
RR [ ] ⌞ ⌟ -

95. [ad-da dam-a-ni-t]a ba-da-gur dam-mu nu-im-me

N [t]a ⌞⌟ - - - - - - -
LL [ ] ⌞ ⌟ - [ ]

Note: LL has remnants of six lines before 95 but they are too fragmentary to be placed.

96. [ama dumu-ni-t]a ba-da-gur dumu-mu nu-im-me

N [gu]r - - - -
LL [t]a - - - du[mu]

97. é zi-da-ke$_4$ é-a-ni mu-un-šub é-mu nu-im-me

J ⌞⌟ - - - - - - - - - - - [ ]
N [u]n - - - - - -
LL [ ] ⌞⌟ - - - - ⌞⌟ [ ]

98. níg-gur$_{11}$ tuku níg-gur$_{11}$-ra-ni-ta giri$_3$ kúr ba-ra-an-[dab$_5$]
J ⌜⌝ - - - - - - - - - - - [ ]
LL [ ] ⌜- - -⌝ b[a-r]a-a[n]

99. u$_4$-ba nam-lugal kalam-ma-ka šu pe-el-lá ba-ab-dug$_4$
J - - - - - - - - * - - - - [ ]
N [ ] ⌜- - -⌝ [ ]
V [ ] - - - ⌜⌝

100. aga men sag-gá gál-la-bi ur-bi ba-ra-a[n-...]
A [me]n - ⌜- -⌝ l[a]
J - - - - - - ba - - - - [ ]
N ⌜- - - -⌝ - - - - - - - x[ ]
V [b]a - a[n]

101. kur-kur-re du$_{10}$-ús dili dab$_5$-ba-bi igi te-en-bi ba-si-il
A [ku]r * ⌜⌝ - - - - - ⌜⌝ - e[n]
J ⌜⌝ - - - - - - - - ⌜⌝ - - - [ ]
N - - * - - - - - - - - - - - - -
V [ ] - - -

102. uri$_5$^{ki} èš nindaba gal-gal-la-ka nindaba-bi ba-d[a$^?$-kúr$^?$]
A [u]ri$_2$^{ki} - - - g[al] / ⌜⌝ - - d[a$^?$]
J [ur]i$_2$^{ki} - - - - ⌜- -⌝ [ ]
N - - - - - - - * - - b[a]
V [ ] dug$_4$

103. ^{d}nanna un u$_8$-gin$_7$ lu-a-na šu bal ba-an-da-ab-ak
A - - ⌜- - -⌝ - - - - - - * - - [ ]
J [ ] ⌜- - -⌝ - - - [ ]
N - - - - - - - - - - - - - - -

104. lugal-bi é-gal ní-te-na zi im-ma-ni-in-gi$_4$
A - - - ga[l t]e - - - - - - - ⌜⌝
J Traces
N - - - - - - - - - - - - -

105. ^{d}i-bí-^{d}en.zu é-gal ní-te-na i-si-iš ba-ni-in-lá-lá
A – – – – – – – – – – / – – – – – – – –
N – – – – – – é-gal-la-na – – – – – ° – –

106. é-nam-ti-la šà ḫúl-la-ka-na ér gig mu-un-še$_8$-še$_8$
A – ⸢– –⸣ – – – – ⸢⸣ – – – – – – –
N – – – – – – – – ni – – – – – –

107. a-ma-ru du$_6$! al-ak-e šu im-ùr-ùr-re
A – – – ki – – – – – – – –
N – – – ki – – – – – – – –

108. u$_4$ gal-gin$_7$ ki-a ur$_5$ mi-ni-ib-ša$_4$ a-ba-a ba-ra-è
A – – – – – – – – in – – – – – – –
N – – – – – – – – – – – – – – – – –

109. uru gul-gul-lu-dè é gul-gul-lu-dè
A – – – – – – – – – – –
N –⸢ki –⸣ – – – – – – – – –

110. lú lul lú zi-da an-ta nú-ù-dè
A – – – – ra – – – – –
N – – l[ú z]i – – – – ° –

111. uri$_3$ lú lul-e lú zi-ra ugu-a-na DU-šè
A – – – – – ra – – – – –
N – – – ⸢– –⸣ [z]i-⸢da⸣ – – – – –

112. ki-ru-gú 1-a-kam
A – – – – – –
N – – g[ú] – [ ]

113. u$_4$-dè mar-ru$_{10}$-gin$_7$ ur-bi ì-gu$_7$-e
A – – – – – – – – – – –
N – – – r[u$_{10}$]

114. giš-gi$_4$-gál ki-ru-gú-da-kam
A - - - - - - - -
N - - - [ ]

115. é kiš^{ki}-a hur-sag-kalam-ma-ka šu hul ba-e-dug$_4$
A - - - - - - - - ⌜⌝ - - - - -
N - - - ⌜⌝ [ ]
LL See discussion pp. 25–26 above.

116. N ^{d}za-ba$_4$-ba$_4$ ki-⌜tuš⌝ [ki-ág-gá-ni giri$_3$ kúr ba-ra-an-dab$_5$]

117. N ama ^{d}ba-Ú ⌜é⌝ u[ru-kù-ga-na ér gig mu-un-še$_8$-še$_8$]

118. N a ⌜uru⌝ [gul-la é gul-la-mu gig-ga-bi im-me]

119. N x[...]

120. [...]

121. [...]

122. [a uru gul-la é gul-la-mu gig-ga-bi im-me]

123. ka-z[al-l]u^{ki} uru ní-ba lu-a šu sùh-a ba-ab-dug$_4$
F - z[al-l]u - - - - - - - - - - - - -
LL [ ]^{ki} - - - - - [ ]

124. ^{d}nu-muš-da uru ki-tuš ki-ág-gá-ni giri$_3$ kúr ba-ra-an-dab$_5$
F ^{d}n[u-m]uš-da - - - - - - - - - - - - -
N [n]u-m[uš]
LL [ ] ⌜⌝ - - - - - [ ]

125. nitadam-a-ni ^{d}nam-ra-at munus sa$_6$-ga-a ér in-še$_8$-še$_8$-e

F - - - - - - - - - - - / - - - - -

N ⸢⸣ ° - ⸢⸣[ ]

LL [ ] ⸢⸣ - ° - - - g[a]

126. F a uru$_2$ gul-la é gul-la-mu gig-ga-bi im-me

N Omits line

LL Omits line

127. íd-bi šà-sù-ga ì-gál a nu-un-dé

F - - - - - - - - - - - -

N ⸢⸣ - - su$_{13}$-g[a]

LL [s]u$_{13}$ - i-im-gál ⸢⸣ [ ]

128. íd ^{d}en-ki-ke$_4$ nam-ku$_5$-rá-gin$_7$ ka-bi-a ba-úš

F - - - - - - - - - - - - - -

LL [k]i - nam ba-an-k[u$_5$]

129. a-šà-ga še gu-nu nu-gál un-e nu-gu$_7$-e

F - - - - - - ° - - - - - -

LL [ ] nu-un-gál [ ]

130. pú ^{giš}kiri$_6$-bi gir$_4$-gin$_7$ ba-ḫur-ḫur eden-bi ság ba-ab-di

F - - - - - - ⸢⸣ - - - - - - - -

LL [g]in$_7$ - - - [ ]

131. F máš-anše níg-úr ⸢limmu$_2$ níg-zi-gál⸣ nu-mu-un-bu-e

132. F níg-úr limmu$_2$ ^{d}⸢šakan$_2$⸣-ke$_4$ ní nu-mu-ni-ib-te-en-te-en

133. F ^{d}lugal-[mara]d-da-ke$_4$ uru-ni-ta bar-ta ba-da-gub

134. F ^{d}nin-zu-a[n-na] ki-tuš ki-ág-gá-ni giri$_3$ kúr ba-ra-an-dab$_5$

135. F a uru$_2$ gul-la é gul-la-na gig-ga-bi im-me

136. i-si-in^{ki} èš kar-re nu-me-a a-e ba-e-dar
F - - - - - - - - - - - - - - - -
N - - ⌜⌝k[i]

137. ^{d}nin-in-si-in-na ama kalam-ma-ke$_4$ ér gig mu-un-še$_8$-še$_8$
F ⌜⌝[1] - - - - - - - - - ì-še$_8$-še$_8$
N - - - - [ ] - - - - - - -

1. Beginning now broken. Langdon's copy has ^{d}ì-si-in-na.

138. a uru gul-la é gul-la-mu gig-ga-bi im-me
F [ ] - - - - na - - - - -
N - - - ⌜⌝ - ⌜ ⌝ - - - - - -
V [] ⌜ ⌝ - - [ ]

139. ^{d}en-líl-le dur-an-ki-ka ^{giš}middu$_2$-a ba-an-sìg
F [nibru]^{ki}-a - - - - - - - - -
N ⌜ - ⌝ - - - - - - - - - - -
V - - - - - ⌜⌝ k[i]

140. ^{d}en-líl-le uru-ni èš nibru^{ki}-a a-nir ba-ab-gar
F [ ] uru-ni nibru^{ki}-a - - - - -
N ^{d}en-líl-le uru^{ki}-ni èš nibru^{ki} kur-re ba-an-gar
V ^{d}en-líl-le uru-ni èš nibru^{k}[^{i}]

141. ama ^{d}nin-líl nin ki-ùr-ra-ke$_4$ ér gig mu-un-še$_8$-še$_8$
F [n]in - - - - - ⌜⌝ - - ì-še$_8$-še$_8$
N - ⌜⌝ - - ⌜⌝ - ⌜ - ⌝ - - - - - -
V - - - - - - - ⌜⌝ k[e$_4$] / - - - - - -

142. F a uru$_2$ gul-la é gul-la-na gig-ga-bi im-me
N Omits line
V Omits line

143. kèš^{ki} an eden-na dili dù-a šu líl-lá ba-ab-dug$_4$
F [kè]š^{ki} - - - - - - - - - - - -
N ⸢⸣ - - - - - - - - - - - -
V - - - - - - - - - - - - -

144. adab^{ki}-bu é íd-dè lá-a-ri a-e ba-da-ab-bu$_x$(PI)
F ⸢⸣ bu^{ki} - - - - - - - - - - -
N - - - - - - - - ⸢- ki⸣ bala-šè ba-ab-dug$_4$
V - - - - - - - - - / ki bala-šè ba-ab-dug$_4$

145. F ⸢muš kur⸣-ra-ke$_4$ ki-ná ba-ni-ib-gar ki bala-šè ba-ab-dug$_4$
N Omits line
V Omits line

146. gu-ti-um^{ki} šà ba-ni-ib-bal-bal numun ba-ni-ib-i-i
F - - - [] - - - * - ⸢⸣ - - - - - -
N - - - - - - - - ⸢⸣ b[al b]a - - - -
V - - - - - - - - - - / - - - - - -
EE [i]b ⸢⸣ - - - - - -[ ]

147. ^{d}nin-tu-re níg-dím-dím-ma-ni-šè ér gig mu-un-še$_8$-še$_8$
F - - ⸢⸣ - - - [ ] - * - - ì-še$_8$-še$_8$
N - - - - - - - m[a m]u - - -
V - - - - - - - - ⸢⸣ - / - - - - š[e$_8$-š]e$_8$
EE [ ] - - - * ⸢- -⸣ m[u-u]n ⸢- -⸣

148. a uru gul-la é gul-la-mu gig-ga-bi im-me
F - uru$_2$ g[ul] - - - - na - - - - - -
N ⸢- - - - -⸣ - ⸢⸣ m[u]
V ⸢⸣ - - - - - - ⸢- - - - - -⸣
EE [ ] - - - g[ig-g]a - - -

149. ki zabala^{ki}-a gi-gun$_4$-na kù-ga šu líl-lá ba-ab-dug$_4$
F ⸢- - -⸣ - - - - - - - - - - - - -
V [k]i - - * - ⸢⸣ [ ]
EE [gu]n$_4$ - - g[a] - - - - - - -

150. unug^{ki}-ta ^{d}inanna ba-da-an-kar ki erim$_2$-e ba-ab-dug$_4$

F – ⸢– –⸣ – – – – – – – – – – – – – –
V [^{k}]^{i} – ⸢–⸣i[nanna]
EE [ ] x x – – – – – –

Note: in the composite text the verbal root is gin. See the commentary to this line.

151. é-an-na èš gi$_6$-par$_4$ kù-ga erim$_2$-e igi i-ni-in-bar

F – – ⸢ ⸣ – – – – – – – – – – – –
EE [ ] – – [ ] – – – mi – – –

152. g[i$_6$-par$_4$] kù nam-en-na-ba šu ba-e-lá-lá

F g[i$_6$-par$_4$] – – – – – – – – – –
N [l]á
EE [na]m – – [ ] – – – – –

153. [en-b]i gi$_6$-par$_4$-ta ba-da-an-kar ki erim$_2$-e ba-ab-de$_6$

F [b]i – – – – – – / [k]i – – – – –
N [t]a ⸢– – ° – –⸣ – – – –
EE [ ] – – – [ ] ⸢– –⸣ – – – de$_6$

154. F [a uru$_2$ g]ul-la é gul-la-na gig-ga-bi im-me

N Omits line
EE Omits line

155. umma^{ki} sig$_4$-kur-šà-ba-ke$_4$ u$_4$ gig-ga ba-e-dal

F ⸢ ⸣ – – – – – – – – – – – – –
N [k]e$_4$ – – – – – –
EE [ ] – ḫur – g[a$^{?}$] ⸢ ⸣ – – [ ] – –

156. [^{d}šara$_2$ é]-maḫ k[i-tuš] ki-ág-gá-ni giri$_3$ kúr ba-ra-an-dab$_5$

N [ ] – – – – / [ ] ⸢ ⸣ – –
EE [ ] – k[i] – – – – – – – – – –

157. EE [^{d}n]in-mul-e uru^{ki} [ḫ]ul-lu-a-na ér gig mu-un-še$_{8}$-⸢še$_{8}$⸣
N [ ]⸢⸣ – * ḫul * – – / [ ] – – ⸢⸣ –

158. EE [uru^{ki}-mu$^{?}$] la-la-bi lú nu-un-gi$_{4}$-a-mu gig-ga-bi im-me
N [ ]⸢– –⸣ / [ ]

159. gír-su^{ki} uru^{ki} ur-sag-gá-e-ne-ke$_{4}$ im-gír-e ba-ab-dug$_{4}$
N [a]b-⸢DU⸣
EE ⸢⸣ – – – – – – – – – – – – – – – – – – –
UU [^{k}]^{i} ⸢– * – – * – – – –⸣ g[ír]

160. ^{d}nin-gír-su-ke$_{4}$ é-ninnu-ta giri$_{3}$ kúr ba-ra-an-dab$_{5}$
B ⸢– –⸣ [ ]
EE – – – – ⸢⸣ – – – – – – – – –
UU ⸢– – –⸣ – – – – – – – – – [ ]

161. ama ^{d}ba-Ú é uru-kù-ga-na ér gig mu-un-še$_{8}$-še$_{8}$
B ⸢⸣ –[ ]
EE – – – – ⸢⸣ – – – – – – – – – – –
UU – ⸢– – –⸣ – – – – ka – – – – – š[e$_{8}$]

162. a uru gul-la é gul-la-mu gig-ga-bi im-me
B – uru$_{2}$ – – – [ ]
EE – –^{ki} – – – – – – – – – – – –
UU ⸢– – –⸣ – – – – – – – – – – –

163. u$_{4}$-ba inim u$_{4}$-dam al-du$_{7}$-du$_{7}$ šà-bi a-ba-a mu-un-zu
B – – – – – a[l]
EE – – – – – – – – – – – – – – – – –
UU ⸢– – –⸣ – ⸢⸣ – – – – –a/ ⸢– – * –⸣ – –

164. inim ^{d}en-líl-lá zi-da gil-èm-dè gùb-bu zu-zu-dè

B - - - - - z[i]
EE - - - - - - - - - - - - - - -
UU [ ] gil-le-èm-e / [z]u-dam

165. ^{d}en-líl lú nam-tar-tar-re-dè a-na bí-in-ak-a-ba

B - - - - - t[ar]
EE [ ] - - - - - - - ⸢⸣ - - - - - - - -
UU [ ] ⸢bí-in⸣-ak-bi

166. ^{d}en-líl-le elam^{ki} lú kúr-ra kur-ta im-ta-an-è

B - - - - - [ ]
EE - - - - - - ⸢⸣ - - - - - - - -
UU [ ] ⸢e$_{11}$?⸣

167. ^{d}nanše dumu gi$_7$ uru bar-ra mu-un-na-TUŠ-àm

B - - - - ur[u$_2$ r]a [ ]
EE - - - - - - - - - - - - -
UU [ ] ⸢- -⸣ [ ]

168. ^{d}nin-mar^{ki}-ra èš gú-ab-ba-ka izi im-ma-da-an-te

B - - - - - ⸢⸣ - - b[a]
I - - - - * - - - - ⸢⸣ [ ]-ma-ni-in-te
EE - - - - - - -⸢a⸣- - - - - - - - -
UU [g]ú a - [ ] / i[zi]-ma-ni-[ ]

169. kù ^{na_4}za-gìn-bi má gal-gal-la bala-šè ì-ak-e

B - - - - - - - - - - š[è]
I - - - - - ^{giš}má - - ⸢⸣ [bal]a ⸢mu?-un?⸣-ak-e
EE ⸢⸣ - - - - - - - e - - - - -

170. nin níg-gur$_{11}$-ra-ni ḫul-lu ti-la-àm kù ^{d}nin-mar^{ki}-ke$_4$

B - - - šè * ⸢⸣ * - - a - - - m[ar]
I - - - šè * - * - - [ ] -
EE - - - - - - - - - - - - - - - -

171. u$_4$-ba u$_4$ KA.NE-gin$_7$ bar$_7$-ra-àm im-ma-da-ab-TAR-re

B nin-e KA.NE-gin$_7$ bar$_7$-a im-⸢ma⸣-⸢da⸣-ra-da-[. . .]
I ⸢nin⸣-e KA.NE-gin$_7$ – x[r]e
EE – – – – – – – – – – – – – – – –

172. ki-lagaša^{ki} elam^{ki} šu-ni-a im-ma-ši-in-gi$_4$

B – – – – – – – – – – – – –
I – – – – – – [š]i ⸢– –⸣
EE – –^{aša}– e – – – – – – – – – – –

173. u$_4$-bi-a nin-e u$_4$-da-a-ni sá nam-ga-mu-ni-ib-dug$_4$

B – – – – – – – ° – – – – – – – – –
I Blank
EE – – – – gá – – – – – – – – – – – –

174. ^{d}ba-Ú lú-u$_{18}$-lu-gin$_7$ u$_4$-da-a-ni sá nam-ga-mu-ni-ib-dug$_4$

B – – – – – – – – – – ° – – – – – – – – –
I Blank
EE – – – – ⸢⸣ ° – – – – – – – – – – – – –

175. me-li-e-a u$_4$-dè šu-ni-a im-ma-ši-in-gi$_4$

B – – – – – – – – – – – – – –
I Blank
EE [l]i – – – – – – – – – – – –

176. u$_4$ uru$_2$ gul-gul-e šu-ni-a im-ma-ši-in-gi$_4$

B – – – [g]ul – – – – – – – – –
I Blank
EE [u]ru – – – – – – – – – – –

177. u$_4$ é gul-gul-e šu-ni-a im-ma-ši-in-gi$_4$

B – – – – – – – – – – – – – –
I Blank
EE [ ] ⸢– –⸣ – – – – – – – – –

178. ^{d}dumu-zi-abzu é-bi ki-nu-nir-šà-ba-ke$_4$ ní im-ma-da-an-te

B	– – – – – – – ∘ – ša^{ki} – – – – – – – – –
I	Blank
N	Traces
EE	[ab]zu ⌈⌉ – – – – – – – ∘ – – – – – t[e]

179. ki-[nu]-nir-šà^{ki} uru nam-dumu gi$_7$-ra-ka-ni kar-kar-re-dè

B	[ ] – – – – – ⌈⌉ – – – – – – –[1] –
I	Blank
N	⌈⌉ [ ] – – ∘ ∘ [k]ar – – –
EE	[ ]x – – – – – ni-gin$_7$ – – ⌈⌉ –

179. *(cont.)* ba-ab-dug$_4$

B	– – –
I	
N	– ⌈⌉ d[ug$_4$]
EE	[ ]

1. Langdon copied rí but the sign is probably ri.

180. ^{d}nanše uru-ni AB×ḪA^{ki}-a kur-re ba-ab-gar

B	[nanš]e – – – – – – – – – –
I	Blank
N	– ⌈ ⌉ki – – – ∘ [k]ur – – – –
EE	[ ] – – – – – – – – [ ]

181. sirara$_3$^{ki} ki-tuš ki-ág-gá-ni ḫul-gál-e ba-an-šúm

B	[ ].NINA.TAG^{ki} – – – – – – – – – – – – – ⌈⌉
I	Blank
N	sirara$_3$^{ki} uru – – – – – – – – – – –
EE	[ ].NINA.TAG^{ki} a – – – – – – giri$_3$ kúr ba-r[a-an-dab$_5$]

182. a uru gul-la é gul-la-mu gig-ga-bi im-me

B [ ] - - - - - - - - - - - -
J [ ] ⌈- - - - -⌉ n[a?]
I - - - - - - - - gá - - - - - -
N - - - - - - - - - ⌈- - - -⌉ [ ]
W [ ] - - na - - - [ ]
EE [g]ul - - - - - - - - - - [ ]

In J and W line is before 185.

183. gi$_6$-par$_4$ kù nam-en-na-ba šu ba-e-lá-lá

B [pa]r$_4$ - - - - - - - - - - -
I - - - - - ⌈-⌉ - - - - - -
N - - - - - - - - ⌈-⌉ [ ]
W [n]a - ⌈- - -⌉ [ ]
EE [k]ù - - - - - - - - - -

184. en-bi gi$_6$-par$_4$-ta ba-da-an-kar ki erim$_2$-e ba-ab-de$_6$

B [ ] - - - - - - - - - - - - - - dug$_4$
I - - - - ⌈- -⌉ - - - - - - - - - -
N - - - - - - - - * - - e[rim$_2$]
W [d]a - - - - ⌈-⌉ [ ]
EE [ ] - - - - - - * gur - - - - - d[ug$_4$]

185. gú íd-nun-na-^{d}nanna-ka á dugud ba-ši-in-DU

B [í]d - - - - - - - - - - -
J [g]ú - - - - - k[a]
I - - - - - - - - - - - - - -
N - - - - - - - šè - - b[a]
W [ ] ⌈- -⌉ kam - - - - - D[U]
EE [n]a - - - - - - - - dé?

186. maš-gana$_2$ maš-gana$_2$ é-dana-^{d}nanna-ka tùr dugud-gin$_7$ ba-gul

B	[ ] – – – – – – dugu[d]
J	[ ] ⌜⌝ – – – – – – [ ]
I	– – ° ° – – – – – – – – – – –
N	– – – – – – – – – ° tù[r] ⌜– – –⌝ [ ]
W	[d]ana – – kam – – – b[a]
EE	[gan]a$_2$ – – – en.zu-na – – – –an–

187. lú kar-ra-bi maš kar-ra-gin$_7$ ur im-me-da

B	[ ] – – – – – –re ba-⌜e⌝-[ ]
J	[ka]r – – – – – – – [ ]
I	– – – b[i] ⌜⌝ – – – – [i]m ⌜– –⌝
N	– – – – – – – – – – – –
W	[r]a – – – – – – – – d[a]
EE	[ ] – ⌜– –⌝ – – – e – – e–

188. ga-eš^{ki} ga-gin$_7$ ur-e ba-an-dé ì-gul-gul-lu-ne

B	[g]a – – re – – – i im – – – –
J	[ ] – – – – – – – – – – g[ul]
I	– – ° – – – – – – – – – – gu[l] x [n]e
N	– – – – – – – – – – – – – – –
W	[g]a – – re – – – ° – – – n[e]
EE	[g]a – – ⌜⌝ – – – – – – – – –

189. alam dím-ma SIG$_7$.ALAM sa$_6$-ga-bi im-zé-er-zé-re-e-ne

B	[A]LAM ⌜⌝ – – – – – – – – – –
J	⌜⌝ – – – – – – – – – – [ ]
I	⌜– – – – –⌝ – – ° mu-uš i-im-/ze-er-ze-er-ne
N	– – – – – – – – – [z]e ⌜⌝ ze – ° –
W	[ ] ⌜⌝ – – – – – ⌜– –⌝ e[r]
EE	[ ] – – – – – [ ] – me ze – ze – ° –

190. a uru gul-la é gul-la-mu gig-ga-bi im-me

B [ ] - - - - - - - - - - -
J Was probably after next line.
I - - - - [ ] - gá - - ⌜⌝ - -
N - - - - - - - - - - g[a b]i - -
W Was probably after next line.
EE Omits line.

191. gi$_6$-par$_4$ kù nam-en-na-ba šu ba-e-lá-lá

B [ ] - - - - - - - - - -
J - - - - - - - - - - - [ ]
I - - - - [ ] ⌜⌝ - - - - -
N - - - - - - - - - ⌜⌝ - -
W [b]a - b[a]
EE [pa]r$_4$ - - - - - ⌜⌝ - - - -
OO [pa]r$_4$ - n[am]

192. en-bi gi$_6$-par$_4$-ta ba-da-an-kar ki-erim$_2$-e ba-ab-de$_6$

B [b]i - - - - - - - - - - - -
I - - - pa[r$_4$] - - - - - - - - -
N - - - - - - - - ° ⌜⌝ - - - b[a a]b-de$_6$
V [ ] ⌞ - - ⌟ -
EE e[n b]i - - - - - - ⌞ ⌟ [k]i - - - - dug$_4$
OO [ ] - - - - - d[a]

193. bara$_2$ an-na-da gíd-da-bi a-nir ba-da-an-di

B [ ] ⌜⌝ - - - - - - - an da -
I - ⌜⌝ - - [b]i ⌜a - - - ⌟ - -
N - - - - - - - a - - - - ° ⌜⌝
V [ ] ab -
EE - ⌜⌝ - - - - ⌞ ⌟[n]ir - - ab si
OO [ ] - - - ⌜⌝ - - ⌜⌝ [ ]

194. ^{giš}gu-za an-na-bi nu-ub-gub sag me-te-a-aš li-bí-ib-gál

B ^{g}[^{iš}] - - ub$^{?}$ - - - - - - - - - -

I - - - - n[a] ⌞ - - - ⌟ - - - ° - -

N - - - - - - - ˹um - ⌟ - - ° ° - - - ⌞⌟

V [ ] ⌞ - ° ⌟

EE ^{gi}[^{š}g]u-za ⌞ - - - um˺ [ ]

OO [g]u - - - - - - - - s[ag]

195. ^{giš}nimbar-gin$_7$ gú-gur$_5$ ba-ab-dug$_4$ ur-bi ba-ra-an-kad$_4$

B ⌞⌟ [ ] ⌞ ⌟ - - - - - - - - -

I ⌞ ⌟ x[. . .] rest of line blank?

N - - - - - - - ⌞⌟ - - - r[a$^{?}$]

V [ ] ⌞ ⌟ ° -

EE - - x[ ] - - [ ] ⌞⌟ - - - -

OO [ ] - - - - - d[ug$_4$]

196. aš-šu^{ki} é íd-dè lá-a-ri a-e ba-da-ab-bu

B a[š] ⌞⌟ [ ] - - - - - - - lá

I - - - - í[d] ⌞ ⌟ - - - ° -

N - - - - ⌞ ⌟ - - - - ⌞⌟ b[a]

V [ ] ⌞?˺

EE - šú ° - í[d] ⌞⌟ - [b]a - an -

OO [ ]- - - ⌞⌟ - - r[i]

197. níg-erim$_2$ nu-dib ^{d}nanna-ka lú erim$_2$-e ba-an-dib

B n[íg] - ⌞⌟ ⌞⌟[ ] - - - - - - -

I - er[im$_2$]x ⌞⌟ - ° - ab -

N [ní]g - - - - ⌞⌟ k[a]

V [ ] e dab$_5$

EE - - [nann]a - - er[im$_2$] - - e -

OO [er]im$_2$ - - - - - [ ]

198.	é	ḫur-re-àm	a-na-àm	ab-ak
B	⸢ ⸣	[	à]m	- -
I	-	⸢- -⸣ [		]x - [?]
N	[ ]	⸢ ⸣ - à[m		]
V	[			a]k?
EE	-	- r[e		] AN.BA /
OO	[ ]	- - *	- - à[m	]

199.	é	pu-úḫ-ru-um-ma	šà-sù-ga	ba-ab-gar
B	-	p[u	]su$_{13}$ -	- an dù
I	-	- ⸢ ⸣ r[u		]
N	[	] ⸢ ⸣ r[u		]
EE	-	- ú[ḫ] -	- - -	- - -
OO	[	] - - - -	- s[ù	]

200.	KI.ABRIG$_2$^{ki}-a	áb	lu	amar	lu-a-ri	tùr	dugud-gin$_7$	ba-gul
B	- [ABRI]G$_2$⸢ ⸣ [		]	-	- - -	-	- -	- -
I	- ABRI[G$_2$							]
EE	- AB[RI]G$_2$-ga^{ki}	x	-	[	]	-	- -	-an-
OO	[ABRI]G$_2$ - *	-	-	⸢ ⸣	- - -	t[ùr		]

201.	^{d}nin-gublaga-ke$_4$	gá-bur-ta	giri$_3$	kúr	ba-ra-an-dab$_5$
B	⸢- -⸣ -	⸢ ⸣ [	gi]ri$_3$	-	- - - -
I	- - [				]
EE	[ ]	- - -	⸢ ⸣	-	- - - ⸢ ⸣
OO	[gubl]aga -	- - ⸢-	-⸣	[	]

202.	^{d}nin-ià-gara$_2$-ke$_4$	ní-te-na	ér	gig	mu-un-še$_8$-še$_8$
B	- - - - -	- [ ] -	-	-	í-še$_8$-še$_8$
I	Traces				
EE	[ga]ra$_2$ -	- - -	-	-	- - - -
OO	[i]à - -	- -⸢a-⸣	[		]

203. a uru gul-la é gul-la-mu gig-ga-bi im-me

B – uru$_2$ – – – – [m]u – – – – –
I [g]a – – –
EE ⌜⌝ u[ru] – – – – – – – – – –
OO [gu]l – – – ⌞ ⌟ g[ig]

204. gi$_6$-par$_4$ kù nam-en-na-ba šu ba-e-lá-lá

B – – – – – n[a] – – – – –
I [ ] ⌜⌝ – – – – –
EE – – – n[am e]n – – – – – – –
OO [k]ù – – – – – [ ]

205. en-bi gi$_6$-par$_4$-ta ba-da-an-kar ki erim$_2$-e ba-ab-de$_6$

B – – – – – – [ ]
I [ ]x ⌞ ⌟ – – – – ° – – –
EE – – – [t]a – – – – – ⌜⌝ – ⌜⌝ – dug$_4$
OO [g]i$_6$ – – – – a[n]

206. ^{d}nin-a-zu é-gíd-da-ke$_4$ ^{giš}tukul ub-ba i-ni-in-gub

B – – – – – gí[d]
EE – – – – ⌜⌝ [ ] – ° – – – – – – – –
OO [z]u – – – – ^{gi}[^{š}]

207. ^{d}nin-ḫur-sag é-nu-tur-ra-ke$_4$ u$_4$ ḫul ba-an-da-dal

B – – – – x[ ]
EE – – – – – n[u] – – – – – – – – –
OO [sa]g – – – – – – ḫ[ul]

208. tu^{mušen}-gin$_7$ ab-làl-ta ba-da-an-dal eden-na bar bí-íb-gub

B – – – [ ]
EE – – – – là[l-t]a – – – – – – – – – –
OO Traces

209. a uru^{ki} gul-la é gul-la-mu gig-ga-bi im-me

B - uru$_{2}$[ ]
AA ⌜⌝ [ ] gu[l]
EE - - - - - - [ ] - - - - - - - -

210. giš-bàn-da é ér-re gál-la-ri gi ér-ra ba-an-mú

B - [ ]
C - - - [gá]l - ⌜- -⌝ [ ]
AA - - [ ]
EE - - - - - [r]e g[ál-l]a - - - - - - -

211. ^{d}nin-giz-zi-da giš-bàn-da giri$_{3}$ kúr ba-ra-an-dab$_{5}$

C - - ⌜- - - -⌝ - - t[a]
AA - - [ ]
EE - - - - - - - d[a[1]] - - - - - - -

1. Space for one more sign after -da.

212. ^{d}á-zi-mú-a nin uru-a-ke$_{4}$ ér gig mu-un-še$_{8}$-še$_{8}$

C -⌜a - - - - -⌝ - - ⌜⌝ [ ]
AA -- z[i]
EE -- - [m]ú - ⌜⌝ - - [ ] ⌜- -⌝ - - -

213. a uru$_{2}$ gul-la é gul-la-mu gig-ga-bi im-me

C - ⌜uru$_{2}$[1] - - -⌝ - ⌜- -⌝ - [ ]
AA - - g[ul]
EE - - ⌜ki⌝ [gu]l ⌜⌝ - - [ ] ⌜⌝ - ⌜- -⌝ -

1. It is impossible to determine what is inscribed, normally this scribe used uru$_{2}$.

214. u$_{4}$-bi-a u$_{18}$-lu lú gi$_{6}$-a ba-an-dúr-ru-ne-eš

C - - - - - - ⌜- - im-ma[1]-[ ]
AA - ba x[ ]
EE [l]u - - - - - - - - -

215. ku᾽ara^{ki} ḫul-ḫul-lu-dè lú gi$_6$-a ba-an-dúr-ru-ne-eš

C ⌜ ⌝ - - - - - ⌜ ⌝ g[i$_6$]

AA - [ ]

EE [ ] - - - - - - - - - ⌜ ⌝ - - -

216. ^{d}nin-é-ḪA-ma ní-te-na ér gig mu-un-še$_8$-še$_8$

C - - - - - - ⌜ ⌝ é[r]

AA -n[in]

EE [m]a-ke$_4$ * * * - - - - - -

217. a uru$_2$ gul-la é gul-la-mu gig-ga-bi im-me

C ⌜ ⌝ - - - - - - - ⌜ ⌝ [ ]

AA - - [ ]

EE [gu]l - - - - - - - - - - -

218. ^{d}asar-lú-ḫi ul$_4$-ul$_4$-la túg ba-an-mu$_4$ LUL.KU mu-un-DU

C - - - - - - - [ ]

AA -a[sar]

EE [ ] - e - - - - - - - - ⌜ ⌝

219. ^{d}lugal-bàn-da ki-tuš ki-ág-gá-ni giri$_3$ kúr ba-ra-an-dab$_5$

C - - - - - - ⌜ ⌝ - [ ]

AA ⌜ ⌝l[ugal]

EE [ ] - - - - - - ⌜ ⌝ - - - - -

219′. AA ⌜d⌝[nin-sún . . .]

220. a uru$_2$ gul-la é gul-la-mu gig-ga-bi im-me

C - - - - - ⌜ - ⌝ [ ]

EE [l]a - - - - - - - - - -

221. eridu^{ki} a gal-la diri-ga a nag-e ba-àm-ugun$^{?}$
C – – – – – – – x x x [ ]
EE [ ] e ⸢⸣ – – – – ⸢⸣ – –
FF – – – – ⸢e⸣ SI[ ]

222. bar-ba eden líl-e dù-a x x[...]
C – ⸢– – –⸣ – – – x x[...]
FF – – – – – – [ ]

223. lú zi ki lul-la x x [...]
C – x ⸢⸣ – – x x [ ]
FF – – – ⸢⸣ x [ ]

224. ^{d}KA-ḫé-gál-la ^{d}igi-ḫé-gál-la [...]
C ^{d}⸢igi-ḫé-gál-la⸣ ^{d}⸢KA-ḫé⸣-[gál-la]
FF ^{d}KA-ḫé-g[ál]

225. guruš me-en u$_4$ nu x la x x mu [x (x)] gul [...]
C – ⸢– ° – – – – – –⸣ – [ ] ⸢⸣ [...]
FF – – – ⸢⸣ [ ]

226. u$_4$ nu-gul-la ḫi-li nu-til-la me-en [...] mu-u[n-...]
C – ⸢– – –⸣ [ ] – – [ ] – u[n-...]
FF ⸢– –⸣ – – ⸢⸣ – – – – – – [ ]

227. x x-gin$_7$ su$^{?}$ sa$_6$-ga-meš ì-[x]-ge-dè-[en-dè-en]
C ⸢– – – – – –⸣ me –[x] ⸢– –⸣ [ ]
FF [ ] – – – ⸢⸣ – – –[ ]

228. x x-gin$_7$ igi gùn-gùn-meš ì-[x-x]x-dè-en-dè-en
C [ ]x – ⸢– – –⸣
FF [ ] – – – – – – –[ ]

229. [ala]n-gin$_7$ kùš-kùš-a dé-a-meš ì-[sì-g]e-dè-en-dè-en
C [ ]x-⸢ra ì⸣-x-[g]e-dè-en-dè-en
FF [ala]n - - - - - - - - - [ ]

230. [gu]-ti-um^{ki} lú ḫa-lam-ma-ke$_4$ me-zé-er-zé-re-ne
C [l]am - - - - - - - - -
FF [ ] - - - - - - - - ka - ⸢ze⸣ [ ]

231. [a-a ^{d}e]n-ki-ra abzu eridu^{ki}-šè šu-a ba-en-dè-en-gi$_4$
C [š]è - - - - - - - -
N [k]i-⸢šè⸣ / [ ]⸢nam⸣
FF [e]n - - - - - - - - - ba-e-dè-e[n]

232. [. . .] a-na im-me-en-da-na a-na bí-in-daḫ-e-da-na
C [ ]x-na-šè - - - * - - - -
N [n]a-šè / [n]am
FF [. . .] ⸢ ⸣ - - - - - - - - - - - - - e[n]

233. [. . .]x a-na im-me-en-da-na a-na bí-in-daḫ-e-da-na
C [d]a - šè - - - * - - - -
N [ ]x / [d]a-nam
FF [. . .]x ⸢- -⸣ - - - - - - - - - - - - da[ḫ]

234. [. . .] eridu^{ki}-ga-ta ḫé-em-da-è$^{?}$-da-na
C [. . .] - - * - - - - - - - -
N [ ]-⸢da⸣-nam
FF [ ] - - ḫ[é] x [ ]

235. [. . .]x ba-gub-bu-da-na gissu ba-x-mu
C [. . .]x ⸢- - - - -⸣ - - - -
FF [ ] gub-bu-un-nam giss[u]

236. gi$_{6}$-a x x-ke$_{4}$ ḫa-ba-gub-bu-da-na u$_{4}$-dè ba-ra-a[n]-tuku

C ⸢– – x x – – – –⸣ b[u] ⸢⸣ – ⸢– – – –⸣ a[n]
N [ ] – ° –
FF [ ] ⸢gub-bu⸣-un-nam – – [ ]

237. u$_{4}$-da-gub sag sìg-ge-me-a-a-na šu ba-ni-ti-en-dè-en

C –
N [ ] ⸢⸣ – –/[d]è –
FF [ ] – – – ba-e-dè-t[i]
OO [ ] – – ⸢– – –⸣ [ ]

238. gi$_{6}$-da-gub ù nu-ku-me-a-a-na ú-gu me-dé-dè-en-dè-[en]

C – – – – – – – – – – – – – ° – [ ]
N [d]è – – °
FF [ ] – – – – – – d[è]
OO [n]u ⸢⸣ – – – – ⸢⸣ g[u]

239. ^{d}en-ki-ke$_{4}$ uru$_{2}$-zu nam ḫa-ba-da-an-ku$_{5}$ ki erim$_{2}$-e

C – – – – – – – – – – – – – – – eri[m$_{2}$
N [eri]m$_{2}$ –
X – – – – ⸢uru⸣[1] – – ⸢⸣ [
FF [ ] ba-e-dè-ku$_{5}$ – – ⸢⸣
OO [ ]x ⸢– –⸣ – – ⸢⸣ – k[i

239. *(cont.)* ḫa-ba-an-šúm

C]
N – – – –
X]
FF [ ]
OO]

1. It is not possible to see if anything is inscribed inside this sign.

240. me-en-dè eridu^{ki}-ta gál-la-da a-na-aš mu-e-dè-lá-e-ne$^{?}$

C ⌜ ⌝ - - - - - - - - - - - - ⌜ ⌝ - - [ ]
N [ ] - - - ⌜?⌝
X - - - [e]n ⌜ ⌝ - šè - ⌜ ⌝ ∗ - [ ]
FF [g]ál - a - - - - ba [ ]
OO [ ] ga - - me - - a[š]

241. ^{giš}nimbar-gin$_7$ šu nu-du$_{11}$-ga-me a-na-aš mu-e-gul-gul-lu-ne

C [ ]x - - - - - - a - - - - - - - - - -
N [ ] ⌜ ⌝ - - - -
X - ⌜ - ⌝ - - x x - - a [ ]
FF [ ] - - - - - - ∗ - - l[u]
OO [ ] - - - - - - - m[u]

242. ^{giš}má gibil-gin$_7$ sa pil-lá nu-ak-e a-na-aš mu-e-zé-er-zé-re-ne

C [ ] - - - - - - - - - - - - - - - - - - - [n]e
J [ ] - -
N [ ] ⌜ ⌝ ze - ze - -
X - - - [ ] ⌜ ⌝ - - ⌜ ⌝ [ ]
FF [n]u - me - - - me-ze-er-z[e]
OO [ ] ⌜ ⌝ ∗ - ⌜ ⌝me - n[a]

243. ^{d}en-ki-ke$_4$ igi-ni ki kúr-ra ba-an-gar-ra-ba

C [k]e$_4$ - - - - - - - - - - -
J [a]n-gar
N [ ] ⌜ba⌝-da-an-gar
X - - - - ⌜ ⌝ - - - [ ]
FF [ku]r - im-ma-d[a]
OO [k]e$_4$ - - - - - [ ]

244. u$_4$ x x nam-tag dugud-da-ke$_4$ giš ḫul mu-un-ne-šum

C [n]am - - - - - - - - - - -
N [u]n-dè-en / [ ] -
X - x x [n]am - - - - - ḫ[ul]
FF [ ] giš ḫul-lu mu-e-n[i]
OO [ ] - - - - - - - [ ]

245. [. . .] UM/DUB$^?$ ba-da-an-zi-ge-eš-a ildu$_2$-ba mu-un-sa$_4$$^?$-eš
C [ ] - - ⸢-⸣ - - - - - - - - - - - -
N [ ] -
X ??
FF [ ]x me-eš - b[a]
OO [d]a - ⌞ - ⌟ * / [ ] ⌞ ⌟

246. [^{d}en-ki]-ke$_4$ eridu^{ki}-ga-ta giri$_3$ kúr ba-ra-an-dab$_5$
C [ ] - - - - ⸢-⸣ - - - - - -
L [ ] - ^{k}[i]
X [k]i - - - g[a (t[a$^?$)]
FF [gi]ri$_3$ - - - - [ ]
OO [a]n ⸢-⸣

247. [^{d}dam-gal]-nun-na ama é-maḫ-a ér gig mu-un-še$_8$-še$_8$
C [ ] ⸢-⸣ - - - ⸢-⸣ - - - - - - -
L [n]a am[a]
FF [ ] ⸢-⸣ - - m[u]
OO [ ] - š[e$_8$]

248. a [uru$_2$ gul-l]a é gul-la-mu gig-ga-bi im-me
C - [l]a - - - - - - - - - -
L [ ] ⸢-⸣ gu[l]
X [l]a ⸢-⸣ [ ]
FF [l]a ⸢-⸣ [ ]
OO [ ] x [ ] - [ ]

249. g[i$_6$]-par$_4$ kù nam-en-na-ba šu ba-e-lá-lá
C g[i$_6$ na]m - - - - - - - -
L [na]m - x[ ]
X [na]m - - - - ⸢-⸣ [ ] ⌞ ⌟
OO [ ] ⌞ ⌟ - e[n] - [ ]

250. en-bi gi_6-par_4-ta ba-da-an-kar ki $erim_2$-e ba-ab-de_6

C – ⌊⌋ [pa]r_4 – – – – – – – – ∘ – – –

L [b]i – – t[a]

X ⌊– – – –⌋ – – – – – – – e[ri]m_2 – – – –

OO [ ] – – – t[a] – [ ] / – – – – [ ]

251. uri_5^{ki}-ma lú ú-šè nu-gin lú a-šè nu-gin

C – ⌊⌋ [ ] ⌊– –⌋ – – – – – – –

L [ur]i_5^{ki}-ma [ ]

X uri_2^{ki} – – – – ⌊– –⌋ – [š]è – –

OO [ur]i_2^{ki} igi-te-en-e nu-ub-[. . .] / su$^?$ (eras$^?$) tab-b[é. . .]

252. ú-šè gin-bi ú-ta ba-gin ur_5 nu-ni-ib-gur-ru

C – – – ⌊– – –⌋ [ ]

L [ ] ⌊– – – –⌋ [ ]

X – – – – – šè – – ⌊⌋ – n[i] – – –

OO [ ] – – šè – g[in]

253. a-šè gin-bi a-ta ba-gin ur_5 nu-ni-ib-gur-ru

C – – – – – – – – – – x[ ]

L [ ] – – – ⌊– – – –⌋ n[u]

X – – – – – šè – – – – n[i] – – –

254. sig-šè elam^{ki}-ma ba-ši-in-gub-bu gaz-dè ì-TIL-e

C – – – ∘ – – – ∘ – – g[az]

L [ela]m – – – – ∘ – – – [ ]

X – – – – – – – – – – – ga[z] – – – ⌊⌋

255. nim-šè ḫa-al-ma lú kúr-ra-ke_4 šu-ni [. . .]x x

C – – – – – – – – – [ ]

L [ ] – – – – kur – [ ]

X – – ⌊⌋ – – – – – ∘ – ⌊⌋ [ ]x x

Note: The original copy of X has -gar at the end of the line. The sign is no longer preserved.

256. ti-id-nu-um^{ki}-e u$_{4}$-šú-uš giš-middu$_{2}$-a úr-ra ba-ni-in-gar

C – – – – – – – – – – – TUK[UL]

L [i]d – – – – – – – – TU[KUL] / [ú]r – – – i[n]

X – ⌜⌝ – – ° – – – e – – – ú[r] ⌜⌝ –

257. sig-šè elam^{ki}-ma ú-a è-a-gin$_{7}$ KU-bi im-[. . .]x-le

C – – – – – – – – – – x[ ]

L [ ] ⌜⌝ – – – – – – i[m]

X – – – – – – – – – – – – – [ ]x –

258. nim-šè in-dal im dal-la-gin$_{7}$ eden-n[a. . .]x

C – – – – – – a – – n[a]

L [ ] – – – – – – [ ]

X – ki – – – – a – ⌜⌝ [ ]x

259. uri$_{5}$^{ki} am gal ù-na-gub-ba-gin$_{7}$ gú ki-š[è ba-ab-gar]

C – – – – – – – – – ° – – š[è]

L [ur]i$_{2}$^{ki}-e – – dab$_{5}$-ba-gin$_{7}$ [ ]

X uri$_{2}$^{ki}-ma – – – – – ⌜⌝ g[in$_{7}$]

260. ^{d}en-líl-le lú nam tar-tar-re-dè a-na [bí-in-ak-a-ba]

C – – – ° – – – – – – – – – [ ]

L [ ] ⌜ ⌝ – – – – – – [ ]

X – – – – – – – – – – – ⌜⌝ n[a]

261. mìn-kam-ma-šè elam^{ki} lú kúr-ra kur-t[a ba-ra-è]

C – – – – – – – – – – t[a]

X – – – – – – – – – – [ ]

L Traces

262. é sag-kal-la giri$_{3}$ dù-a um-ma-[. . .]

C – – – – – – – – – [ ]

X – – – e – – – im-m[a]

263. kisiga^{ki} ḫul-ḫul-lu-dè lú 10 l[ú 5 ...]

C - - - - - - - - l[ú]

X - - - ⌈⌉ - da[m]

264. u$_4$ 3-e gi$_6$ 3-e la-ba-da-te$^?$ x x [...] uru ^{giš}al-e

C - -° - -° - - - - - - - [ ] / - - - -

X - - - - - - [

264. *(cont.)* ba-ab-r[a-aḫ]

C - - r[a-aḫ]

X]

265. kisiga^{ki} ^{d}dumu-zi sag-gin$_7$$^?$ ba-r[a-è] šu-ni ba-da-ab-[dù]

C - - - - - - -$^?$ - r[a] / - - - - - [ ]

X - - - - z[i]

266. X é-šè ki giri$_3$ [...] ⌈a KA⌉ [...]

267. X ⌈zi⌉-ga u$_5$ [...z]i-ga u$_5$ [...] x

268. X [...]-un-DU zi-ga ⌈u$_5$⌉ [...] x

269. X [...s]i gal-gal ba-an-u$_5$-bi x[...]x-DU-eš

270. X [...] si tur-tur máš igi-du-gin$_7$ x[...da]b$_5$$^?$-bé-eš

271. níg-gur$_{11}$-ra-ni-ta ba-da-u$_5$ kur-šè ba-gin

L [t]a ⌈- -⌉ - - - b[a]

X - - - - - - - - - k[ur b]a -

272. i-lu kur kiš-nu-gál-la-ba gal-gal-bi m[i-ni-in-di]

L [n]u - - - - - - m[i]

X - - - - - - - - - g[al]-ab-x-bé

273. ga-ša-an-mèn níg-gur$_{11}$-gá ga-ba-da-[u$_5$ ki]-ba gi$_4$-in dè-mèn
L [ ] – – – – – – [/] – – – d[è]
X – – – – – – – g[a b]a x x ⸢– – –⸣ – ì-mè[n]

274. kù ^{na4}za-gìn-mu-ta ga-ba-e-[da]-u$_5$ ki-ba gi$_4$-in dè-mèn
L [ ] – – – – – – – [ ] / [k]i – – – d[e3]
X – – – – – – – – – ⸢⸣ [ ] ⸢– – –⸣ – – – –

275. ki-ba na-ág-gi$_4$-in nam-lú-ulu$_3$ [x]x SAG a-ba-a ba-ab-ús-e
L [á]g – – ° – – [SA]G – – – ma – ú[s]
X – – – – – – – l[ú]x – – – – – – – ⸢⸣

276. ki-ba na-ág-gi$_4$-in elam^{ki} [x] x a-ba-a ba-ab-ús-e
L [á]g – – – – [ ] x – – – ma – [ ]
X – – – – – – – ⸢⸣ [ ] x – – – – – – –

277. a uru gul-la é gul-la-mu gig-[ga]-bi im-me
L [gu]l – – – [ ]
X – – – – – – – [ ] – – –

278. nin-mu lú kur nu-me-a ku[r$^?$-r]e$^?$ ba-ab-gin
L [l]ú – – – – ku[r$^?$-r]e$^?$ – a[b]
X – – ⸢– –⸣ [b]a – –

279. ^{d}[ama-ušum-ga]l-an-na kisiga[^{ki}....]-gá
L [ga]l – – – [ ] x[x]
X ⸢⸣[ ] –

280. [x-m]u$^?$ uru$_2$-gin$_7$ nu-x[...]
L [m]u$^?$ – – – x[ ]
X [ ]x

281. L ki-r[u-gú 2-kam-ma]

282. L [. . .] x x [. . .]

283. [. . .]

284. [giš-gi$_4$-gál ki-ru-gú-da-kam]

285. [. . .]

286. [. . .]

287. [. . .]

288. [. . .]

289. GG [. . .] ú-a ⸢ba⸣-š[i-in. . .]

290. GG [. . .ú]-a ba-ši-in-x[. . .]

291. GG [. . .gu]b-bu-bi kur$_6$ mah̬-gin$_7$ ba-e-x[. . .]

292. ^{d}en-líl-le [abu]l-la mah̬-ba ^{giš}ig im-ma bí-[in-gub]

X – – – ⸢ ⸣ [ ]

GG [G]AL – – – – – – – – [ ]

293. uri$_2$^{ki}-ma lú ú-šè nu-gin lú a-šè nu-gi[n]

X – ° – [ ]

GG [ ] ⸢ ⸣ – – – – – – – – – – gi[n]

294. un-bi a túl-a dé-a-gin$_7$ šu ì-nigin$^{?}$-ne

X – – – – – ⸢ ⸣ – – ⸢ – ⸣ ni[gin] –

GG [ ] – –[1] lá – – – – – – n[e]

1. In GG túl written LAGAB×BAD.

295. usu-bi ní-bi-a nu-gál giri$_3$-bi ba-ra-an-dab$_5$

X – – – – – – – – – [a]n –

GG [u]su – – – – – – – – – – – –

296. ^{d}en-líl-le šà-gar lú níg-ḫul uru-a ba-an-da-dab$_5$

X – – – – – – – – – – da [ ]x an –

GG [e]n – – – – – – – – – – – – – –

HH –e[n] – – – ⸢– – –⸣ uru^{ki}-ta ba-da-dab$_5$

297. níg uru gul-gul-e níg é gul-gul-e uru-a ba-an-da-dab$_5$

X – – – – ° – – g[ul-gu]l – – [d]a-an –

GG [ní]g – – – – – – – – – – – – – – [ ]

HH – – ^{ki} ⸢– –⸣ ° [ ] – – – ° uru^{ki}-ta ba-da-dab5

298. níg igi-bi-šè ^{giš}tukul-e la-ba-gub-bu-a uru-a ba-an-da-dab$_5$

X – – – ° – – ° – – – ° ° ⸢–⸣ [ ] da-an –

GG [n]íg – – ta – – ° – – – – – – – – – – [ ]

HH – – – – – – – – – ab[ ] uru^{ki}-ta ba-da-dab$_5$

299. šà nu-si-si igi nigin$_2$-bi uru-a ba-an-da-dab$_5$

X – – – – – nigin$_2$-nigin$_2$ x x x [ ]-⸢da⸣-[ ]-⸢dab$_5$⸣

GG [š]à – – – – – – – – – – – [ ]

HH – – – – – – – uru^{ki}-ta ba-da-dab$_5$

300. uri$_5$^{ki}-ma gi dili dù-a-gin$_7$ sag sìg-ge nu-gá-gá

X uri$_2$ – – – – – – – – [ ]

Y x[ ]

GG uri$_2$ – – – – – – – ⸢–⸣ – – – – [ ]

HH – – – – – – – – [sa]g – – – – –

301. un-bi ku$_{6}$ šu dab$_{5}$-ba-gin$_{7}$ zi-bi mi-ni-in-túm-túm-mu

X – – – – nigin$_{2}$-na lu-ga-gin$_{7}$ [ ]
Y ⸢ ⸣ [ ]
GG [u]n– – – dab$_{5}$-ba-gin$_{7}$ – – – – – t[ùm]
HH – – – pú[1] lu-ga-gin$_{7}$ z[i] – – ib – – –

1. Written: . Possibly to be read šu.

302. tur maḫ-bi ì-bara$_{3}$-bara$_{3}$-ge-eš lú nu-um-zi-zi-zi

X [t]ur – – – ⸢– –⸣ – [ ] x x ús
Y ⸢ ⸣ – – [ ] ⸢ ⸣ b[ara$_{3}$]
GG [t]ur – – – – – – – – – – – z[i]
HH – – – – bara$_{x}$-bara$_{x}$[1]-ra-g[e] – – – – – –

1. bara$_{x}$ = KISAL.

303. LUGAL.BI.GUB dub-lá-a u$_{5}$-a níg-gu$_{7}$ la-ba-na-gál

X [LUG]AL – – nu-um-lá-e ° ° – [ ]
Y – – ⸢ ⸣ – nu-um-⸢lá⸣ x[ ]
GG [lu]gal – ° – – ° – – – – – – – gá[l]
HH – – – – – – – – n[íg n]a –

304. lugal níg-sa$_{6}$-ga gu$_{7}$-gu$_{7}$-a kur$_{6}$-re im-ma-an-dab$_{5}$

X [ ] – – – – – [ ]
Y – – – – – – ⸢ ⸣ [ ]
GG [l]ugal – – – – nag – – – – – – [ ]
HH – – – – – – – x[ ]x – –

305. u$_{4}$ im-šú-šú igi im-lá-e šà-ka-tab ì-zu-zu

X ⸢– – – –⸣ – – – – – [ ]
Y – – – – ⸢ ⸣ in – – [ ]
GG [ ] – – – – – – – – – – – – z[u]
HH – – – – – – – – – – t[ab] – –

306. é-lunga-na kaš nu-un-gál munu$_{3}$-bi nu-um-gál

X - ⸢- -⸣ - n[u]

Y - - - x ⸢-⸣ - - - [ ]

GG [ ] - - - - ° - - - - - gá[l]

HH - - - - - - - - [ ] -

In Y x could be -bi.

307. é-gal-la-na níg-gu$_{7}$ la-ba-na-gál tuš-ù-bi nu-ub-du$_{7}$

X - - a - - - [ ]

Y - - - - ⸢- - -⸣ - - gá[l]

GG [n]a ⸢-⸣ - - - - - - - - - u[b]

HH - - - - - - - b[a n]a - [la-b]a-ab-du$_{7}$

308. gá-nun maḫ-a-ni še nu-um-si-si zi-bi la-ba-ši-i[n-túm]-túm-m[u]

X - - - - - š[e]

Y - - - - - - nu-un-⸢gál⸣ [ ]

GG [ ] - - - - - ° - - - - - i[n]

HH - - - - - - [n]u ⸢-⸣ - - - b[i] - m[u]

309. gur$_{7}$-du$_{6}$ gur$_{7}$-maš-a ^{d}nanna-ka ^{d}ašnan nu-u[n]-gál

X - - - m[aš]

Y - - - - - - - k[a]

GG [gu]r$_{7}$ - g[ur$_{7}$] ⸢-⸣ - kam - - - u[n]

HH - - - - e ⸢- -⸣ - - - n[u-u]n -

310. kin-sig unu$_{2}$ gal dingir-re-e-ne-ke$_{4}$ šu ba-e-[l]á-lá

X - - - - - r[e]

Y - - - - - - ° - k[e$_{4}$]

GG [ki]n - ° ° - - ⸢-⸣ [ ]

HH - - ° ° - - - - - x - - [l]á -

311. unu$_{2}$ gal-ba kaš kurun làl mùš im-m[a-ab$^{?}$]-de$_{6}$

X - - - ° - - - [ ]

Y [u]nu$_{2}$ - ⸢-⸣ ° - - - x[ ]

GG [u]nu$_{2}$ - - ° - - x x [ ]

HH - - bi - - - - - m[a-ab$^{?}$] -

312. gír-pa-a gud udu gu$_7$-a ú-šim-e ba-[da$^?$]-ná

X - - - - - ⌜⌝ - ⌜⌝ š[im]
Y [p]a - - - ⌞- -⌟ g[ud]
GG [gí]r - - - - - * gud x[ ]
HH - - - - gu$_7$ - - ra - - - - [ ] -

313. gir$_4$ maḫ-ba gud udu ì-ak-e ir nu-mu-un-u[r$_5$-u]r$_5$-e

X - - - - - - - - [ ]
Y [ ] - - - - - [ ]
GG [g]ir$_4$ - - - - - a[k$^?$]
HH - - - - - nu - - - - - - u[r$_5$-u]r$_5$ -

314. bur-sag á sikil ^{d}nanna-ka za-pa-ág-bi ba-ra-gul

X - - ta - - la - - ⌜⌝ - [ ]
Y [ ] ⌞- -⌟ - - [ ]
GG [bu]r - - - - - kam [ ]
HH - - - - - - - - - - - - - - -

315. é gud-gin$_7$ gù bí-íb-du$_{11}$-ga-a-ri si-ga-bi ba-dù

X - - - - - x x - šè$^?$x[ ]
Y [ ]x ⌞- ib$^!$ [ ]
GG - - - - - in d[u$_{11}$]
HH - - ⌜⌝ - - - - - - - - - - - - -

316. mu-un-DU kù-ga si nu-un-sá-e gar-ra-bi ba-sù-ud

X - * - - - - - - - [ ]
Y Traces
GG mu maḫ - - - nu-mu-u[n]
HH - - - - - [ ] - - - - - - - -

317. ^{na_4}kikkin ^{giš}naga$_3$ ^{giš}gan-na ì-dúr-dúr lú nu-um-ši-gam-e

X - - - - ^{gi}[^{š} ga]m ⌜⌝
GG - - - - - - [ ]
HH - - * - - - - - - - - - - - - -

318. kar-za-gìn-na ^{d}nanna-ka a-e ba-da-lá
X – ⌜–⌝ – – – ⌜–⌝ [a]b-l[á]
GG [k]ar ^{na_4}za-gìn ^{d}nann[a]
HH – – – – – – – – – – – –

319. a ^{giš}má-sag-gá-ke$_4$ gù nu-mu-un-gi$_4$-gi$_4$ asil$_3$-lá nu-mu-un-šub
X – – – – g[á] x nu-um-D[U]
GG [ ] – – – a-ka x[ ]
HH – ° – – – – – – – – – – – – – – – – –

320. unu$_2$-RI-bàn-da ^{d}nanna-ka saḫar ba-da-dub-dub
X – – b[àn]x ⌜ba-da⌝-an-dub[ ]
GG [un]u$_2$ – – [ ]
HH – – – – – – – – – – – –

321. ^{ú}numun$_2$ ba-da-mú ^{ú}numun$_2$ ba-da-mú gir-re-e ba-an-mú
X – – x[nu]mun$_2$ – –an– – ⌜ré⌝ ° – – –
GG [ ] – [ ]
HH – – – – – – – – – – – – – – – – –

322. má má-gur$_8$-ra kar-za-gìn-na mùš im-ma-ab-de$_6$
X – – – [ ] – – – – –
GG [ ] – [ ]
HH – – – – – – – – – – – – –

323. íd má-gur$_8$-ra ba-ab-du$_7$-a-za á nu-un-sù-sù-e
X ⌜– –⌝ [ ] zu – – um ⌜–⌝ ° –
GG [d]u$_7$[ ]
HH – – – – – – – – – – – – – – – – –

324. ezen ki garza-ka giš-ḫur-bi ba-da-kúr
X [b]i – – ⌜–⌝
GG [k]a – [ ]
HH – – – – – – – – ° –

325. má nisag-gá a-a ugu-na-ka nisag nu-mu-un-na-ab-túm

X [n]isag – – – – – tùm
GG [ ] x [ ]
HH – – – – – – – – – – – – ° – –

326. ^{ninda}nindaba-bi ^{d}en-líl nibru^{ki}-šè nu-mu-un-da-an-ku$_4$-ku$_4$

X ⸢ ⸣ – – – – ⸢– –⸣ – – – – ⸢ ⸣ – – – –
HH – – – ° ° ° – – –[1] nu-mu-un-na-da-an-ku$_4$-ku$_4$

1. Written KU.

327. íd-bi šà-su$_{13}$-ga ì-gál má-gur$_8$ nu-mu-un-dib-bé

S – – – – – ⸢i⸣ [ ]
X – – – – – – – [x] – – – – – – – [ ]
Y [ ] ⸢ ⸣ [ ]
HH – – – sù – ì-ni-gál – – – – – – – –

328. gú ^{min_6}min-a-bi giri$_3$ nu-gál ú gíd-da ba-àm-mú

S – – – – – – – – ⸢ ⸣ [ ]
Y [b]i – n[u]
HH – – – – – – – – – – – – – –

329. é-tùr dagal-la ^{d}nanna-ka dub-ba-an-bi ba-si-il

S ⸢ ⸣ – – – – – – [ ]
Y – [dag]al – –nann[a]
HH – – – – – – – – – – – – – – – –

330. gi-sig ^{giš}kiri$_6$-ka šu ba-e-[lá$^?$]-lá gú-giri$_{16}$ ba-an-gar-gar

S [si]g – – ke$_4$ – b[a]
Y – – – – – – – – ⸢ ⸣ [ ]
HH – – – ki[ri$_6$] – – – – – – –

331. áb šilam-ma amar-bi ba-[da-a]b-dab$_5$ ki erim$_2$-e ba-ab-de$_6$

S [ ]x – – b[i]
Y – – – – – – [ ]
HH – – ° – – ⸢da⸣ [a]b – – – – – – –

332.	áb	^{ú}munzur-e	eden	ki	nu-zu-bi	giri$_3$	kúr	ba-ra-an-dab$_5$-bé-eš
S	Traces							
Y	–	– – °	–	[				]
HH	–	– – ⌜⌝	–	–	– – –	–	–	– – – – – –

333.	^{d}ga-a-a-ú	lú	áb	ki-ág-gá	^{giš}tukul	šurim-ma	ba-šub
Y	– – – – –	l[ú					]
HH	– – – – –	–	–	– – –	– –	– –	– –

334.	^{d}šu-ni-dùg	ià	ga-àr-ra	du$_6$-ul-du$_6$-ul-e	ià	ga-àr-ra
Y	– – – d[ùg			] ⌜⌝ [		
HH	– – – –	–	– – –	– – – – –	–	– – –

334. *(cont.)*	nu-du$_6$-ul-du$_6$-ul
Y	]
HH	– – – – –

335.	ià-bi	lú	ià	nu-zu-ne	ì-dun$_5$-dun$_5$-ne
Y	– –	l[ú		n]u – ù[	]
HH	– –	–	–	– – –	– – – –
NN	[	]	–	[	]

336.	ga-bi	lú	ga	nu-zu-ne	ì-im-mùš-mùš-ù-ne
Y	– –	[	g]a	nu-zu-ù-n[e	]
HH	– –	–	–	– – –	– – – – – –
NN	[ ]	⌜⌝	–	[	]

337.	é-tùr-ra	^{dug}šakir$_3$-e	dun$_5$-dun$_5$-e	gù	nun	nu-mu-ni-ib-bé
Y	– ⌜⌝ –	– – ra	– – a	[		]
HH	– – re	– – –	– – –	–	–	– – – – –
NN	[ ] –	– – [				]

338.	ne-mur	dugud-gin$_7$	ì-ra-a-ri	i-bí-bi	ba-gul
Y	n[e-m]ur	– –	– – ba –	[	]
HH	– –	– bi	i – – –	– – –	– –
NN	[ ]x	⌜⌝ bi	– – [		]

339. [. . .]x unu$_2$ gal ^{d}nanna-ka [. . .]

Y [ ] – – – – – [ ]
HH Omits line
NN [ ]x – – –na[nna]

340. ^{d}en.zu-e a-a-ni ^{d}en-líl-ra ér mu-un-na-še$_8$-še$_8$

K – – ⸢⸣ [ ]
Y [ ] ⸢⸣– – ⌞– – –⌟ é[r]
HH – – – – – – – – – – – – – – – – – – –
NN [ ] – – – – – – – r[a?]

341. a-a ugu-mu uru^{ki}-mu a-na-ra-dù? a-na-aš ba-e-da-gur-re-en

K – – – ⸢⸣ ur[u] / – – – – [ ]
Y [ ] ⌞– –⌟ [ ]
HH – – – – – – – – – – – –? – – – – – – – – – – –
NN [ug]u – ⸢⸣ ° – – – x [ ]

342. ^{d}en-líl uri$_5$^{ki}-mu a-na-ra-dù? a-na-aš ba-e-da-gur-re-en

K – – – – ⸢⸣ [ ] / – – [ ]
HH – – – – – – – – – –? – – – – – – – – – – –
NN [ ] – – – – ⌞– x⌟ [ ]

343. má nisag-gá a-a ugu-na-šè nisag nu-mu-un-na-ab-tùm

K – – e [ ]
HH – – – – – – – – – – – – – – – – –
NN [nisa]g –? – – – – [ ]

344. nindaba-zu ^{d}en-líl nibru^{ki}-šè nu-mu-un-na-da-an-ku$_4$-ku$_4$

K ⸢⸣ [ ]
HH ^{ninda}nindaba-zu – – – – – – – – – – – – – – – –
NN ⸢⸣ bi – – – ni[bru]

345.	en	uru	bar-ra	en	uru	šà-ga	líl-e	ḫa-ba-ab-laḫ$_5$-e-eš
K	e[n							]
HH	[ ]	–	– –	–	–	– –	– –	– – – – – –
NN	–	–	– –	–	–	– g[a		]

346.	uri$_5$^{ki}	uru^{ki}	^{giš}al-e	ri-a-gin$_7$	du$_6$-du$_6$-da	ba-šid
K	u[ri$_5$					]
HH	[u]ri$_5$^{ki}	– –	– – –	– – –	– – –	– –
NN	uri$_2$ –	– ⸢–	–⸣ – –	r[i		]

347.	ki-ùr	ki	ní-dúb-bu	^{d}en-líl-lá	èš	líl-lá	ba-ab-gar
G	Traces						
K	⸢– –⸣	[					]
HH	[ ] –	–	– – –	– – ⸢ ⸣ –	–	– –	– – –
NN	[k]i –	–	– ⸢ ⸣ [				]

348.	^{d}en-líl	uru-zu	igi-zu	igi	ba	x	é-ri-a	sù-ga
G	– – –	u[ru z]u	– ⸢ ⸣	[				]
K	– – –	– z[u						]
HH	– – –	– –	– –	–	–	–	– – –	– –

349.	nibru^{ki}	uru-zu	igi-zu	x[. . .	é-ri-a	sù-ga]
G	⸢ ⸣ [	] –	– ⸢ ⸣	x[		]
K	– –	– –	ig[i			]
HH	Omits line					

350.	uri$_5$^{ki}-ma	ur-bi	úr	bàd-da	si-im-si-im	nu-mu-un-ak-e
G	⸢uri$_2$⸣[m]a	– –	–	bà[d		]
K	– – –	– [				]
HH	– – –	– –	–	– –	– – – –	– – – – –

351.	túl	sag	bulug-ga	ganba-bi-a	ki	li-bi-ib-ri-ri-ge
G	tur	–	b[ulug g]a	– – –	–	[ ]
K	tur	–	– –	ga[nba		]
HH	–	–	– –	–^{ba} – –	–	– – – – – –

352. a-a ugu-mu uru-mu dili-bi-ta á-zu-šè nigin$_2$-àm-ši-ib

G – – ug[u] uru$_2$ – – – ° – [ ]

K – – – – – – d[ili]

HH – – – – – ^{ki} – – – – – – – – – – – –

353. ^{d}en-líl uri$_5$^{ki}-mu dili-bi-ta á-zu-šè nigin$_2$-àm-ši-ib

G – – [ ]⌜ ⌝ – – – ° – z[u]

K – – – – – – [ ]

HH – – – – – – – – –^{1} – – – – – – –

1. ta over erased da.

354. é-kiš-nu-gál-mu dili-bi-ta á-zu-šè nigin$_2$-àm-ši-ib

G – [g]ál – – – ° – z[u]

K – – – – – – – x[ ]

HH – – – – la – – – da – – – – – – –

355. uri$_5$^{ki}-ma numun ḫa-ra-ni-ib-è un ḫu-mu-ra-ab-dagal-la

G ur[i$_2$^{k}]^{i}-ma – – – – – x [ ]

K – – e – ḫ[a]

HH – – – ⌜ ⌝ – – – – – – – – – – – – – –

356. me ki-en-gi-ra ba-da-ḫa-lam-e ki-bi ḫa-ra-ab-gi$_4$-gi$_4$

G m[e e]n – – – – – – – – – – [ ]

K ⌜ ⌝ – – – ⌜ ⌝ [ ]

HH – – – – – – – – – – ma – ° – – – – –

357. ki-ru-gú 3-kam-ma

G – – – – – [ ]

K [ ] ⌜ ⌝ [ ]

HH – – – – – –

358. a é zi é zi a lú-bi lú-bi

G ⌜ ⌝ – – – – – – – –

HH – – – – – – – – – –

359. giš-gi$_4$-gál-bi-im
G - - - [ ]
HH - - - - -

360. ^{d}en-líl-le dumu-ni ^{d}en.zu-ra mu-un-na-ni-ib-gi$_4$-gi$_4$
G - - - - - - - - - - - - [ ]
HH - - - - - - - - - - - - - - - - - - -
II [ ] - - - - - - - - - ⸢⸣ - - - - -

361. uru$_2$ líl-lá šà-bi a-nir-ra gi ér-ra ba-àm-mú
G - - - - - - - - - - [ ]
II [ ] ⸢⸣ - - še - - - - - - -

361a. II [šà-b]i a-še-ra gi ér-ra ba-àm-mú

362. šà-bi-a a-nir-ra u$_4$ mi-ni-ib-zal-zal-e
G - - - - - - - - - i[b]
II [ ] - * - še - - - - - - - - -

362a. II [dumu-m]u dumu gi$_7$ IM.ZA-bi-me-en ér-ra ⟨a$^{?}$⟩-na-bi-me-en

363. ^{d}nanna dumu gi$_7$ IM.ZA-bi-me-en ér-ra ⟨a$^{?}$⟩-na-bi-me-en
G - - ⸢⸣ - - - ḫé$^{?}$ - e[n]
II [nan]na - - - - - - - - - - - - - -

364. di-til-la inim pu-úḫ-ru-um-ma-ka šu gi$_4$-gi$_4$ nu-gál
G - - - - - - - - m[a]
II [ ] - - - - - - * - - - - - - - -

365. inim du$_{11}$-ga an ^{d}en-líl-lá-ka šu bal-e nu-zu
G - - - - - - - - - - [ ]
II - - - - - - - - - - - - - - -

366. uri$_5$^{ki}-ma nam-lugal ḫa-ba-šúm bala da-rí la-ba-an-šúm
G uri$_2$ – – – lu[gal] ⸢ ⸣ [ ]
R [r]í – – – –
II – – ° – – – – – – – – – – – –

367. u$_4$ ul kalam ki gar-ra-ta zag un lu-a-šè
G – – – – – – – z[ag]
R [ ] na
II – – – – – – – – – – – –

368. bala nam-lugal-la sag-bi-šè è-a a-ba-a igi im-mi-in-du$_8$-a
G – – – – [ ]
R [D]U – – – ° – mu-un-⸢du$_8$-e$^?$⸣
II – – – – – – – – ° – – – – – – – – – –

369. nam-lugal-bi bala-bi ba-gíd-e-dè šà-kúš-ù-dè
G – – – bal[a]
R [d]è ba-an-kùš-ù-dè-en
II – – – – – – – – – – – – –

370. ^{d}nanna-mu na-an-kúš-kúš-ù-dè uru^{ki}-zu è-bar-ra-ab
G – – – – – [ ]
R [d]è – ° – – ba-ra
II – – – – – – – – – – – – – – – – –

371. u$_4$-ba lugal-mu dumu gi$_7$-ra ur$_5$-ra-ni ba-an-BAD
E – – – – d[umu]
G – – – – – [ ]
R [n]i – ° –
II – – – – – – – ⸢ ⸣ – – – –

372. en ^{d}aš-ím-babbar dumu gi$_7$-ra šà ḫul-lu im-ma-an-dím
E – – ° – – – g[i$_7$]
G – – – – babbar$_2$-r[a]
R [ḫu]l ° – – – –
II – – – – – – – – – – – – – – – –

373. ^{d}nanna lú uru^{ki}-ni ki-ág-gá uru^{ki}-ni ba-ra-è

E – – ° – ° – – [ ]
G ⸢ ⸣ – – – ° – k[i]
R [n]i – – –
II – – – – – – – – – – – – – – –

374. ^{d}en.zu-e uri$_{5}$^{ki} ki-ág-gá giri$_{3}$-ni ba-ra-an-dab$_{5}$

E – – – – – – [ ]
G – – – –x^{1} uri$_{2}$ ⸢ ⸣ [ ]
R [ ] – – – –
II – – – – – – ⸢– –⸣ – ⸢ ⸣ – – – – –

1. x in G is an erased ki.

375. ^{d}nin-gal-e KAS$_{4}$ uru^{ki}-ni-ta ki kúr-šè du-ù-dè

E – – – ° – – ° – t[a]
G – – – – – – ° n[i]
R Traces
II – – – – – – – – ⸢ ⸣ x – – – – – –

376. túg ul$_{4}$-ul$_{4}$-la-bi ba-ra-an-mú uru^{ki}-ta ba-ra-è

E – – – – – im-m[a] x [ ]
G – – – – – im-ma-a[n]
II – – – – – – – – – – – – – – –

377. uri$_{5}$^{ki}-ma ^{d}a-nun-na-bi bar-ra ba-su$_{8}$-ge-eš

E – – – -- – ⸢ ⸣ b[i] – x[ ]
G uri$_{2}$ – – -- – n[a]
II – – – -- – – – ⸢– –⸣ – – – –

378. uri$_{5}$^{ki}-ma NE IM-bi KI x x x a ba-a-te

E – – – – – – – [ ] x x [ ]
G uri$_{2}$ – – ⸢ ⸣ – ba ⸢ ⸣ [ ]
II – – ° x – – x x x x – – – –

379. uri$_5$^{ki}-ma giš-bi tu-ra-àm g[i-b]i tu-ra-àm
E Omits line
G uri$_2$ - - mu - - r[a]
II - - - - - ⌞ ⌟ - g[i-b]i - - -

380. bàd-bi en-na nigin$_2$-na-bi-da a-nir ba-da-di
E ⸢⸣ - - - - - - ta [ ] ⸢⸣ - x[ ]
G - - - - - - - - - - [ ]
II ⸢⸣ - - - - - a - - - - - -

381. u$_4$-šú-uš-e ^{giš}tukul-e igi-bi-šè sag ì-sìg-sìg-ge
E ⸢⸣ [ ] ⸢⸣ - - - - ni ° - - - - g[e]
G ⌞ ⌟ - - - - - - ni - ⸢⸣ [ ]
II ⌞ ⌟ - - - - ⸢⸣ - - - - - - - -

382. uri$_5$^{ki}-ma ^{urudu}ḫa-zi-in gal-gal-e igi-bi-šè ù-sar ì-ak-e
E u[r]i$_5$^{ki}-ma - - - - - - - - ni [ ]
G [ur]i$_2$^{ki}-ma - - - - g[al]
II - - - - - - - - - - - - - - - - -

383. ^{giš}gíd-da á mè-ke$_4$ si bí-ib-sá-sá-e-ne
E - - - - - - - - ba ° - - - [ ]
G [d]a ⌞ - - - - ba$^!$ [ ]
II - - - - - - - - - - - - - -

384. ^{giš}ban gal-gal ^{giš}illar ^{kuš}e-íb-ùr-ra ur im-da-gu$_7$-e
E - - - - - - - - ⌞ - ⌟ - - - ⸢⸣ -
G [ ] - - - ⸢⸣ [ ]
II - - - - - - - - - - - - - - - - - -

385. ^{giš}ti-zú-ke$_4$ muru$_9$ šèg-gá-gin$_7$ bar-ba mi-ni-in-si
E ° - - - - - - - - - - - - -
G [ ] - - - g[in$_7$]
II - - zu - - - ° ⸢⸣ - - àm-mi-íb-si

386. na$_4$ gal-gal-e ní-bi-a pu-ud pa-ad im-mi-ni-ib-za
E – – – – – – – – – – – – – – – –
G [ga]l-bi – – – p[u]
II – – – – – – – – – – – – – – ° íb –

386a. II u$_4$-šú-uš uru^{ki}-ta im ḫul-e mu-un-da-an-gi$_4$-gi$_4$

387. uri$_5$^{ki} nè-bi-ta nir-gál ḫúb-gaz-e ba-gub
E – – – – – – – ⸢e⸣ – – – – –
G [t]a ⸢– –⸣ [ ]
II – – ma usu – – – – – – – – a –

388. un-bi lú erim$_2$-e á bí-íb-gar ^{giš}tukul-e la-ba-su$_8$-ge-eš
E – – níg – – – – ib [g]^{iš} – – – – – – –
II – – – – –[1] – – – – – – – ° – – – –

1. Only half of the sign written.

389. uru ^{giš}tukul-e sag nu-šúm-mu-a šà-gar-e im-ús
E – – – – – – – – – – š[à-ga]r – – –
II – ^{ki} – – – – nu-šúm-ma-šúm-ma-àm – – – ba-e-dab$_5$

390. šà-gar-e uru a-gin$_7$ ba-e-si gá-la nu-um-ta-dag-ge
E – – – – – – – – – – [ ] – – – – – –
II – – – – ^{ki} – – – – – – – – – – – – –

391. šà-gar-e igi-bi im-gam-me-e sa-bi im-lu-gú-ne
E – – – – – – – [ ]x x[ ]
II – – – – – – – – – – – – – – – –

392. un-bi a nigin$_2$-na ba-e-si zi ur$_5$ i-ak-e
E – – – ⸢⸣ – ⸢– –⸣ [ ]
II – – – – – – – – – – – –

393. lugal-bi é-gal ní-te-na-ka zi gig mu-un-pa-an-pa-an
E – – – – – [ ]x ⸢ ⸣ [ ]
II – – – ° – – – – – – – – – – – – –

394. nam-lú-ulu$_3$-bi ^{giš}tukul ba-e-šub ^{giš}tukul ki bí-íb-tag
E – – – lu– – tuku[l šu]b ^{g}[^{iš}]
II – – – – šu-bi – – – – – – – – –

395. šu-bi gú-bi-šè ba-ši-ib-ri-ri ér mu-un-še$_8$-še$_8$-ne
E – – – – ° – – x[1] [ ] x [ ]
II – – – – – – – – – – – – – – – – –

1. Langdon copied NI but this is quite doubtful.

396. ní-bi-a ad mi-ni-ib-gi$_4$-gi$_4$ inim im-šár-šár-e-ne
E – – – – – – ⸢ ⸣ [ ]
II ur – – – – – – – – – – – – – –

397. me-li-e-a du$_{11}$-ga-me nam-mu daḫ-me nam-mu
E – – – – – – m[e] x [ ]
II – – – – – – – – – x – – –
QQ [g]a – – me – – – [ ]

In II the scribe had trouble with DAḪ and tried to erase the BAD sign.

398. èn-šè-àm ka garaš$_2$-a-ka i-im-til-le-dè-en-dè-en
E – – – – ⸢– –⸣ [ ]
II – – – – – – – ° – – la – – – –
QQ – [ga]raš$_2$ – – i-im-til-le-⸢dè⸣-[e]n

399. uri$_5$^{ki}-ma šà-bi nam-ús-àm bar-bi nam-ús-àm
E ⸢– – – – –⸣ n[am]
II – – – – – – – – – – – – –
QQ ur[i$_2$ b]i – – a – ba – – a

– –

400. šà-bi-a níg šà-gar-ra-ka i-im-til-le-dè-en-dè-en

E š[à]
II ⌜⌝ – – – – – – – im-mi-ni-ib-til-e-dè
QQ – – [ ] – – – – – – – – – –

401. bar-bi-a ^{giš}tukul elam^{ki}-ma-ka ga-nam-ba-[e-til-l]e-dè-en-dè-en

II – – – – – – – – – i-im-til-e-dè-en-dè-en
QQ – – – [ ]– – – – – / – [l]e – – – –

402. uri$_5$^{ki}-ma lú erim$_2$ á bí-ib-gar ga-nam-ba-e-til-le-dè-en-dè-en

E [ur]i$_5$^{ki}-ma – – im-m[a]
II – – – – – e im-ma-gub – – – * – e – * – –
QQ uri$_2$^{k}[^{i} l]ú – – – – – / – ⌜⌝ – – – – – – – – –

403. zi-bi murgu-bi-šè ì-ak-e gù-téš-a bí-in-sì-ke-eš

E – – – – – – – ne – t[éš]
II – – – – – – – – – – – – – íb – ge –
QQ – ⌜⌝ mur[gu] – – – – – – – – – – – – –

404. é-gal a ba-šub-ba ba-e-lá-lá giš-si-gar bí-in-bu-bu-uš

E – – – – – – – * – – – – – x[1] [ ]
II abul-la-bi giš-si-gar bí-in-du$_8$-du$_8$-uš giš-ig-bi u$_4$-dè gub-bu
QQ [ ]x – – – – – – – – – – – – –

1. Langdon's copy looks like lí-b[í-. . .]. The tablet has deteriorated and now only si-ga[r. . .] is preserved.

405. elam^{ki}-e a maḫ è-a-gin$_7$ gidim im-ma-ni-íb-gar

E – –ma – ⌜⌝ – – – – – – [ ]
II – – – – – – – – giri$_3$? – – – – –
QQ [ ] ⌜è⌝ maḫ-a-gin$_7$ – – – ši ib –

406. uri$_5^{ki}$-ma ^{giš}tukul ^{dug}saḫar$_2$-gin$_7$ sag-gaz ì-ak-e

E uri$_3^{ki}$-ma – – – – – – – – [ ]

O uri$_2^{ki}$-ma – – – – ra – – – – – ne

II – – – – – e – – – – – – – –

QQ [$^{g]iš}$ – la – – ré – – – – – –

Note: The obverse of O is very worn. Almost all signs are legible, however. I have not used half brackets in the representation of the obverse of this text.

407. lú kar-ra-bi du$_{10}$ nu-um-zil-e bàd zag-ga bí-in-dab$_5$-bé-eš

E maš – – – – – – – – – – – – [ ]

O – – – – – – – – – – ⌜⌝ – – im-dab$_5$?

II – – – – – – – – – – – – – im-tab

QQ [ ]x ⌜– –⌝ – –[1] – – – – –

1. bí- written on top of end of ga.

407a. II ku$_6$ a nigin$_2$-na lu-ga-gin$_7$ zi-bi in-tùm-tùm-mu-ne

407b. II é-kiš-nu-gál ^{d}nanna-ka lú erim$_2$-e ba-e-dab$_5$

407c. II sig an-gar-bi dugud gál-la A.MUŠEN im-ze-er-ze-re-ne

408. alan AN.ZAG-ge si-a-bi gú-gur$_5$ ba-an-ne-eš

E ^{urudu}alan – – – – – – – ⌜⌝ b[a]

O – – – – – – – – – – – – –

II – – – ge$_4$ – – – – – ru ba-ni-in-ak-eš

QQ [ ] ⌜– – –⌝ – –

409. ^{d}nin-ià-gara$_2$ agrig maḫ-e erim$_3$-ma šu bí-in-dag

E – – – – – ⌜⌝ ke$_4$ – ° – – – d[ag]

O – – – – – – ° – ° – – im –

II ⌜⌝ – é – – – – – – – – – – –

QQ [ ] – –

410. giš-gu-za-bi igi-bi-ta ba-e-šú sa$\breve{h}$ar-ra ba-da-an-tuš

E – [b]i – – – – ° – – ta ba-e-da-x[ ]

O – – – – – – – – ° – – ta – – – –

II [ ] – – – – – – – – – – – – – ° –

411. áb ma$\breve{h}$-bi si-mùš-bi ba-ra-an-dab$_{5}$-bé-eš si-bi ba-ra-an-ku$_{5}$

E á[b s]i – – – ° – – – – – – – – – [ ]

O – – – – ⸢ ⸣ – – – – – – – – – – – – – – –

II [ ] – – – – – ta – ° – – – – – – – – – – –

SS [b]i-x[ ] / – x[ ]

412. gud du$_{7}$-du$_{7}$-bi udu ú gu$_{7}$-a-bi ^{giš}tukul-e ba-an-sìg-sìg

E [ ] – – – – – – – ° – – – –

O – – – – – ° gi$_{4}$ – – – – ° ì-in – –

II [d]u$_{7}$ – e – – – ° gin$_{7}$ – – – – – – – –

SS [d]u$_{7}$-gin$_{7}$ – ⸢ ⸣ [ ]

412a. II [^{giš}]nimbar-gin$_{7}$ gú-gur$_{5}$-ru ba-ab-dug$_{4}$ ur-bi ba-ra-an-kad$_{4}$

413. ^{giš}nimbar urudu níg-kala-ga á nam-ur-sag-gá

E [ ] – – – – – – –

O – – – – – – – – – – – –

II [n]imbar – – – – – – – – – –

SS [urud]u – – – [ ]

414. ^{ú}numun$_{2}$-gin$_{7}$ ba-bu ^{ú}numun$_{2}$-gin$_{7}$ ba-zé úr-ba ti mi-ni-ib-bal

E [ ] ⸢ ⸣ – – – – – – – – – – m[i]

O – – – – – – – – – – – – – – – – in –

II ⸢ ⸣ – – – – – – ° – – – – – – – – – –

MM [t]i – – – –

SS [gi]n$_{7}$ – – –[ ]/[ú]r – – [ ]

415. sag saḫar-ra ki ba-ni-ib-ú-ús lú zi-zi la-ba-tuku

E [ ] ⌞⌟ - - - - ⌞⌟ - - - ⌞⌟ [ ]
O - - - - - - - - - - - - - - tuk-tuk
II [sa]g - - - - - - * - - - - - - -
MM [a]n -
SS [ ] - - - i[b]

416. [giš]zé-na-bi gú ba-an-gur$_5$-uš sag šu bí-in-ḫu-ḫu-uz

E [ ] - gú-⌜gur$_5$⌝-uš ba-ab-du[g$_4$ š]u - - - - u[z]
O - - - - gú-gur$_5$ ba-ab-dug$_4$] - - -
II [gi]⌜š⌝zé⌝-na-bi - - - [gu]r$_5$ - - - - - - - / -!
SS [ ] gú-gu[r$_5$]

417. á-an su$_{11}$-lum-ma-bi pú du$_7$-du$_7$ ba-ra-an-BU.BU-dè-eš

E [l]um - - - - - - r[a] ⌞ ⌟ - -
O - - - - - - * ⌜du$_6$-du$_6$-ra - ⌟ a[n] -
II x[1] á - - - - - - - - ba-da-ra-an-BU.BU-dè-eš
SS Traces

1. In II the first sign looks like [g]iš on the copy. The sign is no longer preserved on the original.

418. gi zi NAB? kù-ge mú-a šu ba-e-lá-lá

E [ ] x - - ⌞⌟ - x x ⌞⌟ [b]a - - -
O - - x - - - - -? -? [ ]
II [g]i - ⌞⌟ - ⌞⌟ - - - - - - -
JJ - ⌞⌟ - - ⌞⌟ - - - - - - -
MM [ ] - - giš ki ba-e-lá-[ ]

419. gú-un gal-gal-e mi-ni-in-gar-re-eš-a kur-re ì-íl-íl

E [ ] ⌞ - - - - - - - - - ⌟ - - - -
O - - - - - - - - - - - [ ]
T [í]l ⌞⌟
JJ - - - - - - [ ] - - - - * kúr - - - -
MM [ ]-ni-in-gar-gar-re-eš-a - ré ⌞⌟ [ ]
SS [ ] ⌞ - ⌟ [ ]

420. é-e ^{giš}búr maḫ-bi ba-šub bàd-si-bi ba-gul

E – [ ] ⌞ ⌟ – ⌞⌟ – ⌞ ⌟ – – –
O – a – bú[r]
T [g]ul
JJ – – – – bi ° ° ba-⌜e$^?$⌝-[šu]b – – – – a –
MM [ ]-e-šub – – – ba-e-g[ul]
SS [b]úr-bi ° ° – [ ]

421. máš-anše zi-da gùb-bu-ba gú-da lá-a-bi

E – ⌞⌟ – – ⌞ ⌟ – – ⌞⌟ – – –
O – – z[i]
T [ ] –
JJ ° – e – – – – – – – – ° –
MM [ ] – – – – – – – ba
SS [ ] – – – [ ]

422. ur-sag ur-sag-e gaz-a-gin$_7$ igi-bi-ta ba-šú

E ⌞ ⌟ – – – ⌞⌟ – ⌞ ⌟ – – – –
O – s[ag]
T [ ] – –
JJ – – – – ° – – – – – – – e –
MM [ ]x – – – – – – – e –
SS [u]r ⌞ ⌟ x[ ]

423. ušumgal ka duḫ-a ug-gá ní íl-íl-la-bi

E – – ⌞⌟ – ⌞ – ⌟ – – – –
O – [ ]
T [l]a$^?$-a-bi
JJ un$^?$-gal – – – úg – – gùr-gùr-ru-bi
MM [ ] ug$_7$ – – gùr-gùr-ru-bi

424. am dab$_5$-ba-gin$_7$ saman-e bí-in-šub-bu-ri ki erim$_2$-e ba-ab-de$_6$

E – – – – ⌞⌟ – – – – – – – / – ⌞ – ⌟ – –
O – – – [ ]
T [k]i – – – – d[e$_6$]
JJ – – – – ŠÈ.BU.ŠÈ.TU ba-ra-an-šub-šub-bu – ⌞ – – – ⌟
MM [ ].NUN.TU ba-e-šub-bu-ri – – ° – – –

425. ki-tuš kù ^{d}nanna tir šim ^{giš}eren-na-gin$_7$ ir-si-im-bi ba-gul

E – – – – – – š[im ere]n – ° – – – – – gu[l]
O – – – –[ ]
T [ ] – – – – – – –
JJ – – – – – – – ⸢⸣[ere]n – – – – – ⸢⸣a ba-⸢an⸣-[g]ul
MM [nann]a – – – – – – / – – – – – – –

425a. JJ a-sal-bar-⸢bi⸣ kù-sig$_{17}$ ^{na4}za-gìn ki x x-⸢da⸣ du$_{11}$-ga-a-bi

426. é u$_6$-di-bi ià du$_{10}$-ga-ri u$_6$-di-bi ba-gul

E – – – – – – – r[i b]i – –
O – – [ ]
T [ ] – –
JJ – – ⸢– – – – a – – – –⸣ – – a–
MM [d]i – – – – – – – – – –

427. u$_4$-gin$_7$ kur-kur-ra im-si-a an-usan an-na-gin$_7$ ba-e-dù

E – – – – – – – – – us[an]x ⸢⸣
O – – – – [ ]
T [ ] –
JJ – – – – – i – ⸢⸣ – [ ] ⸢⸣ – – – – – –?
MM [ ] i – – – – u[san]

428. ^{giš}ig-bi mul? an-na x-bi [traces] du$_{11}$-ga-ba

E – ⸢– – – – –⸣ x – [ ]
O – – – [ ]
T [ ]x – –
JJ – – – x ⸢– –⸣ x [ ]x – – a-bi
QQ [ ]x x ⸢– – –⸣

429. ^{urudu}bulug gal-gal-e [?] KA [. . .-g]i$_4$-gi$_4$ ba-ra-an-bu-bu-uš

O ° – – [ ]
T [ ] – – dè-⸢eš⸣
JJ – bulug$_2$[1] – – – x x x x [b]a – – – – dè-eš
QQ [ ]x KA[2] [g]i$_4$ – – – – – – – ⸢–⸣

1. bulug$_2$ = búr.
2. The KA sign is possibly inscribed but it is impossible to determine what, if any, sign was inside. Interpret as sig$_{14}$. . .gi$_4$-gi$_4$?

430. ^{kuš}da/á-si-bi a-ba I[M. . .] LI-bi-šè TÚG.P[I. . .] ba-ab-dug$_4$

M [ ]x ⸢– –⸣ [ ]
O ⸢– – –⸣ [ ]
JJ ° – – – – – I[M] x x x – [ ] –
QQ [ ] ⸢–⸣ – AN [. . .]x – – – / – P[I] – – –

431. ^{giš}nu-kúš-ù-bi-da lú ka[r-r]a-gin$_7$ ér gig ì-še$_8$-še$_8$

M [é]r – – ⸢– –⸣
JJ – – – – – – – LÚ×KÁR-ra-gin$_7$ ⸢– –⸣ mu-un-še$_8$-še$_8$
QQ nam-lú-ulu$_3$-bi-da lú ka[r-r]a – / ⸢– –⸣ – – –

432. ^{giš}[sa]g-kul ^{giš}sa$\breve{h}$ab$_2$ kù-ga ^{giš}ig gal gú bu-i nu-mu-na-ab-bé

M [ ] x x x [g]ú – – – – – – – –
JJ ⸢giš⸣[sa]g – – ⸢– – –⸣ – – ⸢–⸣ – – ° nu-mu-un-na-ak-e

433. ^{giš}ig gú-gíd-da za-pa-ág-bi ba-šub lú gú bu-i la-ba-an-tuku

M [ ] x di-bi za-pa-⸢ág-bi⸣ [l]ú gú bu-i la-ba-an-tuku
JJ ⸢– –⸣ – – – – – – – – ⸢–⸣ l[ú] – ⸢–⸣ ° ⸢la-ba⸣-ab-gar

434. [. . .]x-ba-šè ba-lá-lá sila dagal-la ní-bi ba-ab-gar

M [ ] – – – – – – – [ ] x – – –
JJ [ ]x ⸢– –⸣ – e⸢–⸣ – – – – ⸢– –⸣ [ ]

435. ki x x x KI.LUGAL.GUB-bu-na nindaba-bi ba-kúr

M [luga]l$^?$ - - - - n[a nind]aba - - -

JJ - [. . .luga]l$^?$-da - ⸢⸣ - - ba - - [ ]

436. ki$^?$ kù-ba tigi$_2$ šem$_5$ ^{kuš}á-lá-e gù nun nu-mu-ni-ib-bé

M [ ] - - ⸢⸣ - - - [g]ù - - - - - -

JJ ⸢-$^?$⸣ - - -zabar * - - - - - n[un i]b -

437. ^{giš}tigi$_2$ maḫ-ba ér$^?$ x[. . .]-si-a šìr kù nu-mu-na-ab-bé

M x - - - -$^?$ x[k]ù - - - - -

JJ ⸢⸣ - - [ ] - - - - - - ni [ ]

438. dub-lá-maḫ ki nam-ku$_5$-re-dè ka-inim-ma nu-gál

M - - - - - - - d[a k]a - - - -

JJ - - - - - - - - - - - - g[ál]

439. ^{giš}gu-za ki di ku$_5$-ru-bi nu-mu-un-gub di si nu-um-sá-e

M - - - - - - - - - u[m$^?$] - - - - - -

JJ - - - * - - - - - - - - - - - m[u]

KK ⸢- - -⸣ - - ⸢- -⸣ [ ]

440. ^{d}alamuš-e ^{giš}gidri ba-da-an-šub šu-ni gu$_4$$^?$-ud-gu$_4$-ud

M - ⸢⸣ - -$^?$tukul$^?$ - an d[a š]u - x x dè

JJ - - a - - - - - - - - - - - [u]d

KK - - * * - - an da - - ⸢⸣ [ ]

441. á-ná-da kù ^{d}nanna-ke$_4$ balag šu nu-mu-un-tag-ge-ne

M - n[á-d]a - - - - x[m]u - ⸢⸣ [?]

JJ ⸢⸣ - - -! (za) - - ka ⸢⸣ - na - u[n]

KK - - - - - - ka - - nu x ⸢- - -⸣

442. dub-šen kù lú igi nu-bar-re-dam erim$_{2}$-e igi i-ni-in-bar

M – š[en] – – – – – – – [ ] – – – – –

JJ d[ub-še]n – – – * – – – ⸢⸣ – im-m[i]-⸢ni⸣-i[n]-bar

KK – – – – – – – – – – – – – – – –

443. ^{giš}ná-gi$_{4}$-rin-na nu-um-gub ú za-gìn nu-mu-un-bara$_{3}$

M – n[á-g]i$_{4}$ – bi – – – ⸢⸣ [m]u ⸢⸣ –

JJ ^{giš}[n]á-g[i$_{4}$-r]in-na – un – – za-[gì]n – – ⸢⸣ [bar]a$_{3}$

KK – – – – – – – – – – – – – – – –

444. alan AN.ZAG-ge$_{4}$ si-a-ba gú-gur$_{5}$ ba-an-ne-eš

M – – – – – – ⸢⸣ – g[ur$_{5}$ n]e –

JJ ⸢– – –⸣ – – – bi ⸢⸣ g[ur$_{5}$] x x x x –

KK ^{urudu}alan – – – – – – – – – – –

445. engiz ensi kišib$_{3}$-gál-bi eš-da šu li-bí-in-du$_{7}$-uš

M – – – – x[b]í – – –

JJ [eng]iz ⸢⸣ – ⸢⸣ b[i] ⸢⸣ – – – – *

KK – – – – – – – – – – – – – –

446. gú ki-šè gál-la-bi ba-e-su$_{8}$-su$_{8}$-ge-eš kúr-re ba-ab-laḫ$_{5}$-e-eš

M – – – – – b[i] – x[ ]

JJ g[ú k]i * ⸢⸣ * – – – – – – – – – ⸢⸣ – – ⸢– –⸣ –

KK – – * – – ba ba-⸢e-súg⸣-eš kur – – – – – – –

In JJ this line is after 447.

447. us-ga kù šu-luḫ dadag-ga šà-gada-lá-bi-e-ne

M – – ⸢– – –⸣ [ ]

JJ – – [g]a – ⸢⸣ – – – – ⸢– –⸣ – –

KK – – – – – – –ke$_{4}$– – – – * –

448. giš-hur me kù-ga ba-da-ha-lam-e uru kúr-šè ba-e-re$_7$-eš

M – – ki [ ]
JJ Omits line
KK – – – – – – – – – – – – – – – – –

449. ^{d}en.zu-e šà hul-la-ni a-a-ni-ir ba-ši-in-gin

M – – – x[ ]
JJ [ ] ⌜– –⌝ š[à] gál –a– – – – * – – – –
KK – – – – – – – – – – – – – – – –

450. igi a-a ugu-na ^{d}en-líl-lá-šè du$_{10}$ ki ba-ni-in-ús

M – – – – .– – – [ ]
JJ [ ]– – – – – – – – ib –
KK – – – – – – – – – – – – – – – – –

451. a-a ugu-mu èn-tukum-šè níg-ka$_9$-mu igi erim$_2$-e mu-e-du$_8$

M – – – – ⌜⌝ t[ukum
JJ [ ]x – – – ma bí * – /
KK – – – – – – – – –? * – – – – – –

451. *(cont.)* èn-tukum-šè SAR

M]
JJ – – – –
KK è[n]

452. nam-en nam-lugal šúm-ma-za-àm x mu-e-ši-dé?

M – – – luga[l]
JJ Omits line
KK – – – – – – – – x – – – –

453. a-a ^{d}en-líl lú á-ág-e du$_{11}$-ga zi

M – – – – – – [ ]
JJ Omits line
KK – – – – – – – – – – –

454. M inim kù-zu kalam-m[a...]

JJ Omits line
KK Blank line

455. M [d]i? níg-kúr-zu š[à? ...]

JJ Omits line
KK Blank line

456. šà sú-mu-ug-ga i-zi-gin$_7$ ḫu-luḫ-ḫa-za igi-zi [bar]-mu-un-ši-ib

M - - - u[g m]u-š[i-i]b
JJ - - - - ⸢ ⸣- - ⸢ ⸣x - - / - z[i] ⸢⸣ - - -
KK Blank line

In JJ this line is after 459. x in this line is most probably a badly written ḫu.

457. a-a ^{d}en-líl nam mu-e-tar-ra galga ba-ra-an-du$_8$-du$_8$

M -- --- n[am] ⸢⸣ [ ] ⸢⸣
JJ Omits line
KK -- --- - ---- - - - ⸢ - ⸣

458. siki PA nam-en-na suḫ kéš-da-gá

M ⸢⸣ - - - [n]a - [ ]x - *
JJ - - [ ] -
KK - - - - - - - [ ] -

459. u$_4$ sikil maḫ luḫ-luḫ x x[...]x ^{túg}mu-sír-ra mi-ni-in-mu$_4$

M - - - - - x x[ ] - - - - - - -
JJ - si[kil]x - - - - - - - -
KK Blank line

460. ^{d}en-líl-le dumu-ni ^{d}en.zu-ra inim zi mu-un-na-ab-bé

M -- - [l]e - - -e[n ini]m - - - - ⸢⸣ -
JJ - - - - - - - - - - - - - - ⸢⸣ - - -
KK - - - - - - - - - - - - - - - - - - -

461. dumu-mu uru nam-ḫé giri$_{17}$-zal ša-ra-da-dù-a bala-zu

M [na]m ḫe – – x[ ]x – – – –
JJ Omits line
KK – – – – – – – – – – DU * / – –!

461. *(cont.)* ba-ši-ib-tuku

M – – – ⌞⌟
JJ
KK – – – –

462. uru gul bàd gal bàd-si-bi sì-ke ù-ur$_5$-re bala an-ga-àm

M [ ]x – – b[i] – – – – – àm – –
JJ –^{ki} – – – – – – UD – ge – u[r$_5$-r]e – / – [ ] ⌞⌟
KK – – – – – – ba – – – – – – – – ⌞⌟

463. sá mi-ri-ib-du$_{11}$-ga bala u$_4$ kukku$_2$-ga BI.IR gál-lu ša-ra-da

M [ ] – – – [ ]x – – – – – – –
JJ –[1] – –[2] – – – – – – g[a] ⌞⌟ – [š]a-ra-dug$_4$
KK – – – – – – – – – – – / – – – – – – –

1. Looks like KU. 2. RI written ḪU.

464. dúr-ù-ri ki-tuš é-temen-ní-gùr-ru-za zi-dè-eš dù-dù-àm

M [ ] ⌞– –⌟ [z]i – – – – x x-a-⌜ri⌝
JJ – * * – – – – – – – – ⌞⌟ – – – – ⌞⌟
KK – – – – – – – – – – – – – – – d[ù]

465. uri$_5$^{ki} giri$_{17}$-zal-la ḫé-en-dù un ḫé-en-ši-gam-e

M [ ] – ⌞– – – –⌟
JJ ⌞⌟ – mḫ[a] ⌞⌟ – – – – – – – –
KK uri$_2$ – – – – – – – – – em – g[am]

466. úr-bi-a níg ḫé-en-gál ^{d}ašnan ḫé-éb-da-tuš

M [ḫ]é-da-tuš
JJ – – – – ⌞– –⌟ – – – – – – –
KK – – – – – – – ⌞⌟ – – em – a[n]

467. pa-bi-a giri$_{17}$-zal ḫé-en-gál ^{d}utu ḫé-en-da-ḫúl

M [ ] ⸢⸣ – ∘ – –

JJ – – – – – – ∘ – ^{d}u[tu] – – – –

KK – – – – – – – – ^{d}ut[u] – em – ḫú[l]

468. ^{giš}banšur-ba ḫé-gál ^{d}ašnan-ka gú-da ḫé-em-mi-ib-lá

M [ ] – – – – – – –

O ∘ ⸢⸣ bi-a ⸢⸣ [ ]

JJ X.BA.BI.AN – – – – x – – – / [ ] ⸢⸣ – in –

KK – – – – – – – – – – – – m[i] –

469. uri$_{5}$^{ki} uru an-né nam tar-re ki-bi ḫa-ra-ab-gi$_{4}$-gi$_{4}$

M [b]i – – – – – –

O uri$_{2}$ – ma – – [ ]

JJ – – – – – – – ⸢ré?⸣ – – – – – – – –

KK uri$_{2}$ – – – – – – – – – – – – – – –

470. ^{d}en-líl-le gù zi dé-àm gú an-šè ḫé-en-zi

M [ ] ⸢⸣ ∘ –

O – – – – – [z]i d[é]

JJ – – – – – – [ ] ⸢– – –⸣ –

KK – – – – – – – – – – – – – –

471. ^{d}nanna-ra ma-da sig igi nim-ma gú ḫu-mu-na-ab-si-a

O – ⸢⸣ [ ]

JJ – – – ∘ ∘ – – – – x ⸢ḫé⸣-en-na-si-a

KK – – re – – – ∘ – – – – – – ⸢– si⸣.[?]

472. ^{d}en.zu-ra kaskal kur-ra-ke$_{4}$ si ḫé-en-na-sá-e

O –e[n]

JJ – – – – – – – – [ ] ⸢⸣ – – – –

KK – – – ∘ – – – – – – e[n] ⸢⸣

473. muru$_9$-gin$_7$ ki ús-sa-a-gin$_7$ šu mu-un-na-gá-gá

JJ x – e – – – – x x – – – – – – –
KK – – – – – – – – – x[ ]

474. inim du$_{11}$-ga an ^{d}en-líl-lá-kam šu zi ḫé-gá-gá

JJ – – – – – – – * – – – – – –
KK – – – – – – – – – – z[i]

475. a-a ^{d}nanna uru^{ki}-ni uri$_5$^{ki}-ma sag íl-la mu-un-gin

JJ – – – – – – – – ⌞⌟ – – – – – – –
KK * * – – – * – uri$_2$ – – – – [*[1] m]u x[ ]

1. No space for la.

476. šul ^{d}en.zu é-kiš-nu-gál-la-šè im-ma-da-an-ku$_4$-ku$_4$

O [z]u ⸢e⸣ [ ]
JJ – – – – – – – – – – ⸢na⸣ – – – – – – –
KK * – – – e – – – – – – – – – – – – k[u$_4$]

477. ^{d}nin-gal-e É.NUN-kù-ga-na ní mu-ni-ib-te-en-te-en

O [ ] – – – – – – ⌞⌟ – – – – [ ]
JJ – – – – gá – ⌞⌟ – – – – – – – – – – –
KK – – – – gá – na – – – – – – íb – e[n]

477a. uri$_5$^{ki}-ma é-kiš-nu-gál-la-na im-ma-da-an-ku$_4$-ku$_4$

O Omits line
JJ – – – – – – – – – – – – – – – – –
KK šul ^{d}en.zu – – – ⌞⌟ – š[è i]m – – ⌞⌟ [k]u$_4$ –

478. JJ ki-ru-gú 4-kam-ma

O Omits line
KK Omits line

479. JJ uru^{ki} líl-lá-àm šà-bi a-še-⌜ra⌝ gi ér-ra ba-an-mú

O Omits line
KK Omits line

480. JJ šà-bi a-še-ra gi ér-ra ba-an-mú

O Omits line
KK Omits line

481. JJ un-bi a-še-er-ra u$_4$ mi-ni-ib-zal-zal-e

O Omits line
KK Omits line

482. JJ giš-gi$_4$-gál-bi-im

O Omits line
KK Omits line

483.	u$_4$	gig-ga	u$_4$	gaba-zu	zi-ga-ab	u$_4$	é-za	gi$_4$-bi
D	-	- -	-	- za	z[i			]
O	⌜⌝	- -	-	- -	- - -	-	[	]
JJ	-	- -	-	- -	- - -	-	- -	- -
KK	-	- -	-	- -	- - [	]	uru -	⌜- -⌝

484.	u$_4$	uru$_2$	gul-gul	u$_4$	gaba-zu	zi-ga-ab	u$_4$	é-za	gi$_4$-bi
D	-	-	- -	-	- za	- g[a			]
O	-	-	- -	-	- -	- - -	-	⌜⌝ [	]
KK	-	uru	- -	-	- -	z[i]	-	- -	- -

485.	u$_4$	é	gul-gul	u$_4$	gaba-zu	zi-ga-ab	u$_4$	é-za	[g]i$_4$-[b]i
D	-	-	- -	°	- za	- - -	⌜⌝	[	]
O	-	-	- -	-	- -	- - -	-	- [	]
KK	-	-	- -	-	- -	z[i]	-	[ ] -	[g]i$_4$-[b]i

486.	u$_4$	ki-en-gi-ra	ba-e-zal-la	kur-re	ḫé-eb-zal
D	–	– – – – –	– – – –	– [ ]	⌜– – –⌝
O	–	– – –ki–	– – – – a	– r[e	] ⌜ ⌝ [ ]
KK	–	– – – – –	– * – – a ri	k[ur-ku]r-ra	– – –

487.	u$_4$	ma-da	ba-e-zal-la	kur-re	ḫé-eb-zal
D	–	– –	– – – –	⌜ ⌝ –	– – –
O	–	– –	– – – – a	– ⌜– –⌝	– –
KK	–	– – ke$_4$?	– * – – a ri	kur-kur-ra	ḫ[é-eb-za]l

488.	kur	ti-id-nu-um^{ki}-ma-ka	ḫé-eb-zal	kur-re	ḫé-eb-zal
D	–	– – – – – – –	– ⌜ ⌝ –	– –	– – –
O	–	– – – – * – –	– – za[l	ku]r –	– – –
KK	–	t[i] – – e * *	– – –	– –	ḫ[é] – –

489.	kur	gu-ti-um^{ki}-ma-ka	ḫé-eb-zal	kur-re	ḫé-eb-zal
D	[k]ur	– – – – – –	[ ] ⌜ ⌝ –	– –	ḫ[é-e]b –
O	–	– – – – – – –	– – [z]al	– –	– – –
KK	[	u]m * ⌜ ⌝ –	– – –	[ ]x	– – –

490.	kur	an-ša$_4$-an^{ki}-na-ka	ḫé-eb-zal	kur-re	ḫé-eb-zal
D	–	[š]a$_4$ – – ⌜ ⌝ k[a	e]b –	– –	ḫ[é]
O	–	– – – – – * –	– – [z]al	– –	– – –
KK	[	]– * –	– – –	[ ]	⌜ ⌝ – –

491.	an-ša$_4$-an^{ki}-e	im	ḫul	dal-la-gin$_7$	kuš$_7$	ḫé-ni-ib-su-su
D	a[n]⌜– –⌝	[		] ga –	–	ḫ[é] –
O	– – – – –	–	–	d[al] –	–	– – – – – –
KK	Traces					

492.	šà-gar	lú	níg-ḫul	ḫé-en-da-dab$_5$	un	ḫé-em-ši-ib-gam-e
D	– ⌜ ⌝	[l]ú	– –	⌜ ⌝ – – ⌜ ⌝	–	[ ]
O	– –	–	– –	im * – –	[u]n	– – – – – –

493. me an-na giš-ḫur un gi-né an-né nam-kúr-re

D – – ⸢⸣ – – – – – – – ⸢⸣ [ ]
O – – – – – – – – – – – – –
P [a]n – – – u[n]

494. di-kuru$_5$ ka-aš bar-re un si sá-sá-e an-né nam-kú[r-re]

D – – – – – – – – – – – – ⸢⸣ – kú[r]
P [ ] – – – ° u[n]

495. kaskal kalam-ma-ke$_4$ giri$_3$ gá-gá an-né nam-kúr-r[e]

D – – – – – – – – ⸢– – –⸣ r[e]
P [kala]m ⸢⸣ ka – – [ ]

496. an-né ^{d}en-líl-bi nam-kúr-ru-ne an-né nam-kú[r-re]

D – – – – – ⸢⸣ – – – – ⸢⸣ – ⸢⸣ kú[r]
P [e]n – ⸢– – – ⸢re⸣ [ ]

497. ^{d}en-ki ^{d}nin-maḫ-bi nam-kúr-ru-ne an-né nam-kúr-r[e]

D – – – – – – – – – – [n]e – – ⸢⸣ – r[e]
P [ ] ⸢⸣ – re – [ ]

498. ^{íd}idigna ^{íd}buranun-na a-bi tùm-dè an-né nam-kúr-re

D – – – – – – – ⸢⸣ – – – – – –
P [bura]nun ° – – tù[m]

499. šeg$_x$(IM.A) an-na ki-a še gu-nu an-né nam-kúr-re

D – a[n-n]a – – – – – – ⸢⸣ – – –
P [n]a ⸢– – –⸣ – – a[n]

500. íd a-bi-da a-šà še-bi-da an-né nam-kúr-re

D – – – – – – – – – – – – – –
P [ ] ⸢– –⸣ [ ]

501. D ambar-ambar-re ku$_6$ mušen tùm an-né ⟨nam-kúr-re⟩

502. D ^{giš}gi gi sun gi ⌜h̬enbur⌝ mú-mú-⌜dè⌝ an-né nam-kúr-re

503. D an-né ^{d}en-líl-bi nam-kúr-ru-ne

504. D ^{d}en-ki ^{d}nin-mah̬-bi nam-kúr-ru-ne

505. D pú ^{giš}kiri$_6$ làl geštin ù-tu ⟨an-né nam-kúr-re⟩

506. D an eden-na giš-maš-gurum ⌜ù⌝-[tu] ⟨an-né nam-kúr-re⟩

507. D é-gal-la zi su$_{13}$-ud gál [ù-tu] ⟨an-né nam-kúr-re⟩

508. a-ab-ba h̬é-gál níg ù-tu an-[né nam-kúr-re]
D – – – – – – ⌜⌝[t]u ⟨ ⟩
Z [gá]l ⌜ – – ⌝ [ ]

509. ma-da un lu-a sig igi nim-ma an-[né nam-kúr-re]
D – – – – – – – [ ] ⌜⌝ ⟨ ⟩
Z [u]n – – – – – – – [ ]

510. an-né ^{d}en-líl-bi nam-kúr-re-[ne] an-né nam-kúr-[re]
D – – – – – – – [r]e [ ] ⟨ ⟩
Z [ ] – – – – – – r[e-ne] / ⌜⌝ – – – [ ]

511. ^{d}en-ki ^{d}nin-mah̬-bi nam-kúr-re-n[e an-n]é nam-kúr-re
D – – – – – – – – k[úr n]é – – –
Z [ ] ⌜⌝ – – – ° – – – n[e]

512. D uru dù-dù-a un [šár-šár$^?$]-ra$^?$

513. D an-ki nigin$_2$-na un sa[g s]ì-ga

514. D ^{d}nanna ⸢nam-lugal⸣-zu du$_{10}$-ga-à[m ki-z]a ⸢gi$_{4}$⸣-[n]i-⸢ib⸣

515. uri$_{5}$^{ki}-ma bala du$_{10}$ nam-ḫé u$_{4}$ ḫé-ni-ib-su$_{13}$-ud-dè
D – – ° ⸢–⸣ – – ḫ[é] / – – – – [ ]
KK uri$_{2}$ – – – ° – – – – – – – – –

516. un-bi ú sal-la ḫé-eb-ná e-ne-su$_{13}$-ud ḫé$^{!}$-em-ak$^{?}$
D – – – – – – – [ ]
KK [u]n– – – – – em – – – – – – – –

517. a nam-lú-ulu$_{3}$ ba-ḫúb KU-re egi$_{2}$-re mu-lu ér a-še-re
D – – – – – – [ ] / – bi – – é[r]
KK [ ] – – – – – – – / [e]gi$_{2}$ – – – – – – –

518. ^{d}nanna a uru-zu a é-zu a nam-lú-u$_{18}$-lu$_{7}$-zu
D – ⸢–⸣ – uru$_{2}$⸣[ ]
KK – – – – – – – – / – – – – – –

519. ki-ru-gú 5-kam-ma-à[m]
D [ ] ⸢–⸣ [ ]
KK – – – – – – à[m]

Lexical Index

The index contains a list of all words found in the composite text. Numbers refer to the line in the text in which the word occurs. An asterisk indicates that the word is discussed in the commentary to the line. When a word is discussed in the commentary but does not appear in the line under discussion, the number is in parentheses.

Index of Divine and Royal Names

Index of Geographical and Topographical Names

Introduction to the Figures and Plates

In the figures and plates the obverse of each tablet is followed by the reverse and, in some of the plates, by the edges. When only one side contains readable text, the broken side is not reproduced. The copies and photographs that are included here were generously provided by numerous individuals and institutions who must be acknowledged.

In addition to my own copies, the figures contain the works of two Sumerologists. Figure 11 is by W. W. Hallo. Figures 4 and 8 were copied by S. N. Kramer. The major part of figure 3 was copied, many years ago, by Kramer. Subsequently, two pieces were joined to the tablet. In order to preserve Kramer's excellent copy I have added, in my own hand, the parts from the new joins.

I must also acknowledge the photographs. The reproduction of text A is utilized here by courtesy of the Visitors of the Ashmolean Museum. Texts DD, LL, MM, and NN are reproduced here by permission of the Trustees of the British Museum. The photographs of sources B through T are published by permission of Å. W. Sjöberg, Curator of Sumerian Tablets of the University Museum, and PP by permission of W. W. Hallo, Curator of the Yale Babylonian Collection. Finally, the photographs of text TT, from Larsa, are reproduced here by courtesy of Daniel Arnaud. The photographs of texts B–L, O–T, OO, and QQ were taken by H. Fred Schock, Head Photographer, University Museum, University of Pennsylvania; those of N and RR by Kay Clahassey of the Museum of Anthropology, University of Michigan, Ann Arbor.

The figures are all reproduced at 100% and the plates at approximately 105% (the exact scale of reproduction of fig. 11 and pls. 1, 19, and 24 is unknown).

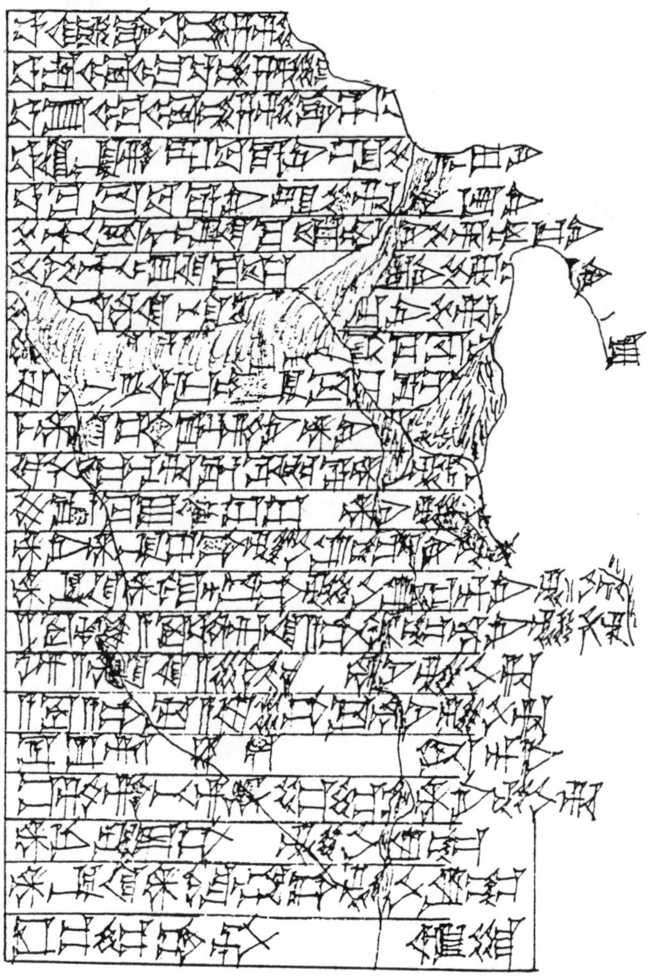

Fig. 1. Text D (Obverse): CBS 2307 + CBS 9204 + CBS 9878 + N 2430

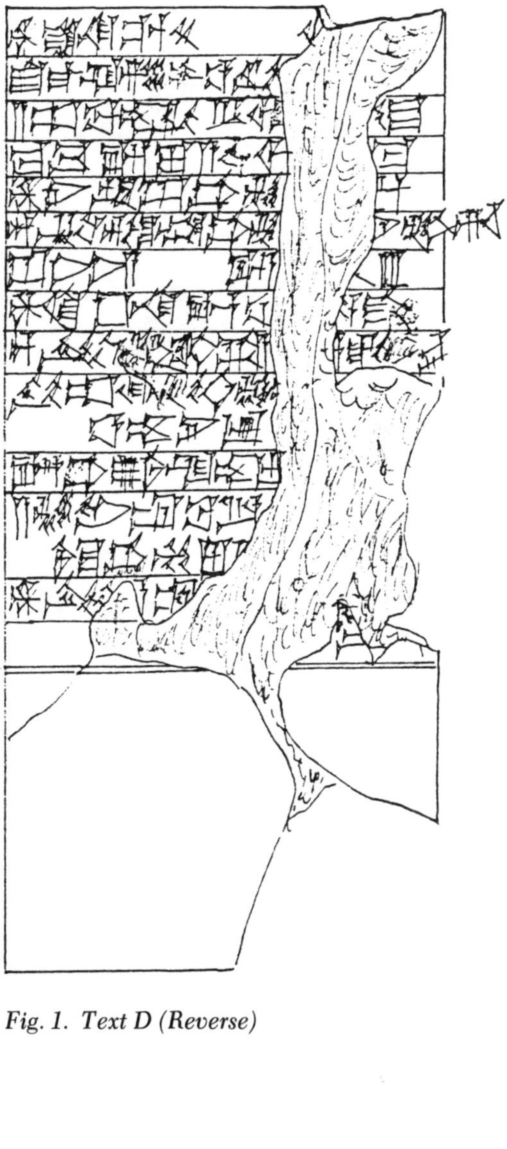

Fig. 1. Text D (Reverse)

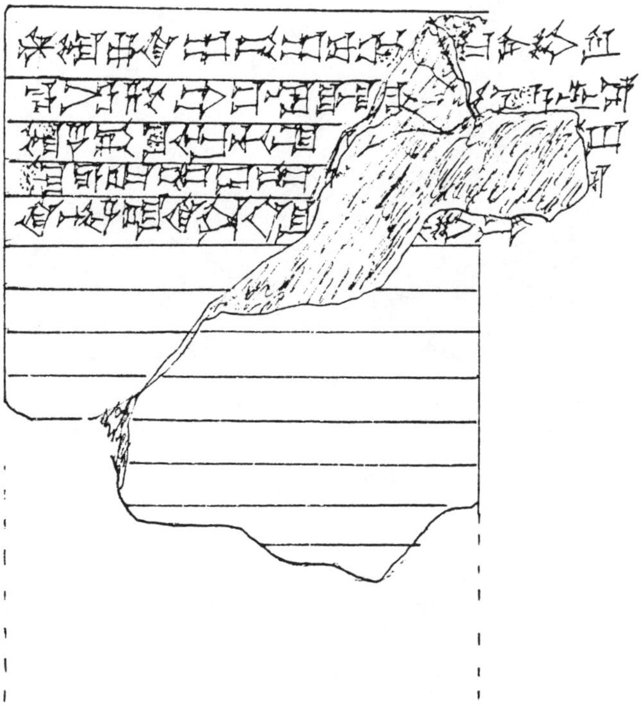

Fig. 2. Text I (Obverse): CBS 9245 [+ CBS 13112]

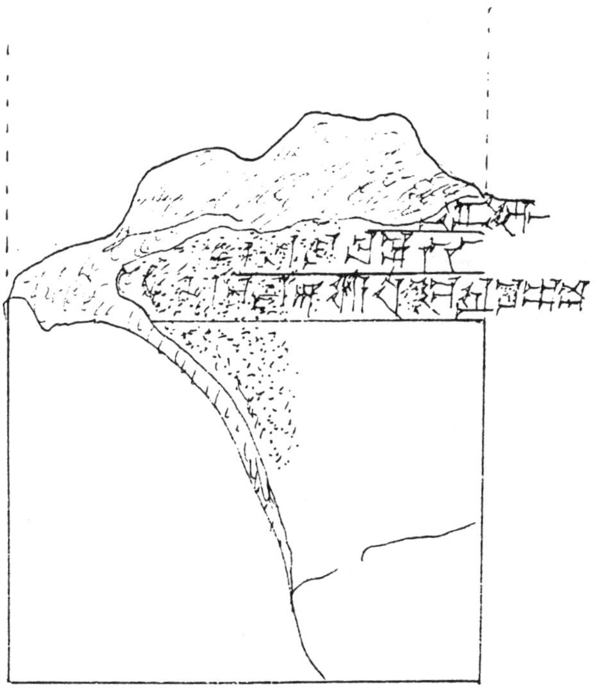

Fig. 2. Text I (Reverse)

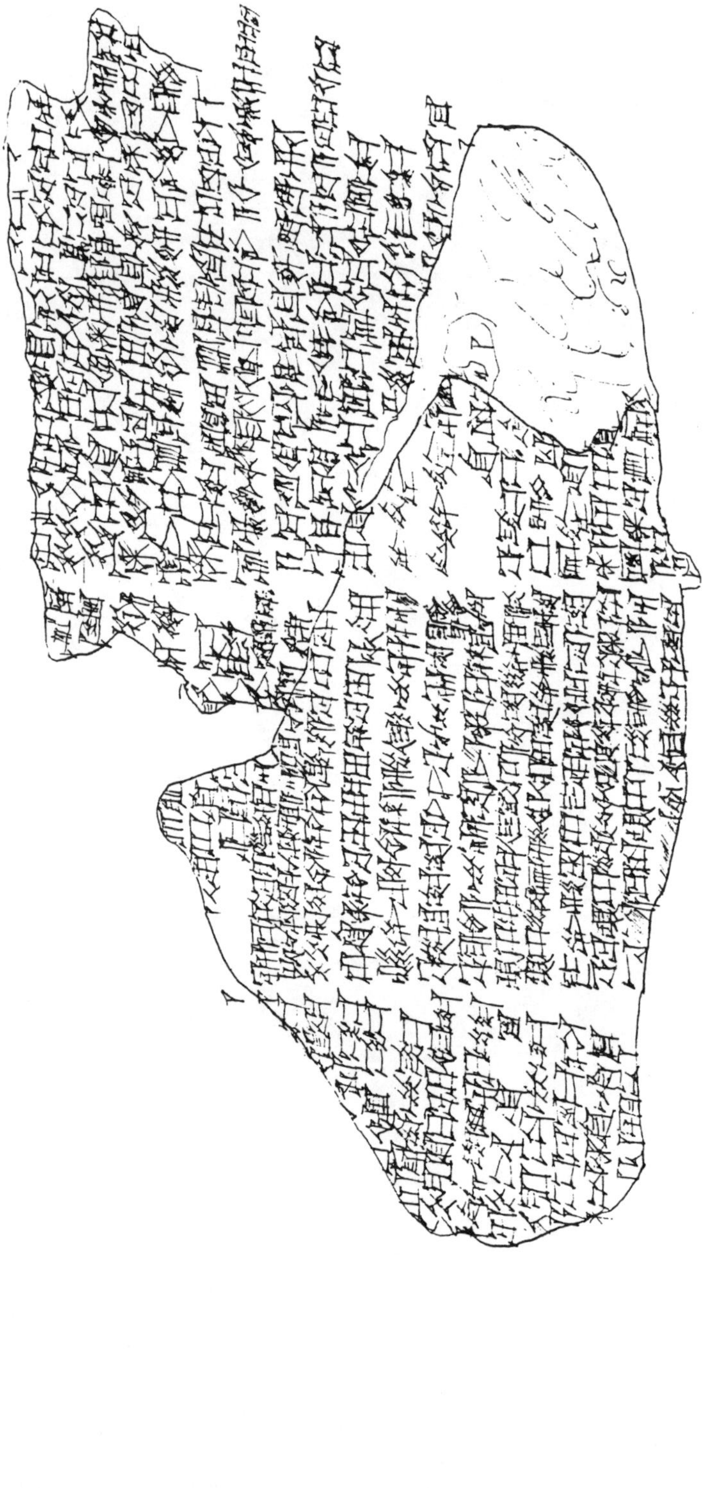

Fig. 3. *Text N (Obverse): N 1735 + N 1764 + N 1783 + N 6287 [+ Ni. 4414]*

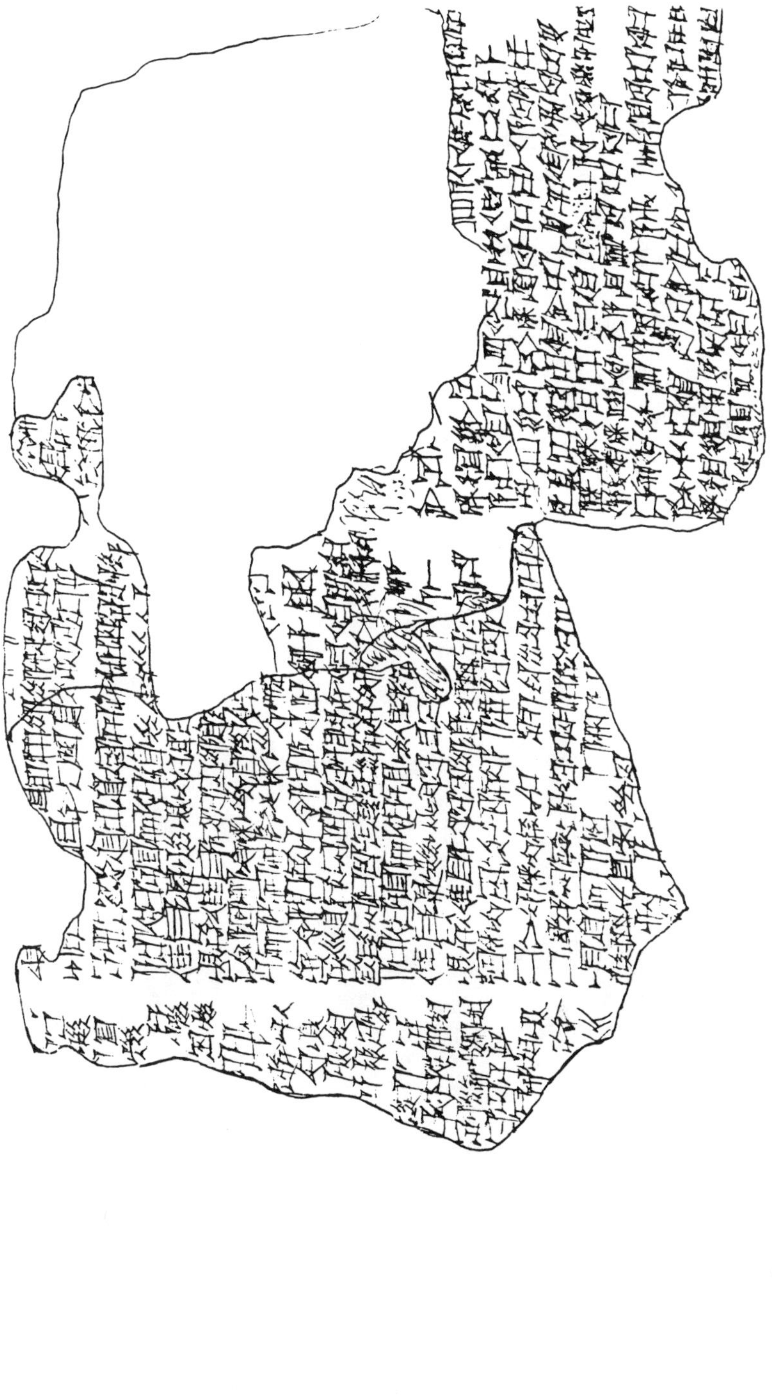

Fig. 3. Text N (Reverse)

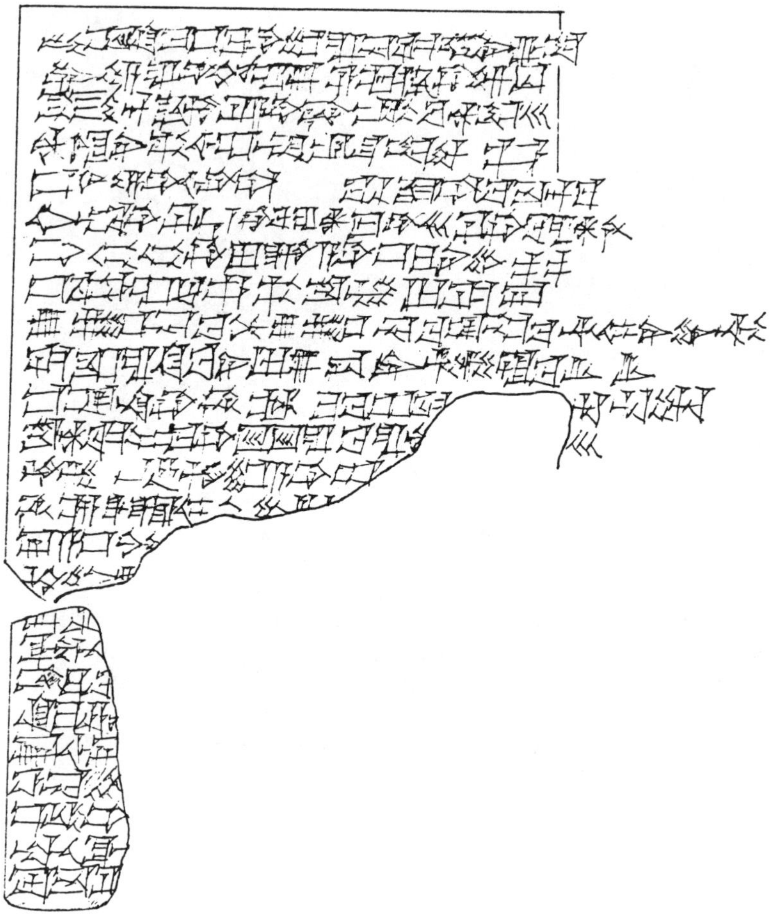

Fig. 4. Text O (Obverse): N 1778 + N 1781

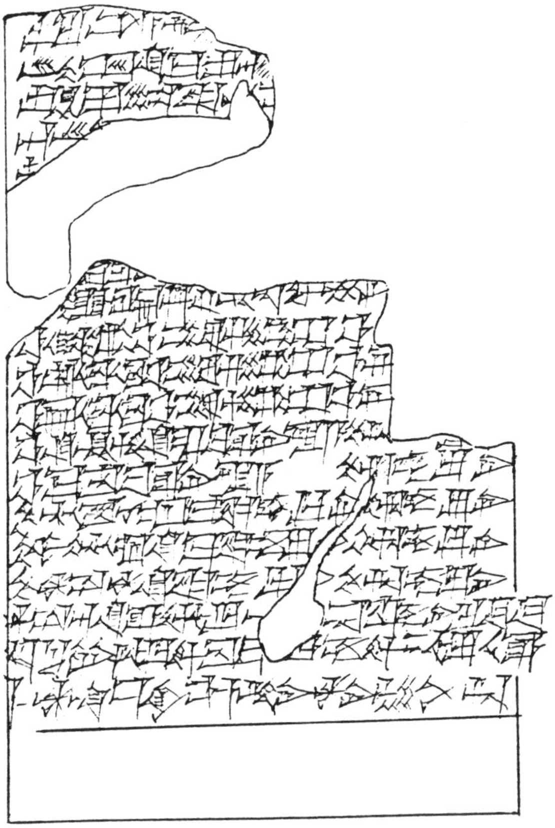

Fig. 4. Text O (Reverse)

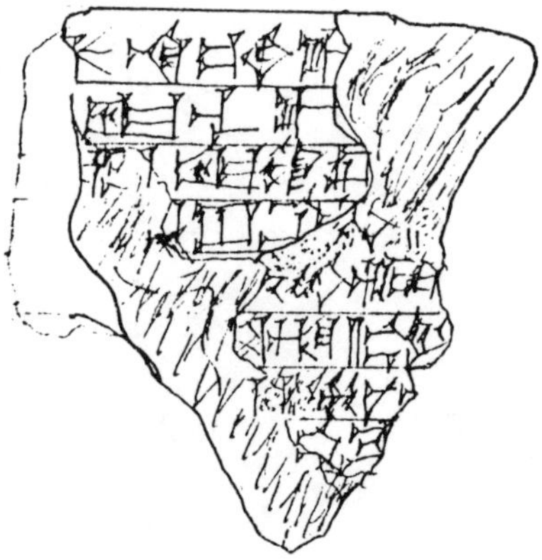

Obverse

Fig. 5. Text P: N 2624 + N 3084

Obverse

Fig. 6. Text Q: N 3123

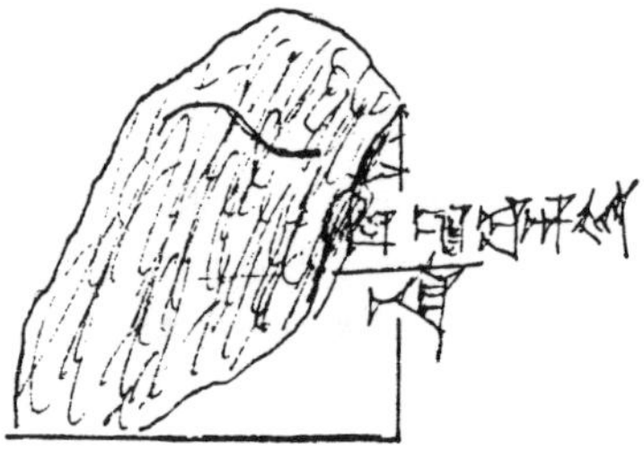

Obverse

Reverse

Fig. 7. Text R: N 3253

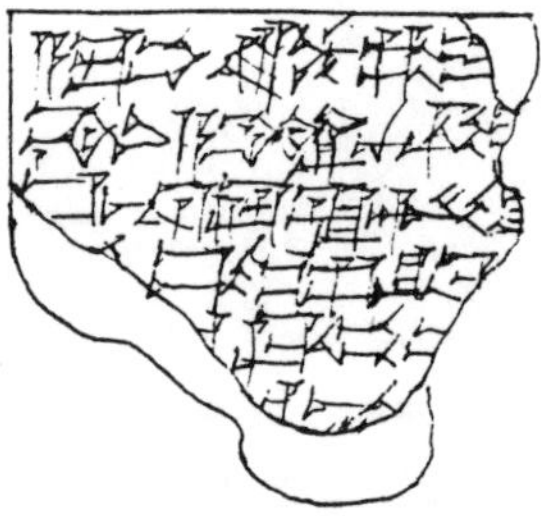

Obverse

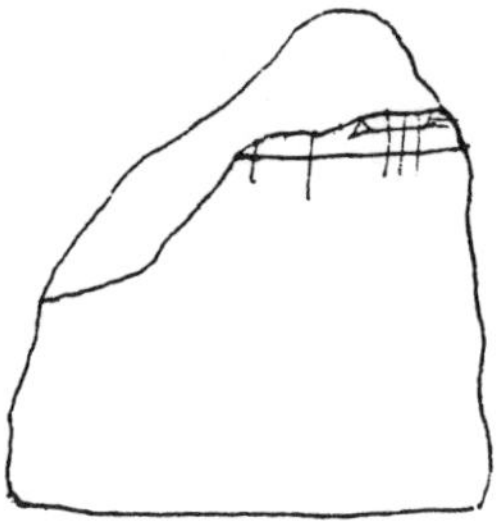

Reverse

Fig. 8. Text S: N 3626

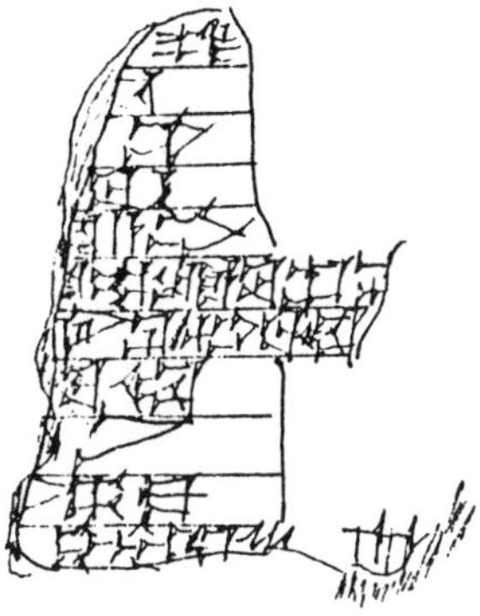

Reverse(?)

Fig. 9. Text T: N 6722

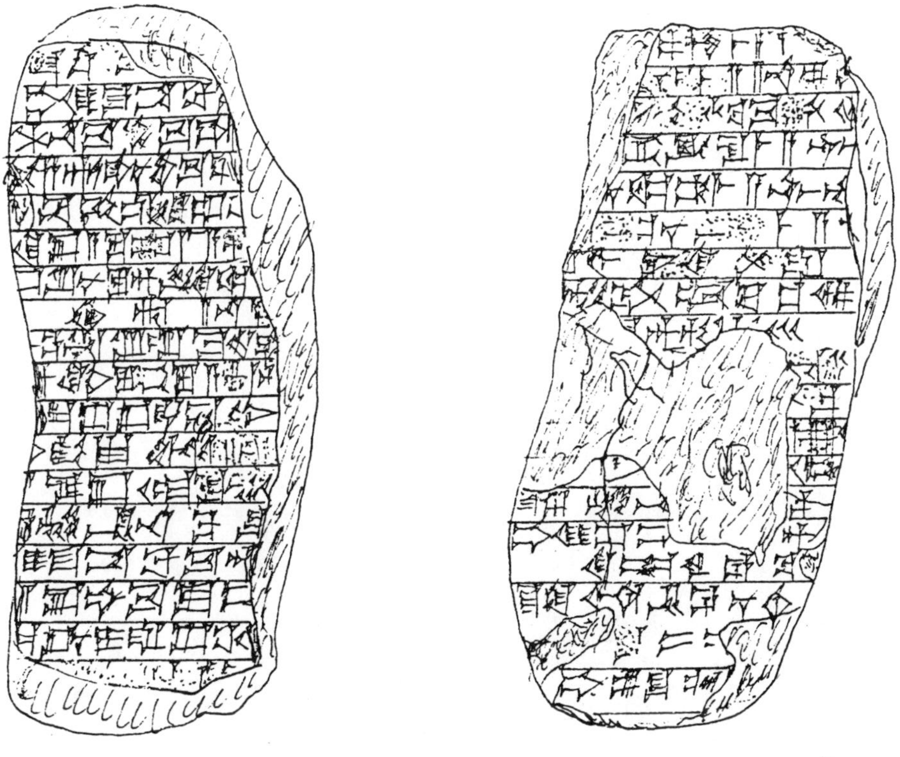

Obverse

Reverse

Fig. 10. Text OO: UM 29-15-414

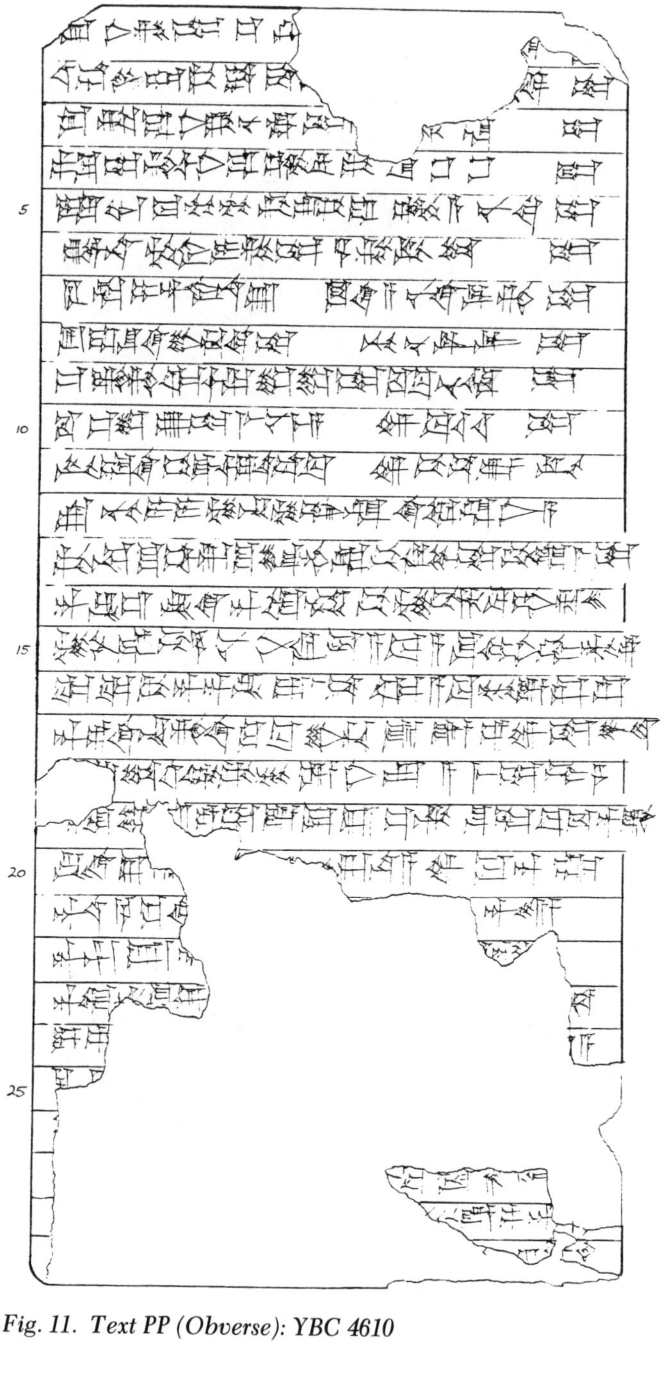

Fig. 11. Text PP (Obverse): YBC 4610

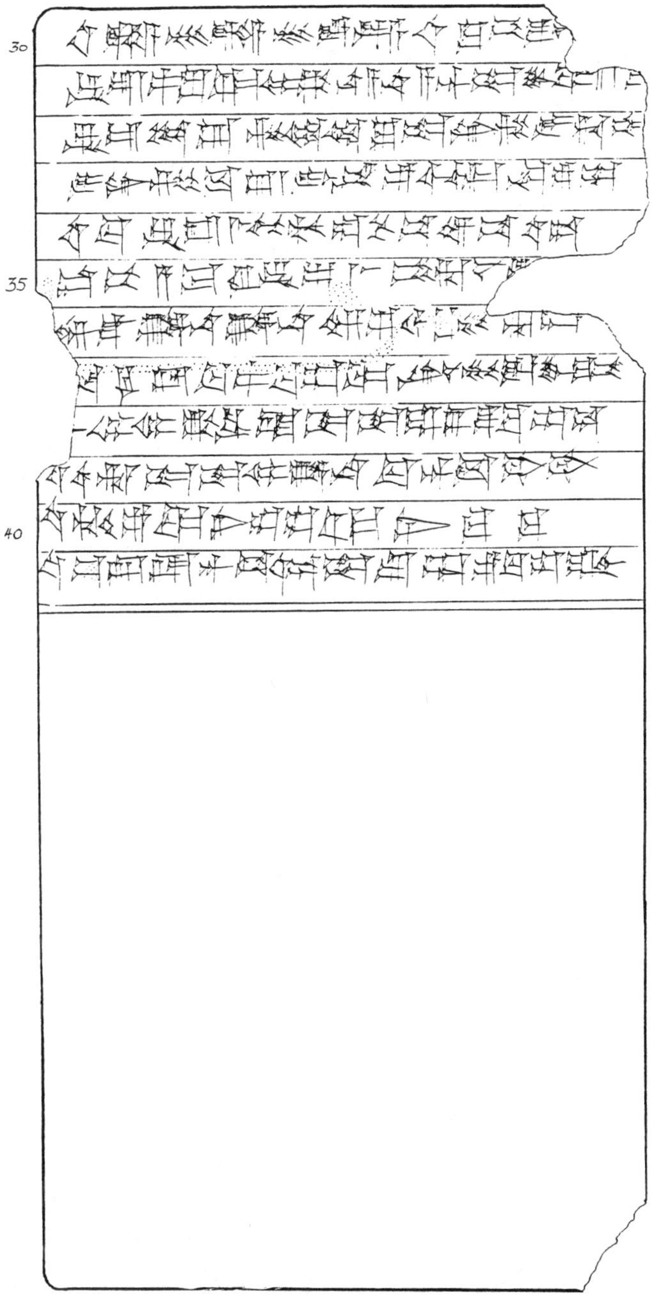

Fig. 11. Text PP (Reverse)

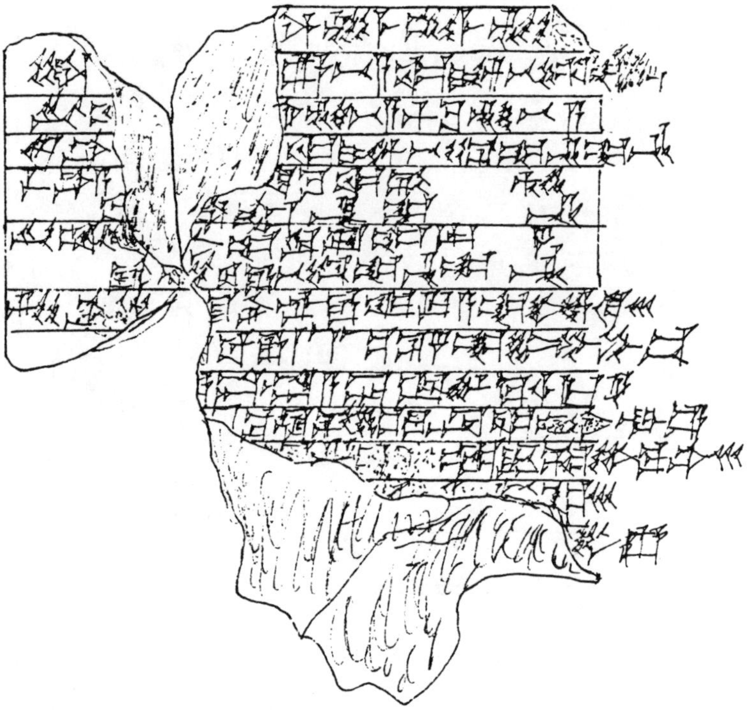

Fig. 12. Text QQ (Obverse): 3 N-T 318B (A 302118B) + 3 N-T 321 (UM 55-21-305)

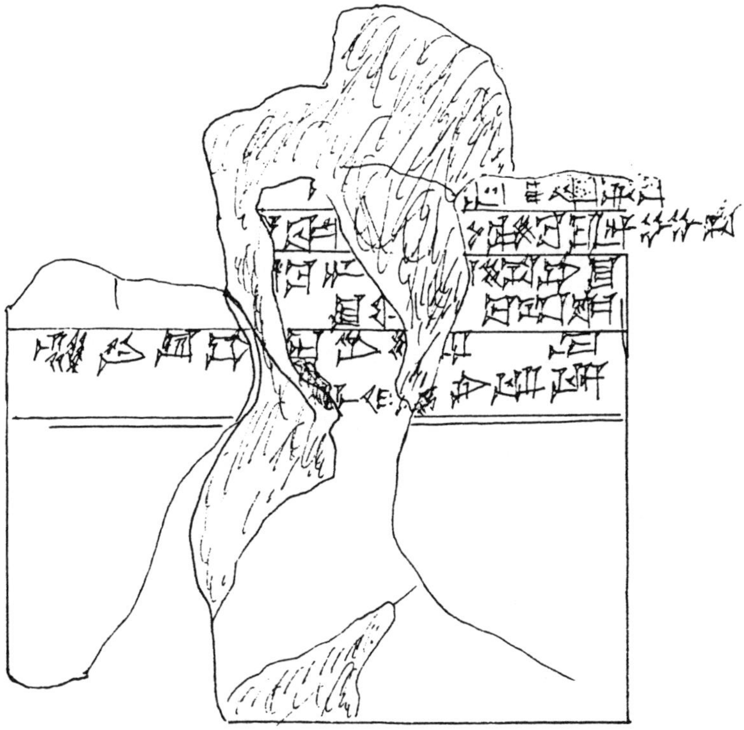

Fig. 12. Text QQ (Reverse)

Fig. 13. Text RR (Obverse): 3 N-T 666 (IM 58605) + 3 N-T 917, 386 + 3 N-T, 402

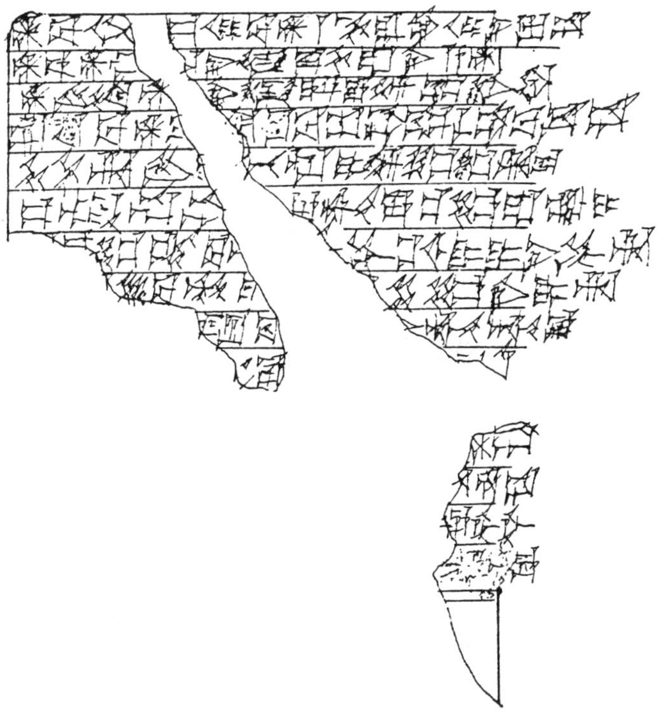

Fig. 13. Text RR (Reverse)

Obverse

Reverse

Right Edge

A = Ash. 1926,396

Plate 2

Right Edge

Reverse

Obverse

B = CBS 2154

Right Edge

Reverse

Obverse

C = CBS 2222 + CBS 2279

Plate 4

Right Edge

Reverse

Obverse

D = CBS 2307 + CBS 9204 + CBS 9878 + N 2430

Plate 5

Right Edge

Reverse

Obverse

E = CBS 2359

Plate 6

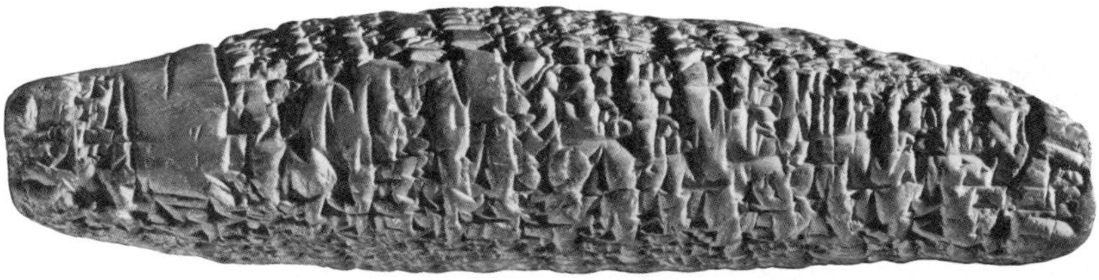

Right Edge

Reverse

Obverse

F = CBS 4577

G = CBS 4593 *Obverse* *Reverse*

H = CBS 8324 *Obverse* *Reverse* *Left Edge*

Plate 8

J = CBS 10342 *Obverse* *Reverse*

K = CBS 12671 *Obverse* *Reverse*

Plate 10

Obverse

Reverse

L = CBS 15178 + CBS 15305

Obverse

N = N 1735 + N 1764 + N 1783 + N 6287

Right Edge

Reverse

N = N 1735 + N 1764 + N 1783 + N 6287

O = N 1778 + N 1781 *Obverse*

Reverse

Right Edge

Left Edge

O = N 1781

Obverse

P = N 2624 + N 3084

Obverse

Q = N 3123

Obverse

Reverse

R = N 3253

Obverse

S = N 3626

Reverse(?)

T = N 6722

Plate 16

Obverse

Reverse

DD = *UET* 6 126 + *UET* 6 127 (+) *UET* 6 *24 + *UET* 6 *139 + *UET* 6 *242 + *UET* 6 *434

Obverse

Reverse

LL = *UET* 6 *21 + *UET* 6 *22

Obverse

Reverse

MM = *UET* 6 *26

Obverse (?)

NN = *UET* 6 *272

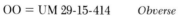

OO = UM 29-15-414 *Obverse* *Reverse*

Plate 19

PP = YBC 4610

Obverse

Reverse

Right Edge

Left Edge

Plate 20

Obverse

Right Edge

QQ = 3 N-T 318B (A 302118B) + 3 N-T 321 (UM 55-21-305)

Reverse

QQ = 3 N-T 318B (A 302118B) + 3 N-T 321 (UM 55-21-305)

Plate 22

Obverse

RR = 3 N-T 666 (IM 58605) + 3 N-T 917, 386 + 3 N-T 917, 402

Reverse

RR = 3 N-T 666 (IM 58605) + 3 N-T 917, 386 + 3 N-T 917, 402

Obverse

Reverse

SS = 3 N-T 900, 3

Plate 24

Obverse

Right Edge

TT = L 74.150 *Left Edge*

Reverse